The importance of a v... pregnancy has long beer... are realising that the benefit for the baby is also greatly enhanced if healthy eating begins well before pregnancy. In this book, Catherine Lewis provides prospective parents with dietary advice illustrated with delicious, wholefood recipes.

Recipes for breakfasts, breads, soups, salads, flans, casseroles, desserts and drinks are included, providing foods rich in nutrients for the growing fetus. And the recommended foods illustrated are designed to be incorporated into daily menus that are ideal for all the family.

With the same well-informed and practical approach that made *Growing Up With Good Food* so successful, Catherine Lewis has compiled a guide to healthy eating in general, and in particular for pregnancy, that will be welcomed by anyone who wants to improve their eating habits naturally.

Good Food Before Birth

CATHERINE LEWIS

London
UNWIN PAPERBACKS
Boston   Sydney

First published by Unwin Paperbacks 1984
This book is copyright under the Berne Convention.
No reproduction without permission. All rights reserved.

UNWIN® PAPERBACKS
40 Museum Street, London WC1A 1LU, UK

Unwin Paperbacks
Park Lane, Hemel Hempstead, Herts HP2 4TE, UK

George Allen & Unwin Australia Pty Ltd
8 Napier Street, North Sydney, NSW 2060, Australia

© Catherine Lewis, 1984

British Library Cataloguing in Publication Data

Lewis, Catherine
Good food before birth.
1. Pregnancy—Nutritional aspects
2. Cookery
I. Title
641.5'63   TX652
ISBN 0-04-641045-7

Set in 10 on 11 point Sabon by Computape (Pickering) Ltd
Reproduced, printed and bound in Great Britain by
Hazell Watson & Viney Limited,
Member of the BPCC Group,
Aylesbury, Bucks

Acknowledgements

My understanding of the value of good food before birth owes most to the organisations and individuals who have been promoting the idea of good preconceptual health in the U.K. over the past five years or so. Conferences organised by the McCarrison Society and by Foresight, talks given by Margaret and Arthur Wynn and their publications have shown why this subject deserves the attention of everyone concerned with the health of babies and their parents.

None of this might ever have come my way had I not edited the cookbook of the Leeds Branch of the NCT, *Growing Up With Good Food* and thereby developed my interest in the importance of a healthy diet for parents and children. To the Branch and all involved in that book I am grateful, as to those members of the wider NCT concerned with nutrition with whom I consequently came in touch, especially Rosemary Fost and Deirdre Mackay, who have helped me with this book too.

Recipes and encouragement have been generously given by Ros Claxton and Jill Kibble, my mother and sister, Margaret and Angela Berry and others. I would like to thank Sally Bunday for help on the topic of hyperactivity and Dr Jonathon Maberly for reading the section on allergy. As is usual, I am responsible for any errors or omissions.

Some kind friends have read drafts and made useful comments, in particular Sylvia Craven and Catherine Richardson as well as those already mentioned including Margaret and Arthur Wynn.

Finally, my thanks are due to proof readers Rachel Howe and my husband, Harry Lewis, who, with my children, tested all the recipes.

Catherine Lewis
Leeds, 1984.

Contents

Acknowledgements	page v
Weights, Measures and Symbols Used	ix
Nourishing a New Life	1
Good Food for Pregnancy	12
Making the Transition to Wholefoods	20
Good Food for Breastfeeding	29
Breakfasts and Breads	32
Fruit at Breakfast	39
Dairy Products	40
Milk Substitutes	41
Breads	44
Soups	61
Hot Dishes	73
Flans	73
Pasta	80
Pizza	83
Cooking with Meat	86
Cooking with Beans and Other Pulses	98
Burgers, Rissoles and Vegetarian Bakes	99
Vegetable Dishes	104
Salads	111
Sprouting Beans and Seeds	113
Dressings	113
Fresh Raw Salads	117
Staple Salads	121
Rice Salads	122
Potato Salads	125
Cooked Vegetable Salads	126
Sweet Things	128
Fruits and Desserts	128
Fruits, Nuts and Seeds	129
Home Baking	143
Picnics and Packed Lunches	156
Picnics	156
Sandwiches	158
Finger Foods and Other Delicacies for a Special Picnic	161

Entertaining Friends — 164
- Friends to 'Coffee' — 165
- Cocktail Parties and Buffets — 165
- Dinners for 6–8 — 171
- Desserts — 183
- Iced Desserts — 184
- Ice Creams — 185
- Three Interesting Flavours — 186

Drinks — 188
- Vegetable Juices — 191
- Herb Teas — 192

Food Allergies and Special Diets — 198
- Hidden Allergies — 199
- Precautions against Hyperactivity — 200
- Gluten-free Diet — 201
- Milk-free Diet — 202
- Vegan Diet — 206

Common Problems in Pregnancy — 207
- Pregnancy Sickness — 207
- Constipation — 209
- Anaemia — 210
- Weight Gain and Fluid Retention — 211
- High Blood Pressure and Toxaemia of Pregnancy — 213

Not Just Nutrition — 215
- Giving Up Smoking — 215
- Pollution — 218
- Contraception — 219
- Alcohol — 220
- Your General Health — 221
- After a Miscarriage — 224
- Infertility — 225

Useful Addresses — 229
Booklist — 232
Index — 236

Weights, Measures and Symbols Used in This Book

The cup measure used is 1 (US) cup = 240ml/8 fl. oz or ½ (US) pint. The tablespoons and teaspoons are level measure spoons 3 teaspoons = 1 tablespoon.

The weight measures are US or imperial (1 lb = 16 oz) and metric (1 kilo = 1000 grams).

The conversions have been calculated to a convenient equivalent for the recipe in question, sometimes rounding up, sometimes rounding down.

CONVERSION TABLES

Weight measurements (exact)
1 oz = 28.35g
2 oz = 56.7g
4 oz = 113.4g
8 oz = 226.8g
12 oz = 340.2g
16 oz = 453.6g = 1 lb

APPROXIMATE CONVERSION

25g = 1 oz
100g = 3½ oz
125g = 4½ oz

250g = 9 oz
500g = 1 lb 1½ oz
1000g = 2 lb 3 oz = 1 kilogram

LIQUID OR VOLUME MEASURES

1 (US) fl. oz = 28 ml
1 (Imp) fl. oz = 28 ml
1 (US) cup = ½ pint = 8 fl. oz = 240 ml

1 (Imp) cup = ½ pint = 10 fl. oz = 280 ml
1 litre = 1000 g/ml = 1¾ (Imp) pints = 35 fl. oz

OVEN TEMPERATURES

	Gas Mark	Fahrenheit	Centigrade
Cool	¼ – ½	250°	121°
Very slow	1	275°	135°
Slow	2 – 3	300–325°	149–163°
Moderate	4 – 5	350–375°	177–190°
Moderately hot	6	400°	205°
Hot	7	425°	218°
Very hot	8 – 9	450–475°	232–246°

HANDY MEASURES

As all the volume measures are standardised to US cups, tablespoons and teaspoons, here are some equivalent weights for certain basic ingredients for those unfamiliar with the American system. Conversely, those unused to weighing things can read the chart in the other direction. If you lack a kitchen measuring jug, containers from cream, yogurt, cottage cheese etc. showing their capacity, may be used instead.

US Cup = 8 fl. oz

1 cup sugar (most kinds) = 225g/8 oz
1 cup honey = 325g/11½ oz
1 cup butter or oil = 225g/8 oz
1 cup white flour = 125g/4 oz
1 cup fine wholewheat flour = 125g/4 oz
1 cup coarse wholewheat flour = 105g/3¾ oz
1 cup polenta (maize meal) = 125g/4 oz
1 cup rolled oats = 85g/3 oz
1 cup sesame seeds = 140g/5 oz
1 cup dry beans = 190g/6¾ oz
1 cup dry red lentils = 180g/6½ oz
1 cup dry brown lentils = 220g/7¾ oz

SYMBOLS USED

Although both cow's milk products and grain products containing gluten are very good and cheap foods for most people, those aware of the possibility of allergy in their families may wish to eat less or need to exclude these foods from their diets. To help such people, as well as those following a vegan diet (using no animal products at all), we have used the following symbols to mark suitable recipes throughout the book.

- **GF** gluten free
- **MF** milk free
- **VEG** vegan
- ***** An asterisk after these symbols indicates that the recipe is suitable provided appropriate modifications are made to any asterisked item, such as omitting an optional ingredient or substituting a suitable one.

Recipes given are, unless otherwise specified, designed for four average servings.

Nourishing a New Life

It is wonderful to see how rapidly a fertilised egg grows. In a week or so there are over a hundred cells. Within six weeks we have a recognisable human baby with eyes, nose, lips, tongue and limbs curled up in its tiny walnut-sized sac in the uterus. A lot is now known about how the baby develops in the womb.

> 'The prize is that we can try to be as intelligent about "intra-uterine" mothering as we try to be today about the care of our children after they are born. This increased awareness can also bear the fruit of increased enjoyment.'
> (Geraldine Lux Flanagan, *The First Nine Months of Life*.)

NURTURING YOUR BABY

Nurturing the baby can extend back to the time before birth. When we start to think about the nutritional requirements of the new baby, we realise that some of the most biologically demanding moments occur in the earliest stages, when cells divide and become different sorts of cells for the various body systems.

What tells some cells to become the placenta? What tells others to turn into the brain and nervous system? How do others 'know' to develop the digestive tract and associated organs? And another set of cells to produce the skeleton, heart, blood vessels and muscles? The genes on the chromosomes which form part of the initial fertilised cell carry this code. To express their message they need a specific biochemical environment. This is where nutrition is important.

Preparing for pregnancy

Your baby will look for what it needs not only from what you eat now but from reserves in your body as well. In order to build up these reserves it is a good idea to start eating good food before you conceive. A good diet of fresh food and wholefoods is important for the prospective father too, in order to ensure that the sperm is healthy. Then your baby will be well provided for at this crucial time, right at the beginning, before you know or can be sure you are pregnant. Your baby will set off in the right direction.

A good time to improve one's diet

This is a good time to think of making changes in one's diet, for most diets can be improved, whether by eating more wholewheat bread, salads, fresh fruit, or by cutting down on sugar, fried foods and manufactured foods and drinks (including alcoholic ones). The changes made can then help develop good eating habits for good health generally. By the time your baby comes to join in family meals, they will be the kind of meals which will give him good eating habits too.

Food preferences often change in pregnancy. Take advantage of this to find out what really tastes good to you. The body of a pregnant woman functions more efficiently than usual in terms of making the nutritional elements she needs available to herself and to her developing baby. So it is worthwhile thinking about your diet, both in pregnancy and in the period before, if you know you want to conceive.

When should one start?

It's never too late to start! Ideally, however, a preparation time of at least six months is a suitable span especially if you have been using the contraceptive pill. Oral contraceptives lower the levels of certain B vitamins, vitamin C and zinc. It is important to take other contraceptive measures at this stage. Natural methods of fertility-control help one get in tune with one's body. (See p. 219 and titles in the Booklist.)

Other factors which may affect your starting point include whether either partner smokes, drinks more than ten drinks a week, or is in the habit of taking drugs, including quite common ones like sleeping pills, tranquillisers, headache pills or aspirin. It may take some time for your body to function well without any of these items, all of which affect the way the body uses food. (For more information, turn to the section entitled *Not Just Nutrition* p. 215.)

Looking at your diet

There are three points to bear in mind when you consider your diet. One is the special needs of the baby; the second is its sensitivity to substances which an adult can tolerate reasonably well, and the third is the possibility that your diet may be deficient in some area. Modern manufactured food is likely to lack many nutrients important for healthy sperm and for the environment the fertilised egg will grow in. It may actually be deficient in vitamins and minerals, or it may use up your stores as the body gets rid of things it does not need like some food additives, lead or other toxic substances.

A vegetarian or vegan diet with little or no animal sources of food could be low on zinc or vitamin B12. People who live far from the sea can suffer iodine deficiency if care is not taken. Any diet with little variety may be missing some of the thirty to sixty nutrients the body needs for cell replication and cell differentiation in the earliest days of embryonic growth.

The biological demands of reproduction mean that your reserves need to be well built up. The recipes here have been based on foods which will help you to increase these reserves, to nourish your baby once you are pregnant. When it is born you will be living on less sleep, whether you breastfeed or not, and a good reserve of nutritional supplies will stand you in good stead during this time.

If you look for the nutrients needed, such as vitamins of the B complex, vitamin C, zinc, iron and other minerals in food (rather than supplements) you will also be taking many other valuable nutrients with them. All the things a mother eats which would sustain growth — seeds, kernels, grains, beans, eggs, cod roe, potatoes and other tubers — contain many of the things the baby needs too for its growth.

Do you need supplements?

On the whole, it should not be necessary to take extra vitamin or mineral supplements. You will most likely get what you need from your healthy diet. However, if you do not feel particularly healthy, then you might be wise to have your vitamin and mineral status checked. This is recommended for anyone who is always getting colds or other infections, or if you are trying to build yourself up after a miscarriage, or if you had problems in a previous pregnancy such as pre-eclamptic toxaemia or had the misfortune to have had a baby with some defect. *Foresight*, the Association for the Promotion of Preconceptual Care, would be able to help you here (see Address list, page 229). *Foresight* has prepared a vitamin and mineral supplement especially for pregnancy. One circumstance where it could be a sensible precaution to take it, is if you were required to spend some time in hospital during your pregnancy.

Your good health is your baby's best ally

It is undoubtedly true that, on a broad scale, healthy parents have healthy children. Conversely, populations which are not well nourished have a higher perinatal mortality rate, a higher rate of severe handicap among their babies, or children who are just less healthy and more prone to infection and medical troubles throughout life. At the same time, it is important to recognise the fact that accidents can happen to anyone. A sophisticated understanding includes the knowledge that it is impossible to influence every factor. Looking after your own health and eating well makes sense because this is something you can do to improve your chances of having a good pregnancy, an easy birth and a lovely baby. In this way you can help put luck on your side. But it is as well to take note of the many other factors involved.

Seeing things in perspective: from genes to birth

A baby will be the product of many different things: its genes, its development in the womb, the circumstances of its birth are a few of them.

Each parent will bring a certain genetic inheritance to the baby. The precise composition of each contribution will be unknown. The baby has many genes to choose from and no one knows which ones it will pick. It takes only half from each parent. Each half will be affected, to some extent, by the other half in the fertilised egg which becomes implanted in the womb and so brings about a pregnancy.

The way the pregnancy develops will in turn be influenced by other factors. These include the way the mother's body functions, her metabolism, the secretion of hormones and enzymes which inter-react with emotional factors and other things around in her environment, such as the water in her area, lead in the atmosphere and food, radiation and so on. Her own propensities will make a contribution to these processes, for example, if she has a tendency to develop high blood pressure or to become anaemic. Some of these will be unknown, some may become known during the pregnancy, whereas conditions such as diabetes or asthma may be known in advance. Many can be helped by good medical care. It is difficult to know exactly which factors are helping and which are hindering the development of a particular embryo as it begins its many cell divisions and starts growing its various organs and body structures.

The sheer number of factors involved in the development of the baby make it impossible to predict in advance that everything will be all right. What you want to know is that you are putting in as many positive elements as you can and, at the same time removing some of the potential bad factors. But the ground on which they are operating remains essentially unknown. Our knowledge is based on general understanding only. An individual can use this and have good reason to hope that it will work for the best in her case.

The actual circumstances of the labour and birth will also play a role in the condition of the newborn baby. You are more likely to be able to give birth naturally without the use of drugs or anaesthesia if you have looked after your health. When a mother is helped to do this, she can feel confident that her baby has had the best chance. Where birth is not straightforward, compromises may be necessary, and it is still rational to hope that they will be for the best.

What if you still have problems?

It is bound to be very disappointing if you really try hard to do everything right and still have a miscarriage, a problem pregnancy or a baby with a birth defect. You are likely to feel cheated. You may feel resentment or even anger. You may blame yourself. The thought will occur and recur, 'Why us?' These are to be expected as natural reactions, especially at first.

Gradually you may be able to get beyond these feelings as you come to realise that it is not surprising that things sometimes go wrong. Some of those who have suffered in this way have gone on to find out more about nutrition and its role in reproductive health. They may be able to help you. There are groups which can help you with this situation (some are mentioned in the Address list, p. 229.)

Do some people do all the wrong things and get away with it?
You will hear about those who smoked or drank heavily, lived a stressful life and still ended up with a baby of good birthweight. This may give rise to scepticism. People will say, 'Does it make any difference anyway?' And you may wonder whether there is any point in bothering at all. Some are careful and still have problems. Others carry on cheerfully in their less healthy way and seem to get away with it.

People have different constitutions. Some manage birth more easily than others. Some babies are stronger than others. There is no denying the differences that exist, not only between people, but also between different pregnancies in the same person. Remembering this should make it less surprising that all these things happen. Nobody can make predictions about individuals, but we can get information about probabilities from statistics. This information justifies the endeavour to provide the best environment for all the many reproductive processes to take place. The biochemistry of the 'here and now' is what we hope to favour by eating well, being relaxed and well exercised and all the health measures we can take. If there are negative factors in the picture we can hope to outweigh them and tip the balance in our favour. But we do not know how the balance was loaded from the beginning.

It's up to you to decide what you would like to do. If you remain happy to trust to luck, then may fortune smile on you. If you want to have a go at giving yourself the advantage of a good diet, read on! At least statistics are on your side.

A parenthesis giving some statistics follows. Interested readers can pursue the topic further in Barbara Pickard's *Food, Health and Having a Baby* (in the Booklist, page 233).

SOME STATISTICS ON THE ROLE OF NUTRITION IN PREGNANCY

1 *Better births for women with food supplements*
In Toronto General Hospital from 1938–41 Ebbs and others divided pregnant women into two classes: well nourished and

poorly nourished. The second was sub-divided into two groups: those left on their diet and those given food supplements (30fl.oz milk, 1 orange, 1 egg, 2 tablespoons wheatgerm and a vitamin D capsule – 2000 units – daily; and a weekly allowance of 8oz cheese and 32oz canned tomatoes) from 12 weeks' gestation until 6 weeks post-partum. They were also counselled on wise buys with a limited income for the rest of their food.

Complications and outcomes

	Poor diet (120 mothers)	Supplemented (90 mothers)	Good diet (170 mothers)
Miscarriages	1.0%	0%	1.2%
Premature births	8.0%	2.2%	3.0%
Stillbirths	3.4%	0%	0.6%
Long labour	7.0%	3.4%	9.0%
Uterine inertia	9.5%	1.1%	7.7%
Required blood	2.6%	0%	0.6%
No complications	58.6%	84.0%	68.0%
Duration of labour (primipara)	21.8hrs.	16.6hrs.	20.2hrs.
Breastfeeding at 6 wks	59.0%	86.0%	71.0%

From Ebbs *et al.* C.M.A.J., Jan. 1942 (quoted by G. Bonham, *Nutrition and Health*, Vol. 1, No 3/4, 1983).

2 Birthweight increased and perinatal mortality reduced through food supplements and nutrition counselling

Agnes Higgins at the Montreal Diet Dispensary worked from 1963–72 with the Royal Victoria Hospital public maternity clinic, providing nutritional care for women with a poor obstetrical history, poor nutritional status, two-thirds of whom were below the poverty line. They were given food supplements (milk, eggs, oranges, vitamin and mineral supplements) from 20 weeks' gestation and counselling on good nutrition.

The average birthweight was 3418g/7½lb and the low birthweight (under 2500g/5½lb) rate was 3.31%. There were 6 perinatal deaths among 712 births of women supplemented for 21 weeks or more, which gives a perinatal mortality rate of 11.9 per 1,000 (comparable to the better rates in the U.K. in 1980 and better than the prevailing rate in the local community at the time).

3 Healthier babies through counselling on nutrition, smoking, alcohol and drug abuse

The Vancouver Perinatal Project involved health workers at all levels collaborating on a 'lifestyle' – oriented health programme for pregnancy. Community counsellors recorded the food habits, smoking, alcohol and drug abuse of each couple and gave advice at home. The women received a computer analysis of their diets showing its adequacy/deficiency profile which proved a powerful motivation for change.

Among the 156 pregnancies, a low birthweight rate of 3.8% was recorded, with the average birthweight at 3440/7.6lb.

Breastfeeding and infant illness

	Women in the project (156)	Comparison (353)
% breastfeeding		
at discharge	93%	68%
at 3 months	74%	47%
at 6 months	52%	42%
% ill (requiring a prescription drug)		
0–3 months	7%	23%
3–6 months	17%	36%

Bonham, *Nutrition and Health*, Vol. 1, No 3/4, 1983. The project was conducted in the late 1970s.

4 More supporting evidence

Studies in the UK and elsewhere corroborate the evidence shown in these Canadian projects. A recent comparison of women in Hackney and Hampstead in London showed that the better nourished group had a mean birthweight of 3313g/7.3lb compared with 3026g/6.7lb among the Hackney group. There were no low birthweight babies in the Hampstead group, but 11.8% below 2500g/5½lb in the group with inadequate calorie intake. The national rate in Britain in the 1970s was around 7.0%.

Babies of low birthweight account for 70% of perinatal deaths, and many of the remaining 30% will be handicapped to a greater or lesser extent, whether born pre-term or of low birthweight from fetal growth retardation.

COMMENTS

It is remarkable to see in the Ebbs study that the supplemented women had better outcomes than those on a good diet. This could show that intervention is beneficial in itself – it is a most helpful thing to make a new mother feel special and cared for.

Another striking feature is how successful these programmes were in increasing birthweight, considering that the supplements were not given until the fourth or fifth month of pregnancy. The single fertilised cell must double 46 times during pregnancy: there are 30 doublings in the first 10 weeks, 16 in the next 20 weeks and in the last 10 weeks the cells double only once. This suggests that attention to the peri-conceptional period would bring even better results.

NOTES ON THE MEASURES USED

1. *Birthweight* The weight of babies is always recorded at birth. This enables comparisons to be made between communities around the world. Although weight is not the only significant factor, it is one way of assessing satisfactory fetal growth in which nutrition plays an important part.
2. *Perinatal Mortality* This covers deaths from 28 weeks of pregnancy up to 7 days after birth, (neonatal mortality covers the period from birth to 4 weeks afterwards). Again, this affords a standard of comparison, as records are kept in most countries. The UK is well down the international league table. It gives some measure of the health of the baby as well as of obstetric and paediatric practice. Rates are always higher among groups who are poorly nourished. However, malnutrition rarely exists in isolation, but usually goes with other deprivations, such as low income, poor housing, or social stress. Good nutrition can help offset some of these factors, as the Canadian studies show.
3. *Length of breastfeeding* One way to look at the mother-infant relationship is to measure the time breastfeeding continues.

It testifies to satisfactory nutrition in the mother and gives the baby a good start in life. It does not mean that babies who are breastfed for a shorter time or not at all are inevitably doomed! There are many ways to compensate.

4. *Visits to the doctor or hospital admissions* The need to visit the doctor, to receive a prescription drug or to be hospitalised, although obviously a crude measure (social customs vary) does give some indication of factors influenced by nutrition such as general immune competence, congenital handicap (even minor), and susceptibility to stress.

5. *Other measures?* It would be a great help to be able to see more evidence of the well-nourished baby's capacity to love, to learn, to be happy and to be successful in life (however one assesses success), but formal studies rarely attempt such evaluations.

There are however two very small studies involving 17 and 21 children. The first, carried out by Chavez and others during the 1970s in a poor Mexican village, studied children supplemented from the third trimester of pregnancy through to the age of seven. Compared with controls, they grew faster, slept less in favour of more physical activity, the mother responded more quickly, and there was more talking and play from the parents, including fathers.

The second study by Hicks and others, in Louisiana in 1982, matched supplemented children with an older sibling considered to be at nutritional risk. It appeared that they did considerably better on a range of cognitive tests. These are both reported by Dr D. Rush, 'Protein and Calorie Supplementation during Pregnancy' in *Nutrition in Pregnancy* (Royal College of Obstetrics and Gynaecology, London, 1983).

EVIDENCE ON THE ROLE OF PERI-CONCEPTIONAL NUTRITION

There are still relatively few controlled studies on the value of good nutrition around the time of conception in women. The understanding of its importance is based on other evidence.

1 Epidemiological evidence from large scale events like famines, wartime food regulations, correlations of certain birth defects

with aspects of national diet and knowledge of environmental deficiencies (such as lack of iodine in Switzerland linked with a high rate of cretinism in the late nineteenth century).

2 Understanding of the physiology of normal reproduction, such as the rate of doubling of the cells, the timing of the development of different organs and body systems in the embryonic period (the first eight weeks of life) and of the placenta which will mediate nutrition to the fetus for the rest of the pregnancy.

3 Nutritional deficiencies can be experimentally studied in animals where diet can be controlled. This is neither practical nor ethical with people. However, blood, blood serum and hair can all be tested prior to conception to reveal deficiencies of vitamins and minerals, which can then be corrected through diet or supplementation, and ensuing pregnancies studied.

4 Links between nutritional deficiencies (and the presence of anti-nutritional elements such as lead, mercury, cadmium, aluminium) and certain birth defects, or a high incidence of miscarriage or pre-term birth can be made by testing various fetal and maternal tissues, and studying stillborn babies or aborted fetuses (spontaneous or intentional). Derek Bryce-Smith of Reading University is engaged in such a study now.

5 The effects of such things as smoking, alcohol, the Pill and other drugs on reproductive capability can be studied in what happens anyway. Results can be correlated with knowledge from controlled experiments with animals. This has led to the understanding that effects are synergistic (always worse in combination with each other), and that ill-effects can be offset to some extent by good nutrition.

6 Interventions to prevent specific defects have met with some success. Smithells, in Leeds, noted vitamin and mineral deficiencies in women who had given birth to babies with neural tube defects (spina bifida and anencephaly), and attempted to prevent a recurrence by giving supplements prior to conception and afterwards. The rate was significantly reduced.

Good Food for Pregnancy

What is a good balanced diet?
A good balanced diet may mean many things. One way to make sense of it is to look at the balance of nutrients right across the spectrum and to choose foods which cover as broad a range as possible, and thus are balanced in themselves.

Some people find it useful to think in terms of food groups and to recommend a balance of the different groups such as grains and pulses, milk and dairy products, fruit and vegetables, meats and fish.

Others find in the principles of yin and yang an idea of balance centering on the wholegrains and swinging on the yin side to pulses, sea vegetables, land vegetables and fruit, and on the yang side to animal products such as butter, milk, fish, fowl, cheese, eggs and meat. The one side needs balancing from the other, and the staples should form the greater part of the diet.

On the other hand, we may be told to eat calcium foods for bones and teeth, protein foods for muscles and organs, iron and certain vitamins for blood, other vitamins and minerals for general health and foods high in carbohydrate for energy. This seems to me less useful. Really most foods combine a number of these different elements and it is artificial to separate them in this way, just as it is inadvisable to refine foods so that they do represent mainly one substance (such as white sugar). It can lead people to regard, say, potatoes as an 'energy food' whereas they contain as much protein as breastmilk (though not as well balanced for a baby's needs) and, because of the quantity in which they are eaten, contribute a significant amount of vitamin C to many diets.

The balance of protein to calories is very near our average requirement in the potato, wholegrains and pulses, and indeed in many vegetables such as cabbage or broccoli.

'The only catch here is that as soon as there is a departure from a diet of whole, natural food and, for example, a piece of fudge or two is taken or a bit of jam with bread, one is in trouble ... An immediate nutrient "debt" is incurred. In this case it is a "protein debt" ... And in the case of sugar and refined flour, a vitamin and mineral debt ... '
(Rudolph Ballentine, *Diet and Nutrition a holistic approach*)

This would need to be balanced with foods such as meat or eggs, fish or dairy products. Because few people would never depart from a diet of whole natural food, it is wise to make allowance for indulgences by building in such foods to one's balanced diet. Vegetable proteins can be balanced with respect to so-called 'reference protein' (the ideal proportions of the essential amino acids) by combining pulses with seeds or grains (and milk products if these are used). The ideal proportions for achieving complete protein are given in the diagram for complementing proteins. (The proportions for milk can be scaled down when cheese is used.)

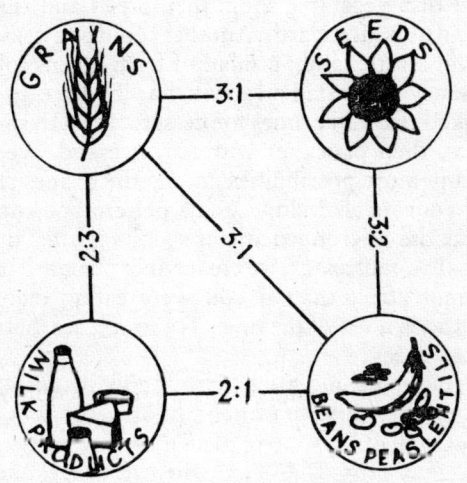

Complementing Proteins

Which foods should one eat?

The best general guidelines for thinking about the foods one should eat and how to construct one's daily diet are to say you will be having good balanced diet if

1. the bulk of your calories are coming from Beans, Pulses, Whole Grains and Potatoes,
2. Vegetables are added ad lib – as many different kinds as possible, preferably fresh and seasonal and some raw each day,
3. Meat, Fish, Eggs, Milk and Dairy Products (cheese, yogurt, cream) are taken in moderation and as flavouring, binding, sauce or topping to the staple,
4. Fruits, Seeds, Nuts are eaten for snacks or desserts,
5. and Herbs and Spices are used as healthy condiments (replacing synthetic flavourings or food additives). Sugar, if used as a spice, can be added to enhance some dishes.

(This suggested plan is recommended by Colin Tudge in *Future Cook – A Taste of Things to Come*, see Booklist page 234.) Many different patterns can be shaped from these ingredients. One meal might consist of a vegetable soup, then bread and cheese, with dried fruits and nuts afterwards. Another could be a couscous with chick peas and a little lamb, a salad of fresh greens followed by yogurt and honey; or a salad meal with hardboiled eggs or a pulse salad and baked rice and prunes for dessert. Try a fresh vegetable hors d'oeuvre, then pancakes with savoury and sweet fillings. There are many more possibilities among the recipes given here.

If most of your meals follow such a pattern you can be fairly confident that the micronutrients are looking after themselves. The occasional bought snack, ice cream or chocolate bar will have a very different effect than if you were eating manufactured convenience foods most of the time. Try to restrict these foods to once or twice a week.

These general guidelines are easy to follow. It saves having to calculate the usable grams of protein, calorie counts or having to delve into the detail of the sources of all the many nutrients needed for successful fetal growth. In fact, when you check out some of them, you find that they are well catered for by these rules of thumb.

GOOD FOOD FOR PREGNANCY

Broccoli, Brussels sprouts, cabbage, runner beans are all good sources of folate, pyridoxine (vitamin B6) and manganese; wholewheat flour is a good source of all these together with zinc and most of the other B vitamins. Vitamin B12, only found in animal foods and bacteria growing on some fungi and seaweeds or used in fermenting soya products such as miso, although required in tiny amounts, is in eggs (more in free range), milk and cheese, fish, kidney and liver. Needless to say, these foods are rich in many other valuable nutrients, including those already mentioned and lots of others. Nuts, seeds and leafy greens are rich in the essential fatty acids important for brain and nervous system development and many other functions. The pulses (peas, lentils and beans) provide many vitamins and minerals as well as protein. Root vegetables, fruits of all kinds, peanuts, potatoes, sweetcorn, mushrooms, onions, garlic and black pepper all add to the range of micronutrients needed in pregnancy as well as contributing to the diet in other ways. (See *Supplementary Chapters to Guidelines for Future Parents* from *Foresight* in the Address list, page 229 for more detail.)

Looking at other dietary recommendations about fat and fibre, we find these guidelines conform. To take more than half one's calories from vegetable sources (grains, pulses, potatoes and fresh vegetables – with a good proportion raw) would have to mean that the proportion of fat was between 25–30%, especially if it was coming from the fat in nuts and seeds, meat, eggs, milk products to a large extent. It would also be extremely difficult not to be getting adequate fibre on the diet recommended. Even an elevated protein requirement for pregnancy and breastfeeding would be easily met. Therefore it is safe to conclude that it would be healthy in all respects *and* good food for pregnancy.

At this point, however, one has to consider whether there are any foods which should be restricted in pregnancy.

Are there any foods to avoid?

There are some foods best excluded from a healthy diet for pregnancy, and some to be reduced to a minimum. These recommendations need to be added to the positive ones to ensure that certain risks are excluded as far as possible.

Any food containing additives which could be mutagenic (i.e.

would hinder or damage the DNA in the growing cells of the baby) is best avoided. Foods which may be contaminated through pollution of air or water with toxins such as heavy metals (lead, cadmium, mercury) or pesticides (DDT, 245-T, aldicarb etc) should also be left out. Alcohol, which can be harmful in itself, caffeine, if too much is taken, and sugar, which is unnecessary should be added to the list. Natural toxins from moulds and fungal growths on food, blight etc can also be harmful. The best thing is to eat only food which will decay and deteriorate, but eat it before it does. The longer the shelf life, the less the food value of a product – take a cue from the micro-organisms! Here are some more detailed warnings.

1. Bacon, ham, corned beef, sausages, salami, garlic sausage, all cured or pickled meats, patés, spreads etc most likely contain sodium nitrite as a preservative. This has mutagenic potential, particularly in conjunction with some fermented soya products.
2. Shellfish, seafoods such as prawns or crabmeat, tinned fish such as tuna, inland water fish and fish that feed near the shore are likely to contain heavy metals. Big fish may have larger quantities of cumulative poisons, being higher on the food chain. (They eat smaller fish, who eat plankton, and so on down the line, all of which may carry a dose if the water is polluted.)
3. Liver and kidney, though full of valuable 'friendly' minerals (and therefore often recommended to be taken frequently in pregnancy) are nevertheless the part of an animal's body where waste toxic substances accumulate, waiting to be excreted. Animals who feed close to busy roads may well get too much lead into their systems. Sheep are more likely to graze on marginal land further from roads, such as hillsides. Does the good outweigh the danger of lead in liver? Some think so, others would say not. A middle course might be to eat an occasional lamb's liver or kidney once every three weeks.
4. Foods containing colour dyes are best excluded. An official committee has recommended that dyes should not be added to baby foods. This recommendation should apply with greater force to the more sensitive fetus. Look at the label of any

manufactured food to see if a 'permitted' colour is present (now usually given its EEC standardised code number, e.g. E102 for tartrazine). Even some 'natural' foods may be dyed. The skins of citrus fruits usually dyed and coated with mineral oil. Egg yolks are sometimes coloured from a dye added to the feed of battery hens.

5 All food additives are best avoided where possible. Although they are said to be 'safe', the method of testing them takes each one singly, whereas there could be effects that take place when they are in combination with one another. Even if they are not positively harmful, food additives are likely to use up valuable nutrients in the body's effort to get rid of them. They are also likely to be in foods which have already been depleted of the nutrients needed. Highly processed manufactured foods are therefore best kept to a minimum.

The *Hyperactive Children's Support Group* (see Address list, page 230) will supply a list of foods free of additives, including colour dyes.

6 Artificial sweeteners such as saccharin or aspartame are best avoided. These are found in low calorie or 'diet' sweet foods and drinks, or as sweeteners to add to hot drinks.

7 Sugar, especially white sugar, is an unnecessary 'additive' to a healthy diet. It also uses up good things as the body metabolises it, such as your B vitamins, so lowering your immune status, if the supply of these is limited. This could leave your baby more prone to infections and allergy as a result, or even cancer. Sugar is not harmless 'empty calories' but a definite minus to the system. This is apart from any effects on the teeth, on obesity and on the good foods it displaces in the day's calories which may prevent you taking sufficient dietary fibre, vitamins and minerals.

Try to restrict your sugar intake to 25g/1oz a day (or less), including hidden sugar in manufactured foods. Read the labels: sugar is not just found in jam, biscuits, ice cream, but also tomato ketchup, baked beans, chutneys, tinned soup and in many other places where you might not expect it!

8 Alcohol should be high on the list of things to avoid in the period of preparation for pregnancy (for both man and woman) and during pregnancy (for the mother). It affects the reproductive system of men as well as of women and can

reduce fertility (see p. 220). This is unfortunate if it has become part of your lifestyle. Remember it is still good to cut down even if you cannot cut it out completely. There are many ways you can help yourself do this in the section on drinks, (see also p. 188).

You may begin to wonder whether you are going to be able to carry out all this advice. Perhaps the diet sketched looks very different from the way you have been eating. Well, you can only start from where you are! *Any* improvement is an improvement and well worth it. If you try the different things suggested here, your own tastes will guide you, and gradually your movement for change will gather its own momentum. It is much better to grow to like healthy food gradually. Do not expect to convert your diet radically overnight. It would be unkind to your body; your system needs time to adjust.

Pregnancy, in particular, is a time when you suddenly get a taste for different things (occasionally quite funny fads, but usually sensible fancies). Here are lots of good things to choose – experiment with new recipes, have fun and may your baby benefit!

Anyone already acquainted with *Growing Up With Good Food* will see that this is a more radical book. If you are just beginning to think about a more healthy diet you may find it useful to use recipes from that book together with those here. The following section is written to show how it is perfectly possible to make up recipes using part white flour, pasta or rice. Just do what you feel happy with. It is important to enjoy your food too.

There are also ideas in the section, on page 215, entitled Not Just Nutrition, on other health tips which are worth considering as you prepare for pregnancy. Possibly some of them will provide a more acceptable starting point. Later you can turn back to the question of food.

You may feel you need the incentive of actually being pregnant to help you make any improvements in your lifestyle. Although it is obviously better to start sooner rather than later, it is never too late to begin. The time when you are introducing a mixed diet to your baby may be the first occasion you really look at the food you eat.

Making the Transition to Wholefoods

A daily menu based on the principles already given might look like this.

Breakfast: orange or grapefruit or fruit juice
muesli or porridge or wheatflakes with milk or yogurt
a slice of wholewheat toast with peanut butter or sesame or sunflower spread, sugarless jam or yeast extract spread (Marmite, Barmene etc)

Lunch: corn on the cob, wholewheat roll, fresh fruit
a fresh salad and a staple salad
a jacket potato with cheese or cream cheese and chives,
a green leaf salad, dried figs or apricots
a vegetable soup and wholewheat roll, nuts and seeds or fresh fruit
a wholewheat sandwich with cheese or egg and salad,
fresh or dried fruit

Dinner: Stir-fried rice with beans or meat, other vegetables not used in stir-fry in a raw salad with seeds or nuts
vegetable soup, meat or fish with potatoes and a green salad
pasta with cheese or egg (if not already taken) and a salad
bean or meat casserole with rice or potatoes and salad

Snacks: fresh or dried fruit (to make up 3 pieces a day), carrot or celery sticks, nuts or seeds (to make up 25g/1oz a day), wholewheat bread with spreads as for breakfast (count peanut butter or seed spreads as part of daily allowance), a glass of milk, cottage cheese or cheese (to make up 25g/1oz a day) — wholewheat biscuits, scones, cakes etc (preferably low in fat and sugar), occasional carob bar, plain crisps, for a treat.

In pregnancy you should be taking in about 2000 calories a day (a little more as time goes on). This would be made up as follows:

800 from grains, beans and potatoes = 40% of daily calories
300 from vegetables (about 1kg/2lb a day) = 15%
500 from 1 helping meat or fish or egg (4–5 per week), 300ml/½ pint milk or yogurt and 25g/1oz cheese, 25g/1oz butter or cream (about 250g/½lb butter per week) = 25%
A vegan should take more from the beans, nuts and seeds, soya products such as tofu etc.
400 from fruit (3 pieces a day, fresh or dried), nuts and seeds (25g/1oz a day), 3 tablespoons seed oil (300ml/½pint per week) = 20%

As you can allow yourself a little more, choose your extra 100–500 calories from sugar, extra snacks, extra wholegrain products and the occasional treat.

Now the diet is set out in some detail, it may look even less like your daily menu. If you still eat white bread, white flour, chips, packet soups and so on, consider taking some supplements while gradually making the transition to wholefoods. Wheatgerm, brewer's yeast, kelp tablets, fish liver oil capsules would all enrich your diet with a good variety of necessary nutrients. Have liver or kidney once a fortnight instead of the suggested once in 3–4 weeks.

Here are some ideas on how to start introducing more wholefoods to your diet.

FLOUR

There are many differences between things made with white flour and those made with wholewheat flour beside the nutritional difference. Things look different, they taste different and the texture is different too. These aspects all contribute to the unfamiliarity of wholewheat baking for someone used to refined flour and all need respecting.

Start by using unbleached flour, then a tablespoon of wheatgerm added to your usual recipes. The wheatgerm is not as coarse nor as brown as the bran, yet it will be adding goodness. When, finally, you are used to wholewheat flour, there will be no special point in using wheatgerm as a separate product. But at first it can be a gentle way to start accustoming your palate to the new taste and your eye to the new look. Before long, you will be used to the nuttier flavour and could then use a little more, or start adding a small proportion of wholewheat flour to your pastry, bread, biscuits, pancakes or 'white' sauce. Gradually work up until you are using half and half.

If your family is resistant to this change, but you still want to persuade them, try using the wholewheat flour only in recipes where it will not be so apparent, say in gingerbread, chocolate cake, hazelnut cake or flan bases. Remember that things always taste better hot and fresh from the oven, especially bread!

RICE AND PASTA

When it comes to rice and pasta you can proceed with the same gradual approach. The brown rice will need to cook longer so start it off 10–15 minutes before adding the white rice. Use the proportions which are acceptable to you and those at your table. As you get used to speckled rice, you can go on increasing the proportion of brown, and enjoying the chewiness, which is very satisfying.

Spaghetti, macaroni, buckwheat pasta or other pastas can be treated similarly. Try a striped lasagne, layers of white, green and brown! If you find the wholewheat pasta needs longer cooking, start it off first, as before, but 5 minutes extra cooking should be enough.

THE POINT OF GRADUAL CHANGE

If you are starting from a completely refined diet, expect the change to take some months. Do not hurry on beyond the point where you feel comfortable. It could take two years before you are completely at home with your new diet. This is another reason to start early, before you are pregnant. Perhaps the main beneficiary will be your next baby!

Another reason to take things slowly is to let your body get used to new habits. The gut flora need to become accustomed to your new diet too. At first you may find that an increase in the fibre content of your food and added pulses makes some wind. There are remedies for this (ginger, coriander and cardamom all help, as does peppermint tea afterwards), but the long-term answer is to grow new gut flora, the ones that like digesting this sort of food for you. You will find they develop naturally.

SUGAR

It may be that the idea of reducing sugar appeals more than moving over to brown flour. If this is the case, then make sugar reduction your starting point.

On the other hand, any sweet-toothed initiates to the new diet may have great cravings for sweet things. Take that slowly too, by just using a little less on all the occasions you want sugar, whether on your breakfast cereal, in tea and coffee or in cakes and puddings. After a while, you may find you can remove your sugar bowl from the breakfast table and substitute a bowl of sultanas or raisins to go on your cereal, or use a sweeter cereal, such as crunchy granola as a topping. Some people like sugar in coffee but not in tea (or vice versa). In this case try to cut down to one a day of your sugared drink and take fruit juice, herb teas or carob drink on the other occasions (see Drinks, page 188).

Another way to reduce sugar if you normally have a pudding every day, is to alternate with fresh fruit, dried fruit and nuts or cheese and biscuits. A pudding every second day, may then slip down to twice a week with a fresh fruit salad using juice as a sweetener on the third day.

FAT

Another difference in the proposed diet, which could be a big difference, is that it probably contains considerably less fat. Here it is important to remember that the quality of the fat matters as well as the quantity. Perhaps a first step may be to get used to good butter (without added colour) and to cold-pressed seed oils. Cream need not be despised – it is no doubt better for you than synthetic toppings and packet custards. Make a sauce like custard from cornflour (and a little sugar, flavoured with vanilla or a piece of lemon rind) which will be free of colour and additives. Also try using plain yogurt or homemade egg custard on desserts.

If you are keen on fried foods and reluctant to give them up, try shallow frying instead of deep frying, or oven frying (works well with chips) or grilling fish and meat. Thick-cut chips absorb less fat per potato.

Another point to remember if you want to reduce your fat consumption is that there is a lot of fat in foods such as cheese, oily fish, nuts and meat (even lean meat). Cutting down on these while you are still having fried food would help. In general, it is better to get fat from foods such as these rather than from the butter dish. Other fatty foods such as pastry, especially flaky pastry, bacon (on the elimination list for other reasons), sausages, crisps, salad cream, cream crackers, ice cream and chocolate can all be left out of one's diet quite safely, provided you are happy about it, or just cut down if this list includes some firm favourites.

As with the other changes you are considering, let yourself in gently to new ways of cooking and eating. In this way, the new habits are likely to stay with you. Remember too, that the fats which are the most valuable in pregnancy are the essential fatty acids found in leaves, nuts and seeds and in 'long chain derivatives' in liver, organ meats especially brain, and other meats and fish. Honeycomb contains 'long chain' waxes which, like vitamin E, stabilise the polyunsaturated compounds.

MEAT

Meat is a costly item in many food budgets. Maybe you could reduce the amount you eat, supplying more pulses and wholegrain staples to fill the gap. Many meats are not well-raised, and the hormones or antibiotics given to the animals are no good for you. All processed meats are best kept to a minimum in pregnancy, so there could be a real health advantage as well as a

MAKING THE TRANSITION TO WHOLEFOODS

financial one in eating less meat. Just one roasting joint or chicken per week (and eating smaller portions should leave enough for a cold meal), one stew, casserole, curry or mince dish (with less meat, filling it out with beans or lentils), and a fish or liver meal once a week, would be plenty of meat. Instead of having something cheap like sausages (or whatever) for other meals, try a vegetarian meal or one based on eggs or cheese (such as a flan), which could well work out even cheaper. There are lots of suggestions among the recipes for such dishes, see also Cooking With Meat page 86.

MANUFACTURED FOODS

The person with very conservative tastes who not only prefers manufactured foods, but even particular brands, may find the idea of any change particularly daunting.

Assuming such a person is at least partly convinced that there may be some advantage in healthier food, then look for the things already being eaten that are healthier, and increase those at the expense of some less healthy items. Perhaps it is tomatoes or apples or other 'straight' fruits or vegetables. Perhaps traditionally-made cheese is really preferred but processed is found more convenient. Maybe fresh juices are liked but you have squash because you find it cheaper. Everybody's preferences will be different, so you will have to find for yourself the points at which you, and those in your household, can make contact with the good ordinary foods. The whole pattern of your eating is bound up with likes and dislikes, often compromised to fit in with other members of the family, as well as many other factors such as convenience and cost. You may not be particularly interested in which things are good for you and which not. Such an interest may appear to have some unwelcome consequences! You will have to weigh the whole thing up and make your own decision about it. Look again at the comments on additives (on page 16-17).

Very few people eat only wholefoods. Most of us, even those committed to the wholefood idea, do use some processed foods, have takeaway meals on occasion or ice creams, even if only on holiday, and eat what other people provide in their houses. To cut these things out altogether is quite unacceptable to most people. It is really a question of the amount of these foods you consume on average. See what proportion they form in your diet as a whole.

CHOOSING MANUFACTURED FOODS

★ Pick those with fewest additives (preferably none!). Ingredients are listed on the label in descending order of weight. Notice how many, even savoury foods, contain sugar!
★ Some processing is better than others. For example, frozen foods may have less done to them than tinned; tinned may be less processed and have fewer additives than dried food in packets. In general, the more processed and the longer the shelf life, the less the food value of the product.

IMPROVING THEM

★ See if you can add some fresh ingredients as you make up packet foods. Add some grated carrot or chopped herbs to a soup. Extend a packet burger with your own ground nuts, mashed cooked beans or cooked rice, oatmeal or such like.
★ Use stored vegetable water or stock to make up a sauce or soup.
★ You may find that you can use some things in weaker concentrations than suggested, for example, stock cubes could be halved, or the amount of water increased.

BALANCING THE MEAL

If your meal is going to have as its main course a takeaway or tin, then think about what goes with it.

★ Serve it with your own brown rice or wholemeal pasta.
★ Make a fresh green salad or even add just some cress or grated carrot at the side.
★ For dessert why not a piece of fresh fruit or a quick simple fruit salad?

★ If you keep in mind that the things likely to be lacking in convenience foods are the vitamins, minerals and fibre, you will find ways of adding fresh, raw and wholefoods to your meal.

A NOTE ON COSTS

Many manufactured foods are expensive. A change from, say, bottled fizzy drinks to pure juice may not be as costly as you imagine. Some people regard fresh fruit as expensive. So are sweets, chocolate and bought desserts, including fruit yogurts. Were you to replace such snacks or desserts with fresh fruit you would probably not be paying more – it could be quite a lot less. But the value per calorie would be much greater in nutritional terms. As already mentioned, replacing some of the meat you eat with pulses also has a cost advantage.

ORGANICALLY GROWN

The same goes for organically grown food. It is well worth the extra money in terms of food value. It is not always easy to obtain. Indeed, it is only recently that the big chains of supermarkets have been stocking wholemeal bread and flour, brown rice and wholewheat pasta. Asking for it to be organically grown too may seem to be asking too much! Cigarettes and alcohol are expensive indulgences too. If you are able to cut these out, or to cut down your consumption, convert the money into real value for yourself, and, when you have the choice, take the organically grown product or the free range eggs.

INTERESTING EXERCISES

It could be an interesting exercise for you to keep a note of your expenses on food as you make a transition to a more wholefood diet. There will be a good deal of balancing out but many people find they end up spending less overall. You could form a buying co-op with friends and neighbours if you are able to get bulk supplies from a wholesale merchant. This would be another way to cut costs.

Another interesting experiment might be to segregate your rubbish. Collect paper, tins and bottles, fruit and vegetable waste (for garden compost possibly) separately. Notice how the proportions change. You were paying for all those packets and tins! It is likely you will end up with less to throw away.

Finally, expect there to be ups and downs in your progress. Some of your experiments will fail. Don't be discouraged! If you can work out what it was that went wrong, you can do it a different way next time, or simply turn to something else to try. Get ideas from friends, magazines or books on how to use up the rest of whatever your family did not like the first time you served it. There are so many approaches. Only you can find the right one for your family. Every little improvement is worth it. Keep enjoying your food – it helps digestion!

Good Food for Breastfeeding

A new mother needs mothering. If there are people about you who can do this for you, so much the better. You will find it easier to give the mothering your baby needs to him or her. Breastfeeding is one of the most enjoyable ways of doing this in the early days (and later) for both mother and baby. Cuddling, looking at each other, plenty of skin-to-skin contact are also mutually rewarding for the baby with either parent. Should you lack someone who can mother you, then pamper yourself as much as you can, with no guilt: this is doing the best for your baby. Stay in bed, rest, play with the baby, listen to music, indulge yourself with delicious snacks. Your pleasure in the early days with your new baby is something too important to miss and really worth fostering.

Before the birth
Your good diet will help build up the reserves you need for breastfeeding. Fat is laid down in the latter months by both mother and baby in preparation for the post-partum period.

Fresh air and sunshine on the nipples helps to strengthen the skin and will be the best way to prevent sore nipples when the baby starts suckling. Although it is important to wash well, too much soap can interfere with the natural oils produced in the areola around the nipple. Rolling the nipple between finger and thumb can help stimulate the production of the natural oils. You can rub in a little seed oil or calendula or chamomile cream, and these are good things to use afterwards if the area becomes tender, and fresh air alone does not work.

After the birth
Even if you are not intending to breastfeed for very long, it is worth letting the baby have the colostrum produced in the first days before the milk comes in. This more watery-looking sub-

stance is the most beneficial first food for the baby, containing, apart from all the important nutrients it needs, in the right proportions, valuable antibodies which line the gut and protect against adverse allergic reactions later, and against infections. It helps prepare the baby's digestive processes for the task they have not yet undertaken of assimilating food through the digestive tract, since it has been fed through the umbilical cord until birth.

Breastfeeding stimulates the hormones which make the uterus contract back to its former size. It also helps get your figure back by using up the deposition of fat laid down for the purpose. You need to continue eating well, as in pregnancy, for the baby will require between 600–800 calories a day. The balance of nutrients is fairly similar to those of pregnancy, with just a little more zinc, a little more vitamin A and C, some of the B vitamins (riboflavin and niacin) and iodine. The baby's biological tasks are slightly different now. For example, in terms of growth the brain was completed 70% before birth. The remaining 30% is only a small part of the brain's post-natal development, which mainly consists in making connections between all the neurones (brain and nerve cells), each being capable of 10,000 connections! The composition of the breastmilk reflects these biological needs. Two-thirds of brain matter consists of structural fat, for which the essential fatty acids, linoleic (found in seeds) and linolenic (found in green leaves) and the 'long chain derivatives' of these polyunsaturates in animal foods such as fish and meat, are needed.

What to eat

The diet sketched for pregnancy should adequately meet these needs. Perhaps you could increase the allowance of nuts and seeds, and have fish a little more frequently (if you eat it), but otherwise the wholegrains, leafy greens and all the other vegetables and sea vegetable, the pulses, soya products, eggs and dairy products, meat and fruit will all give you the right things. Notice if your baby seems unsettled or has an unusual dirty nappy after you have eaten some new seasonal fruit (such as strawberries), or something spicy or unusual for you. Discontinue the food for the time being, if you can identify it, and re-introduce it later, just as you would when weaning the baby. Tastes pass through into the breastmilk, and this is one way the baby becomes familiar with ordinary food, and why it will make weaning easier if the food you eat is good food your baby can share when mixed feeding begins (after six months or so).

Should you have any reason to suspect an allergy in the baby, such as to cow's milk, look at the section on this topic, on pages 202–5. The ideas there on Instant Nourishment for a Breastfeeding Mother, may be useful in any event.

What to drink

You are likely to feel thirstier than usual when breastfeeding. Water is a good drink, bottled or filtered if you worry about the possible lead content, and many other healthy drinks are given in the section on Drinks, page 188.

Have a drink beside you while you are feeding the baby; it can relax you as well as supplying your needs. Fresh whole milk is an excellent 'instant' food for those who can take it. But there is no special need to drink milk, unless you like it. Your body can make good breastmilk from all the other components of your diet.

Any problems?

It is usually reassuring to talk with someone about any problems that arise, although there are many good books on breastfeeding which may well provide an answer to your query. Some are to be found in the booklist. There are also many useful leaflets provided by the *National Childbirth Trust* and *La Leche League* or the *Association of Breastfeeding Mothers* (equivalents exist in most countries). Addresses are given on page 229–30. The NCT (and some other organisations) also train breastfeeding counsellors who are happy to be telephoned about any problems, and usually able to visit you at home too, to give practical advice, help and support whenever it is needed.

Breakfasts and Breads

Breakfast is a good place for the whole grain cereals in your diet. These can be eaten as breakfast cereals or as bread. Fruits, nuts and seeds can all be added together with various dairy products including milk, yogurt, cheese and eggs.

If you have been in the habit of skipping breakfast or just grabbing something quick on your way out, now is the time to think again about the role the first meal of the day should play.

Spacing the day's calories out evenly could be a first step. It is better for you to consume them before you use them, than to take in the bulk of your calories at the end of the day and then store them. The last meal should really be the lightest and it is good to finish eating at least three hours before sleeping. This will give you a good appetite at breakfast time.

Getting up in time for a leisurely breakfast may also seem a problem. Perhaps adjustments in your meal pattern will help. But if you have a long way to travel to work, or for some other reason this is not feasible, you will have to work out the best compromise. In any case it is a good idea to be up and about for an hour or so before eating breakfast. Perhaps you could take a packed breakfast to work with you. (A carton of muesli and a carton of yogurt or milk and a piece of fruit would travel well. More suggestions follow in this section.)

Wholegrains, nuts and dried fruits are a good idea because the energy is released slowly as they are digested, sustaining you through to the next meal. The range of B vitamins (including folate) and minerals and trace elements they supply mean they should play a significant part in one's daily food.

Of the seven grains: wheat, oats, rye, barley, millet, rice and maize, the first two are easiest to accommodate in breakfast menus. The others (possibly excluding maize) can all be used in muesli and other ways.

WHOLEGRAINS FOR BREAKFAST

WHEAT

Wheat is a most nutritious grain, especially when organically grown and the whole grain is used. Only those suffering from gluten allergy need to exclude wheat (see p. 201). However, since wheatflour is used widely in manufactured foods as thickeners, cereal in sausages and other prepared meat products, in sauces, and as a base in such things as mustard and monosodium glutamate, it is no doubt a good idea to take an opportunity to vary the grains eaten. Breakfast offers the chance to sample other grains such as oats, or rye or a mixture in muesli or granola.

CEREALS

Now that people are more conscious of the value of dietary fibre, manufacturers are offering more variety in whole grain cereals. Those using wheat are the most numerous. Generally speaking, the less it looks like a wheat grain, the more processed the cereal will be and the lower the food value. Sometimes a sort of porridge is made, then extruded into shapes and baked. Much more has happened to those wheat grains than simply being rolled into flakes.

There is plenty of bran, left over from all the white bread on the market, which manufacturers find ways of using. Extra bran is not needed if wholegrain products are used. Too much can cause loss of minerals in the digestive tract, both chemically and mechanically, as it hastens the passage of food through. So just use it occasionally, if at all, when suffering from constipation (see page 209–10).

BREAD

Bread is an obvious way to use wholewheat flour at breakfast, as it is delicious toasted. For a topping there is honey and marmalade (look for no-sugar kinds) for a sweet flavour, or yeast extract spreads (Marmite, Barmene – a brand which contains vitamin B12), peanut butter, sesame or sunflower spread (combining a seed spread with peanut butter complements the protein) or cheese.

Hot, freshly baked rolls or muffins are a special treat. You could also make pancakes for a change at weekends or on holidays.

WHEAT BERRIES

Here are two ways of eating the whole wheat berries or grains themselves.

MF* FRUMENTY

This traditional porridge comes from the days of ranges kept in all night. It should cook at least 8–10 hours.

After dinner take a cup of wheat grains and soak them for two or three hours. Before going to bed, bring them to the boil in three cups of water and add some raisins. Place in an ovenproof casserole, cover and leave to bake slowly in the oven at 200°/gas mark ½/130°C. When all the water has been absorbed by morning the grains will be swollen and creamy inside.* Treat yourself to a little top of the milk poured over them, or puréed or fresh fruit.

MF VEG SPROUTED WHEAT

Eating sprouted wheat for breakfast will really exercise your jaw! A dentist recommended it.

Soak the wheat grains in water for a few hours. Drain, rinse the grains in fresh water. Place in a glass jar with some muslin held over the top with a rubber band. Find a warm, dark place for it. Rinse with fresh water two or three times a day until you see the sprout just beginning to appear. Your sprouted wheat is ready. Use or store in a refrigerator. When the shoot is longer the grain tastes sweet and rather odd. If this happens a change of plan can save it. Lay some kitchen towels folded over several times on a flat dish or in a cress container, or put pieces of cotton wool in one half of an egg container. Moisten the water-holding medium and scatter your grains over it close together but not on top of each other. Let the shoots grow at least an inch, but not more than about three inches (7cm) in the light. Cut them to mix in with green salads or for a garnish on soups. Children will be amazed to see so much grow out of the little seeds. This will help them understand why there is so much goodness in grains.

Try eating the grain sprouts with grated apple and orange juice, or add to your usual breakfast cereal.

OATS

Oats are recommended as good for the nerves and as a tonic when you lack strength and energy. Smaller flakes are made for porridge, the jumbo flakes are used in muesli. Oatmeal can be added to bread for a tasty loaf with a pleasant texture. Instant rolled oats have been subjected to greater heat in the processing with consequent nutrient loss.

MF* VEG*   **PORRIDGE**

For two small helpings or one generous serving, take one cup of cold water

½ cup rolled porridge oats (increasing quantities in this proportion for more people)

optional additions include,
a little salt
a handful of raisins, currants or sultanas
other flakes can be used to replace some of the oats; try barley, rye, millet or wheat flakes or mixed muesli base.

Place the cold water in a heavy based pan and sprinkle the oats in and stir. Bring to the boil slowly, stirring occasionally, and simmer on a low heat for 5 minutes.

Should you need to reheat the porridge, add a little milk. It mixes in better than water.

Some like a teaspoon of muscovado sugar served with it, but the raisins should be a sufficient sweetener. Many like porridge simply because it is not too sweet. Instead of salt you could try roast crushed seaweeds or gomasio (toasted ground sesame seeds mixed with sea salt, anything from 10–20 parts seeds to 1 of salt, depending on taste).

Many like porridge served with milk. *Alternatives are almond milk or cream see p. 192 soya milk, or simply make the porridge creamy by soaking the flakes overnight and cooking for 15–20 minutes in more water.

MF* VEG*   **BIRCHER MUESLI**

Dr Bircher-Benner, who discovered the muesli made by Swiss shepherds, recommended a simple mixture using only oats. At his clinic (now run by his descendants) it is served twice daily. One does not tire of the less elaborate recipe, they say. (See Ruth Bircher, *Eating Your Way to Health*, *The Bircher-Benner Health Guide*, in the Booklist, page 232.)

Per serving: 1 tablespoon rolled oats or medium oatmeal soaked for 12 hours in 3 tablespoons water,
1 tablespoon lemon juice

1 grated apple
1 tablespoon condensed milk* or 1 tablespoon honey with yogurt*
1 tablespoon nut cream or grated hazelnuts or almonds

In summer you can substitute plums, apricots or berry fruits for the apple.

Mix ingredients together and top with the grated nuts. The use of condensed milk may seem odd, but it is something to remember when camping. Using less lemon juice would reduce the need for an added sweetener.

MF* VEG*   **OTHER MUESLIS**

Oats are still the base for other mueslis. You can make your own from muesli base bought at wholefood shops, or even make your own base using the proportion of different cereal flakes you like. It can be a new mix each time. If buying a commercial muesli, look at the quantity of sugar added. You can dilute it by adding up to equal quantities of porridge oats or porridge oats mixed with jumbo oats. It may still taste too sweet!

In a large storage jar or airtight plastic box put your oats up to half way. These can be all jumbo flakes or part porridge oats. A third of oats may be enough if you have many other flakes. Mix with other cereal flakes, barley, rye, millet or wheat, up to three-quarters full, or more.

Add some dried fruit both vine fruit (currants, sultanas, raisins) and tree fruit (dried chopped apricots, figs, dates, peaches, pears), a cupful all told should be enough.

Add two or three tablespoons of crunchy seeds or millet pearls, (sunflower, sesame or pumpkin seeds are all suitable).

And half a cup or so of nuts. Whole hazelnuts and almonds can be used, or chop them if you prefer, also walnuts, Brazils, cashews and a little desiccated coconut if liked.

Other variations include adding toasted flakes or nuts, or some crunchy granola. You could keep these separate to add when serving.

Grain flakes should be well chewed. This aids digestion and gives good exercise to teeth and jaws (one of the reasons this is such a satisfying breakfast). If you find the muesli too chewy, you can soak it overnight in milk or water, or simply add the milk 15 minutes before eating it. Another way is to pour some boiling water over it, just enough for it to be all absorbed in about 10 minutes and serve with yogurt or top of the milk, or nut milks (page 192).*

As can be seen, this recipe is extremely flexible. Part of the fun is finding new variations. So just use what you have and do not worry if all the ingredients suggested are not to hand.

MF VEG   **GRANOLA**

Here, too, great variety is possible. The difference between granola and muesli lies in the toasting. Remember that there is always loss of nutrients with heat, so just use this as a topping to muesli or other breakfast cereals. It is nice to nibble for a snack too. You can also serve it as a topping to fresh or stewed fruit or other desserts.

Start with about 3–4 cups rolled oats or 3 of oats and 1 cup of another grain flake
1 cup wheatgerm, wholewheat flour or soya flour
½–1 cup sesame or sunflower seeds
½–1 cup chopped almonds, walnuts, hazelnuts, Brazils, or cashews
½ cup coconut (if liked)
Spices can be added for variation, try cinnamon or for chocolate flavour you could add ½ cup carob powder

Mix together ½ cup water and ½ cup seed oil, adding, if you wish 1–2 tablespoons honey and flavouring it with vanilla (optional).

At the end of baking some sultanas or chopped dried fruit can be added.

Spread the dry ingredients out in a baking tray and pour over the mixed water and oil (with honey or vanilla mixed in). Bake in a slow oven at 300°/gas mark 2 for an hour, turning the mixture from time to time. Alternatively, start at 350°F/gas mark 4/180°C to brown for 15 minutes and then turn down to 225°F/gas mark ½/120°C for the rest of the time. Allow to cool and store in an airtight container.

RYE AND OTHER GRAINS

Rye flour, barley flour, millet flakes or pearls and cooked rice can all be added to bread (see pages 53–5). One uses maize flour for coating muffins. Pancakes can be made with part barley flour, or buckwheat flour. (Although buckwheat is not a true grain, botanically speaking, it behaves like one from the culinary point of view.) Soya flour can also be added for extra protein or in place of an egg.

GF Corn on the cob is another idea to try.

Rye bread keeps well and is usually easy to cut finely. Use it or rye crackers to try a Scandinavian breakfast for a change.

SCANDINAVIAN BREAKFAST

On your slice of rye bread or rye cracker place thinly sliced Dutch or mild Cheddar cheese and top with slices of tomato or cucumber. You could serve slices of hardboiled egg for a change.

This would make a good packed breakfast. In Scandinavia the traditional accompaniment would be a glass of milk and a cup of black coffee. If you are not drinking coffee just omit that part — authenticity on this point is not compulsory!

FRUIT AT BREAKFAST

GF MF VEG   **JUICE**

A glass of juice is refreshing in the morning and a good place to add vitamin C powder if you are taking a supplement. (It is best to take it occasionally when you feel low or can sense a cold coming on, rather than taking it habitually.)

Juice can be squeezed freshly from oranges or grapefruit (though why not eat the fruit and get the roughage too?). It is also conveniently available in cartons and bottles. Clear glass will let light in which can cause vitamins to deteriorate, but it is a very inert substance which will not be affected by the acid content of the juice. Juice in cartons is usually heated to sterilise it without additives. Frozen may have the best vitamin content after fresh. As usual one has to weigh up different snags and benefits when deciding what to choose. Vegetable juices can provide a change from fruit juice.

GF MF VEG   **FRESH FRUIT**

Fresh fruit is a good addition to most beakfasts. You can eat it on its own, with cereals or yogurt. Apple is easily grated. Rub the skin clean (some pesticides are potentiated by water!) and grate the apple, skin and all. Peaches are delicious and other seasonal fruit all add variety. Bananas make a substantial course in breakfast and go well with cereals.

GF MF VEG   **COMPOTE OF FRUIT**

Stewed fruit makes a change and is a way of using windfalls and fruit unsuitable for raw use. Dried prunes, apricots, peaches and pears are nutritious and delicious stewed too. Soak for a while before stewing and you will not need to cook them so long.

DAIRY PRODUCTS

Milk, yogurt and cheese from either cows or goats all have a place at breakfast. The calcium (together with that in dried fruits, nuts and seeds) is necessary for stores before pregnancy, for the bones and teeth of the baby during pregnancy, and later if you breastfeed. It is also likely to protect one from assimilating too much lead. Vitamin C and protein also play this protective role. If you suspect an allergy to cow's milk, and if goat's milk is no better, there are other substitutes (see below). Eggs are a part of the traditional cooked breakfast. They can also be used hardboiled. It may be some time since you had cooked breakfasts, and it may not appeal at all. But it is a way of ringing the changes, especially if you do not particularly like cereals.

GF   **MILK**

Untreated milk (from a brucellosis-accredited herd) has undoubtedly the best food value. Most people use pasteurised milk but there may be a trend towards sterilised and ultra-heat treated milk as more comes on the market. It suits manufacturers and distributors to deal in longer life milk. You can choose what seems best to you. Goat's milk for a baby should be scalded as its production is not supervised in the same way as cow's milk.

GF   **YOGURT**

There is a recipe on pp. 131–2. It is easy to make your own and is much cheaper. When buying fruit yogurts look for those flavoured with fruit alone and without colour, sugar or preservatives. You can eat it on its own, with cereals, fresh, dried or stewed fruit. If you find a place where you can get goat's milk it will probably sell goat's yogurt too.

GF*	CHEESE

The lactose in both cheese and yogurt is converted into lactic acid, which makes it easier to digest for many people. 'Cooked' cheese like Edam, Gruyère etc tends to be higher in salt. For vegetarians there are rennet-free cheeses, which tend to be milder, but will be well made. Goat's cheese tends to be more crumbly. Hot cheese is said to be less digestible, but many people like cheese cooked on toast.* If you are making it for a few people you can grate it into a beaten egg and make a version of Welsh rarebit.

MF GF*	EGGS

Free range eggs give better food value, including more vitamin B12 (which is important for vegetarians). It is worth finding a source of good eggs, even if you cannot go there all the time. Do not be misled by signs such as 'Fresh Farm Eggs' (it may be a battery farm!), but ask if the hens are free range or 'deep litter' – the next best thing.

For breakfast (or other meals) they may be served with toast (or gluten-free bread*) boiled, poached, fried, baked in ramekins in the oven, scrambled or made into an omelette. However you cook them, do not overcook them. If you do not cook them, as for use in egg flips etc, then just place the egg for 30 seconds in boiling water. This will prevent the avidin in the white from counteracting the valuable biotin in the yolk, but it will not coagulate the white. You can whizz it up with orange juice* or milk for a nutritious drink which should be easy to take.

MILK SUBSTITUTES

MF GF VEG	SOYA MILK

There are several brands of soya milk easily available at health and wholefood shops, or sections of supermarkets. It is less easy to find one which does not contain added sugar. A Chinese or

Japanese delicatessen might be the place to look, if the brand you are using is too sweet. Broadly speaking, you can use soya milk as you would cow's milk, but it will taste different.

MF GF VEG   ALMOND, HAZELNUT OR OTHER NUT MILKS

These are easy to make at home if you have a blender. The recipe is given on page 192. Nut milks go well with cereals, but not for adding to tea or coffee. It would be better to drink juice or lemon or herb teas if you are on a milk-free diet. Carob may suit a coffee habitué.

MF GF VEG   FRUIT JUICE

An acceptable substitute for milk with cereals may be found in orange juice or other juices. Find the combinations you like, for not all juices will be best with all cereals.

PACKED BREAKFASTS

Here are a few ideas of a breakfast that could be taken to work.

MF* VEG* GF*   1. Some crunchy granola in a container, an orange and a sandwich.*

2. Some muesli in a container with a lid from which you can eat, a carton of yogurt or milk and a piece of fruit.

MF*   3. A hardboiled egg, a bread and butter* sandwich or roll and a piece of fruit.

VEG   4. A carton of fruit juice and some oatcakes or rye crackers and honey or ginger marmalade (if you are feeling a bit sick).

GF   5. Some yogurt and honey in a container. If you are able to heat water, you could take a sachet of herb tea such as chamomile.

BREAKFAST WHEN SUFFERING FROM PREGNANCY SICKNESS

On the 'little and often' principle, divide your breakfast into several courses and do something in between each course. Your morning could go like this:

On waking before you get up have a drink of juice, chamomile or ginger tea (see page 193). It could be made the night before and be ready by the bed, as it is perfectly nice cold. Perhaps someone would make you hot tea or herb tea if that seems better. Try to eat a digestive biscuit or an oatcake.

After getting up and perhaps dressing, about half to one hour later, you could have another drink of juice, chamomile or ginger tea, or ordinary weak tea, possibly varying it from the first drink, with some toast and honey or ginger marmalade (if you find ginger helps).

About an hour later, after reading the paper, going to work, taking the children to school or doing some household job, any of the following might be taken: a piece of fruit, some stewed apple, pear or prunes, a yogurt and honey or some thin porridge, or one of the last two packed breakfast suggestions.

Breads

Those new to bread making should read these notes before trying any of the recipes.

The explanations are designed to help you understand the processes at work, so you can soon get a 'feel' for bread making.

Any attempts which are not crowned with success are bound to be discouraging. Do not be put off making bread. Everyone has failures sometimes. The difference between you and someone with more experience is that the experienced cook knows how to correct mistakes! If you cannot work out for yourself what went wrong, ask a friend who bakes or read a good book, such as Elizabeth David's *English Bread and Yeast Cookery*, see Booklist, page 232.

An introduction to making brown yeast-risen bread and sour dough bread is offered in *Growing Up With Good Food*. Here you will find ways of varying these basic loaves.

NOTES ON INGREDIENTS AND METHODS

Ingredients

The minimum ingredients for a bread dough are flour, water and yeast. In a moist and warm environment, the yeast feeds on the starch in the flour, and in the process carbon dioxide gas is released and some alcohol is formed – this is the process of fermentation. In bread-making the important product of fermentation is the gas, which expands in pockets formed by the gluten, which swell and cause the whole dough to increase in volume and so to rise. The small quantity of alcohol produced boils away in the oven when the dough is baked.

Flour

Where the kind of flour is not specified in the recipe, you may use anything from all white ('unbleached' flour if you can get it) to all wholewheat. ('Strong' flour is preferred for bread. It is made from wheat higher in gluten, and it is gluten that makes up the structure of the loaf.) If you are used to white bread, but wish to make wholewheat bread to improve your diet, it is quite a good idea to change the mixture gradually from (say) one third wholewheat flour, over a matter of weeks, towards wholewheat.

Differences between home-made and commercial bread
Home-made bread will not rise as much as most commercial bread because the latter is made (in the UK) by the industrial 'Chorleywood' process which (as they say) 'makes water stand up'. Extra gluten may also be added to factory-made wholewheat bread. So if you are new to home-baking, you may wish to get used progressively to the denser texture. Loaves made with wholewheat flour rise less and are denser than loaves made with strong white bread flour because the wholewheat flour is (with rare exceptions) lower in the gluten that makes the rise possible, and because the flour contains other (nutritious) solid matter that breaks up the gluten strands.

Handling different doughs
If you make in succession doughs with white and with wholewheat flour you will find that that they handle very differently as you mix and knead them. Wholewheat dough is less smooth – by comparison, white feels almost silky – and does not become as springy as a well-kneaded white dough. In fact a dough with more than half wholewheat flour can be 'handled' a lot less – kneaded lightly and put straight into tins for a first and only proving (see below), whereas a white flour dough will develop a finer texture and a bigger rise if it is proved twice, once in the bowl and once in the tin (or on the baking sheet).

Keeping qualities
Another important difference between white and wholewheat flour is in storage. Wholewheat flour should be used quickly after purchase (we are not the only creatures to appreciate the extra nutrition it contains). Within two months is a generally safe guide. It is best to buy it in small quantities and use it within days. Very fresh wholewheat flour – within a couple of hours of milling – contains volatile oils that otherwise escape into the atmosphere,

and bread made from it has an even better flavour and does not dry out as quickly. So if you are able to find a source of fresh-milled flour, cultivate it; and use the flour as soon as you get it home if you can. (Electric stone-grinding flour mills can be bought for home use, and grain, unlike the flour milled from it, stores well for months.)

Not only do you capture the valuable volatile oils, but those which would remain have no chance to go rancid.

Different flours on the market

Strong white bread flour, unbleached white flour are 70% extraction (the wheatgerm and the bran are both removed).

Wheatmeal or brown flour is around 81–85% extraction. The packet may tell you if it is made from 'hard', 'durum' or 'strong' wheat, or if this has been added for bread making.

Wholewheat flour should be 100% wheat (nothing added and nothing removed), compost-grown or organically grown kinds are to be preferred.

'Granary' flour is based on a strong white flour with added malt and cracked toasted wheat grains (and occasionally other flours, such as rye). The malt makes it sticky to use on its own, but mixed half and half with plain flour it will handle more easily, and the resulting loaf will still retain the distinctive malt flavour.

'Gluten' flour is powdered wheat gluten which can (if available) be used to 'strengthen' softer flours for breadmaking.

Rye or barley flour and oatmeal all have less gluten, so are used sparingly together with wheatflour to give the bread some rise.

Gluten-free bread recipes can be found in titles given in the Booklist, page 234.

Yeast

Unless otherwise indicated, the yeast quantities in the recipes are for fresh or 'compressed' (US) yeast. Under normal conditions 28g/1oz fresh yeast will serve to give a rise to a dough made with 1kg 350g/3lb of flour, and warm water (100°F), in about 2 hours. The quantity of yeast is not kept proportional to the flour, 450g/1lb of flour requires 15g/½oz of yeast, 2kg 700g/6lb requires 40g/1½oz, for similar performance.

It is worth grasping the several factors that affect the speed of rising of a yeast dough, as the commonest fault of newcomers to bread-making is to allow inadequate time for rising.

Yeast acts quite differently from baking powder or other sodium bicarbonate/acid mixtures used to raise soda bread and most cakes. The latter are put in the oven immediately after mixing lest the rise be lost. An unrisen yeast dough, on the other hand, needs *time* before it goes into the oven. A cold unrisen dough put into a hot oven may rise faster for a time, but long before the yeast has done its work it will be killed off (at around 130°F).

Factors influencing the speed of the rise

Cold ingredients (flour and water), or a cold place to rise will slow the rise, so too will less yeast. Some of the finest breads are made with an overnight rise, with 1/4 to 1/3 of the usual quantity of yeast. But this method is not really suitable for doughs with a significant proportion of wholewheat flour.

To speed a rise with cold flour (from a cellar, for example), you can allow it to reach room temperature before you begin. It could be placed in a warm bowl, or heated briefly in an oven on minimum heat. The temperature of the water can also compensate, so long as you are sure it is below 120°F/50°C, lest you kill off the yeast. Conversely there is a limit to how much the rising of a yeast dough can be speeded up by increasing the quantity of yeast. It is not advisable to increase the quantities of yeast given in the recipes.

The addition of vitamin C (ascorbic acid) to a dough will speed up the action of the yeast. This is part of the 'Chorleywood' process. It is not recommended except for possible occasional use, as it does not improve the nutritional quality of the bread. None of the vitamin is left and the speeding up results in more phytic acid which binds some of the calcium otherwise available so that less is available for absorption in the body.

Different types of yeast

If you want to keep fresh yeast, the best way is to freeze batch-sized bits, wrapped separately. They will keep several months and should be thawed out for 15 minutes or so before use.

There are two kinds of dried yeast. Read the instructions on your pack to find out whether it is granular dried yeast (which is to be reconstituted with liquid), or Fermipan or similar (sometimes repackaged with other brand names) which can be added to the flour directly. The proportions needed also differ: about half the quantity of fresh yeast, if it is granular, about one quarter, if it is the Fermipan type. So: 30g/1oz fresh yeast = 15g/½oz granular dried yeast (or 2 tablespoons – slightly heaped) = 1 slightly heaped tablespoon of Fermipan (or similar yeast). It is difficult to weigh tiny amounts like 1/4oz or 7g, so the tablespoon measure is given. Use a proper measuring spoon, not the tablespoon that goes with your cutlery set (see Weights and measures page ix).

These measures may be less than is recommended by the instructions on the yeast sachet, but an excess of dried yeast makes for an unsatisfactory loaf.

Once the dried yeast container has been broached, keep it tightly closed when not in use. Granular dried yeast lasts a few months, whereas Fermipan, if transferred to a clean screw-top jar and kept in a cool dry place, retains its potency for at least a year.

Liquid

The recipes usually call for plain water, or a water and milk mixture. A dough made with milk (which actually is composed mainly of water) as the only liquid gives a softer bread, and the small amount of fat in the milk slows the rise a little.

Forms of soured milk such as buttermilk or yogurt may be used to replace a proportion of the water in the dough; like milk, these will also help the bread to keep its freshness longer.

Whey (left over from making soft cheese, see page 142) can also be used.

Naturally, those on a milk-free diet must omit milk from any recipe. If you want to increase the protein content of your loaf add a tablespoon of soya flour for every 250g/½lb flour and remove a tablespoon of flour. This will add many other nutrients, including calcium too.

Salt

In bread salt is not only a flavouring; it also affects fermentation, by slowing it a little. Most people are used to quite salty bread, and find bread with no salt insipid; but in bread as in other things, it is good to use as little salt as possible, and to reduce the amount progressively as you become accustomed to less. The recipes allow a moderate amount; it is best not to use more, and to try to use less.

Using sea salt, dissolve it in the liquid first as the grains are large. The finer cooking or table salt can be added to the dried ingredients.

METHODS

General points

To make yeast-leavened bread, the most important step is to combine ingredients *thoroughly*, ensuring in particular that the components essential to the working of the yeast – gluten, liquid, and the yeast – are evenly distributed in the dough, together with any salt which also affects the fermentation (see note above); and then to knead the mixture to develop the gluten strands. After that, the dough must be left alone to rise or 'prove'. When it has risen, it may be baked immediately.

With loaves baked from wholewheat flour, this minimum method – as far as possible leaving the yeast to do its work unhindered – is recommended. And so, when a recipe calls for *two* periods of proving, they may be reduced to one if using only or mostly wholewheat flour. The dough once kneaded may be formed into loaves and put into tins or onto baking trays to rise.

Always *preheat* the oven for bread to 450°F/gas mark 8/230°C to start the bread in a hot oven. To ensure that the loaf is baked right through without burning on the outside, the temperature should be progressively reduced (see notes under *Baking* on page 52), during the baking time.

Mixing

Thorough mixing is important, or you will get an uneven rise and a lumpy loaf. The usual method is to mix together all the dry ingredients (including Fermipan yeast if used), likewise all the liquid ingredients (including, if used, the fresh yeast or reactivated dried granular yeast) separately and then to combine them. Put the flour mixture into a suitably large bowl; make a well in the centre and pour in the liquid. Stir the liquid with a wooden spoon and gradually incorporate more and more dry flour into the mixture. The mixture will thicken to a batter and eventually stirring will be possible no longer. This is the point at which to abandon the wooden spoon and to attack the mixture, now on the point of becoming a fully fledged dough, with bare (but clean) hands. Squeeze handfuls of the mixture through your fingers and combine everything thoroughly. The dough at this stage will be moist and quite sticky but should not be sloppy. The mixing process to this point takes only a couple of minutes. With all the ingredients now evenly and thoroughly combined, the process passes imperceptibly from mixing to kneading.

Kneading

Kneading, which is the magical transformation of an inert lump of dough to a springy and coherent structure of gluten pockets with their local yeast cells ready to feed on the starch, is a mechanical process. It causes the gluten in the mixture to form long strands and sheets. The astonishing elasticity of wheat gluten is known to anyone who has made mille-feuille pastry, apple strudel or croissants.

The lump of dough, still in the bowl, is sticky and difficult to handle. In a big enough bowl it should be possible to fold it over on itself a few times, before turning it out on to a floured board or work surface.

Do not worry about the dough sticking to your fingers, but settle to serious kneading, folding and turning the dough. After two to three minutes you will already detect a change in the texture. The lump will begin to feel springy and to peel off the stray bits from your fingers. If making a wholewheat loaf, move immediately to forming your loaf and leaving it to prove. Mixtures based on white flour will reward a longer labour – anything up to 10 minutes' kneading, before returning the dough, now no longer at all sticky, to the bowl.

A note on machinery

If you have a heavy-duty mixer with a dough hook, or a food processor, the machine will perform the mixing and kneading for you. There is no obligation to use only the maker's recipes, but do observe maximum limits on the amount of dough that can be processed and the mixing time, as kneading is heavy work, even for machines.

Proving

Cover the dough, in its bowl or tin, with a damp cloth or with a sheet of polythene, or in a large polythene bag, leaving space for rising, and leave the yeast to do its work. The cover keeps in moisture, stops the surface of the dough drying out and setting – remember flour and water is a glue – which would inhibit the rise. If using a plastic cover, you will notice extra moisture, another by-product of fermentation, on its inside surface.

The recipes give approximate proving times, for flour at room temperature (here assumed to be 60–70°F/15–20°C), water at blood heat, proving at room temperature. It is common to advise 'leave to prove until doubled in size', but most of us cannot easily estimate doubling precisely, especially in containers such as bowls, where a doubling in volume is nothing like a doubling in height. A properly proved dough will certainly look bigger, and if poked with the finger will be light and airy, not the dense mass that was kneaded. There is such a thing as 'over-proving' – stretching the gluten past breaking point, which releases the carbon dioxide from its gluten balloons, so that the dough falls back and collapses sadly. The rather tedious remedy is to mix in, very thoroughly, flour and water in proportion – say one-third of the quantities in the recipe you are using – and knead all over again; and avoid over-proving a second time!

For a twice-risen dough, leave the dough in its mixing bowl for the first proving; then 'knock it down' (a single punch will cause it to collapse) and knead lightly (1–2 minutes is all that is needed this time) before shaping it into loaves.

A once-risen loaf goes straight into the oven when it is adequately proved.

Shaping

It is tempting to stuff the dough into its baking tin without ceremony. But a moment's trouble is well-rewarded at this point; particularly for round loaves and other free-form shapes baked on a tray. If the dough is flattened, by hand or with a rolling pin, and then rolled up like a carpet, at least once (or a second time too, after a 90° turn) it is given a structure which will help it to bake evenly and to hold itself up. The ends of the 'carpet' can be flattened and tucked under for a tin loaf; a little rounding at the ends and folding under is all that a round loaf needs.

The recipes suggest the use of oil for baking tins and trays – a good quality but not strong-tasting oil such as sunflower or safflower is recommended. You should have no trouble with your loaves sticking to a lightly oiled tin; but if using ovenproof ceramic vessels, e.g. for a rounded loaf, a thorough oiling is required. Bread tins are best kept just for bread, as they 'season' themselves and develop a non-stick surface. They come away from their loaves clean and need no washing – they should *not* be scoured.

Making cuts

Decorate your loaf with cuts about 15 minutes before it is due to go into the oven. Use a serrated knife or a pair of scissors, and any design of your choice. Quite deep cuts of 1cm/½inch may be used – they will open out to reveal the structure of the dough during baking.

For an extra crisp crust, spray the loaf with water just before you put it into the oven.

Baking

Always preheat the oven; but hold the loaf back until it is nicely proved *before* committing it to the heat. Only thus can you remain in control. It will rise a little more in the oven, but then become fixed by the heat. Typical baking times for a 450g/1lb loaf are: white dough, 45 minutes; wholewheat dough, 55 minutes; in the centre of the oven at 450°F/gas mark 8/230°C for the first 15 minutes, reduced to 375–400°F/gas mark 5–6/190–200°C for the rest of the time. It is good to turn out a tin loaf onto the shelf for the last 5 minutes.

Cooling

After baking, set the loaves to cool on a rack (to allow free circulation around the crust, which will otherwise become soggy) but away from draughts which would cool the exterior too rapidly and cause cracking. As it cools, the bread 'sets'; fresh from the oven, the contrast between the crisp crust and the soft interior is very marked. If you release bread fresh from the oven to the family table, be prepared for a large increase in bread consumption in your family!

BREADS

Keeping

Once cool, loaves not to be consumed immediately should be wrapped in a cloth (e.g. a spare teacloth) – but not refrigerated or kept in plastic unless frozen. Freezing (after sealing in plastic) *is* a good way to keep bread.

MF* VEG*	OATMEAL BREAD

One tin loaf

340g/12oz flour
110g/4oz fine or medium oatmeal
1 tablespoon salt

15g/½oz fresh yeast (*or* 1/4oz/1 US package dried yeast *or* 2 teaspoons Fermipan) see *Yeast* page 46–8
275ml/10fl oz water (or milk/water mixture)*

Preheat oven to 425–450°F/gas mark 7–8/220–230°C

Warm water to blood heat (a drop on the inside of the wrist should not feel warm or cold).

If using dried yeast, reconstitute with a little of the water and a pinch of sugar. Leave for about 10 minutes, until frothy.

If using Fermipan, mix into the dry flour. Fresh yeast should be mixed into the water.

Combine flour and oatmeal and salt in a large mixing bowl. Make a well in the centre, add liquid and mix, gathering up the flour gradually to make the dough. When mixing is no longer possible, knead with the hands, first in the bowl then on a suitable clean flat surface dusted with flour to prevent sticking. Replace dough in the bowl and prove in a warm place, covered, until well risen. (Even with strong white flour this dough will rise less because of the oatmeal.)

Then knock down and shape into one or two loaves to fit the tin(s) available. Prove until well rounded. (This will be faster than the first proving.) Bake for ½ hour, then for another ½ hour at 300–350°F/gas mark 3–4/170–180°C. Remove from tin(s) and cool on a wire tray.

MF* VEG*	POTATO BREAD

Two round loaves

900g/2lb flour	30g/1oz fresh yeast (or
250g/½lb mashed potatoes	equivalents, see page 48)
30g/1oz salt	570ml/1 pint liquid (potato water or milk* and water)

Preheat oven to 425°F/gas mark 7/220°C

Clean a generous ½lb of potatoes; cook in their skins; peel carefully and mash thoroughly while still warm.

Have ready the liquid – not *more* than 120°F/230°C if using the potato water – but not cooler than blood heat. Cream fresh yeast with a little of it, or proceed as indicated with other yeasts. Mix flour and salt in a bowl. Make a well in the centre, add yeast liquid (if used) and about half the warm water. When the mixture in the well is of the consistency of a batter, add the mashed potato gradually, mix it in well and then add most of the remaining water, but hold some back until you are sure the dough needs it, after thorough mixing. (It should be moist and take up all the dry flour – but not sloppy.)

Then turn out on to a floured board and knead thoroughly. Return to bowl, cover well and leave to prove for 2 hours.

Knock down and knead for a minute or two; divide into two equally sized lumps (scales can help here, if you find it difficult to judge by eye). Form into round loaves by flattening the piece of dough and rolling it up like a Swiss roll, now in one direction, then across, and shape the result into a ball by tucking the ends under, pinching together and forming them with your hands.

Place loaves on an oiled baking tray, covered for half an hour. Decorative cuts on top of the loaves may be made 15 minutes before they are due to go into the oven. Bake at a slightly reduced temperature (400°F/gas mark 6/200°C) for one hour.

MF VEG	RICE BREAD

Two tin loaves
Like potato bread, rice bread keeps well and stays moist.

Follow the instructions for potato bread, but substitute for the mashed potato, 110g/4oz rice (uncooked weight). Brown short grain is best. Cook the rice until just done, but not sticky; add it to the flour and salt and mix thoroughly *before* adding the other ingredients to make the dough.

Because the rice grains break up the dough rather more than does mashed potato, the added support given by the tin in baking is probably to be preferred.

MF VEG   **SPROUTED SEED BREAD**

One tin loaf

450g/1lb flour
50g/2oz sprouted sesame or sunflower seeds
15g/½oz salt
15g/½oz fresh yeast (or equivalents, see page 48)
275ml/10fl oz water

Preheat oven to 450°F/gas mark 8/230°C

Sprouted seeds can be used to very good effect in bread doughs. For this use, the seeds should be allowed to develop only until the shoots are making their first appearance – a little white protuberance (see Sprouting Seeds page 113). Rinse and drain the seeds.

Mix flour and salt in a bowl; have the water ready and warmed. Add seeds to flour, mix in thoroughly. Cream fresh yeast with a little water (or proceed as indicated with other yeasts). Make a well in the flour mixture, add yeast liquid (if used) and some water. Combine the liquids with the flour, adding more water as the flour is taken up. When you can mix no longer, turn out on to a floured surface and knead for at least 5 minutes, until the dough becomes elastic and is no longer sticky. Return to bowl; leave to prove (covered) 1½–2 hours.

Knock down, knead lightly; flatten and roll up; press into an oiled tin, seam up, then empty it out onto your hand and put it back in, seam down. Allow to prove until clearly rising again for about 45 minutes. Bake in the centre of the oven for 20 minutes, then reduce the temperature to 350°F/gas mark 4/180°C and bake for a further 25 minutes. Cool on a rack.

ONION AND HERB BREAD

One tin loaf

450g/1lb flour
15g/½oz fresh yeast (or equivalents, see page 48)
150ml/5fl oz yogurt
150ml/5fl oz water
1 teaspoon salt

1 small onion
1 teaspoon thyme
1 teaspoon oregano (or other herbs of your choice, fresh or dried sage and rosemary are good – use 1 teaspoon if fresh.)

Preheat oven to 450°F/gas mark 8/230°C

Add water to yogurt and warm, stirring to mix (it does no harm if it does separate). Cream fresh yeast with a little of this liquid and mix in with the remainder (or proceed as indicated with other yeasts).

Chop the onion into small bits. Add with the salt and herbs to the flour and combine well in the bowl. Hold back a little of the onion to sprinkle on the loaf – just before baking.

Make a well in the middle of the flour mixture, pour in the liquid, stir in the flour and mix very well. When all the flour is taken up, knead in the bowl, then on a lightly floured board; return to bowl, cover and leave to prove for about two hours.

Knock down, knead lightly, flatten and roll up, press into an oiled baking tin (olive oil is good), sprinkle with chopped onion. Leave to rise in tin until well rounded.

Bake for 20 minutes, then reduce temperature to 400°F/gas mark 6/200°C for 20 minutes. Remove loaf from tin and replace in oven for 5 minutes. Cool on rack.

MF VEG ## BROWN BAGUETTES

Three baguettes

450g/1lb wheatmeal flour (or ½ wholewheat, ½ strong white or unbleached flour)
275ml/½ pint water

15g/½oz fresh yeast (or equivalents, see page 48)
up to 15g/½oz salt

Preheat oven to 450°F/gas mark 8/230°C

Warm the water to blood heat. Have the flour ready in the mixing bowl. Mix in the salt. Cream fresh yeast with a little of the water and add back to the rest of the water (or proceed as indicated with other yeasts). Make a well in the flour.

Add liquid slowly to flour, mixing all the time until too stiff to mix. Lightly flour a board or work surface. Oil a large flat baking tray. Work mixture thoroughly with your hands in the bowl. Turn out on to surface and knead lightly.

Divide into 3 lumps (weighing on scales if you want them exactly equal). Taking each lump in turn, flatten it with your hands (or a rolling pin if you prefer) to about 1cm/½ inch thickness. Make it the length of your baking tray. Roll up tightly into a long stick and squeeze in the seams with your fingers. Tuck flattened ends under and squeeze seams. Lay out on the baking tray.

Allow the baguettes to rise for about an hour.

Score loaves diagonally at intervals. Bake for half an hour.

Note

If you are fond of the baguette shape you may wish to invest in a 'corrugated' baking tray, specially made for the purpose, that gives a rounded bottom and support at the sides.

MF* VEG*   **HOT GARLIC BREAD**

For each baguette:

50g/2oz butter (softened) or   1 clove garlic (pressed)
  whey-free margarine*

Preheat oven to 400°F/gas mark 6/200°C

Add pepper and salt if you wish, or some fresh chopped parsley or other herbs for interesting variations (optional).

Pound garlic (and other ingredients if used) into the butter and mix well. Slash the baguette into thick slices, taking care not to cut right through. Open each slice carefully and butter with the mixture. Close up and wrap in tinfoil. Heat the garlic bread for 10–15 minutes. Serve hot, cutting through the slices completely or breaking them off. Delicious with soups or salads.

SODA BREAD

One round loaf or four buns

Bread leavened with baking powder has a different consistency from bread made with a yeast dough. It is not kneaded and because of the need to get the mixture into the oven quickly, it is not left to prove: thus the gluten in the flour has no chance to form the structure that holds a yeast dough together. The result has a lumpy appearance like a rock bun, and it does not keep well. However soda rolls or loaves can be useful if you are caught in an emergency; and with the right flour can be delicious when eaten fresh from the oven.

450g/1lb wholewheat flour
Approximately 25ml/10fl oz milk and water mixture
3 teaspoons baking powder
1 teaspoon salt

Preheat the oven to 450°F/gas mark 8/230°C

Oil a flat baking tray. Mix the salt and baking powder thoroughly with the flour in a bowl. Make a well and add enough liquid to mix to a soft but not sloppy dough. Form into a round loaf and turn out onto the baking sheet. Bake for 45 minutes. Cool on a rack for a few moments before serving hot.

An attractive shape for this bread is made by cutting across the round and again at right angles to make four wedges. Alternatively, shape into four buns and bake for 30 minutes.

FRUIT PLAIT A LA TASSAJARA

(from *The Tassajara Bread Book*, by Edward Espe Brown, see Booklist, page 232).

Any yeasted bread dough can be made into fruit-filled loaves braided on top. Make any sized loaf.

Preheat oven to 350°F/gas mark 4/180°C.

Flatten dough into a rectangle about 1cm/½inch thick by rolling, pressing and/or stretching.

Arrange sliced fruit pieces (apple, banana, peach, plum, pear, apricot, nectarine or some dried fruits mixed in) down the centre third of the dough.

Sprinkle on some brown sugar, if you like, and your choice of spices such as cinnamon, allspice, nutmeg, mace, anise.

Make diagonal cuts in the dough about 1cm/½inch apart from near the fruit to the edge on both sides.

Fold the strips alternately from each side over the fruit, stretching and twisting slightly to form a compact loaf.

Place in a baking pan or greased baking sheet. Let rise 20 minutes.

Brush with egg wash (one egg beaten with 4–5fl oz/120–150ml water or milk). Sprinkle poppy seed on top if liked.

Bake for one hour until golden brown.

Serve as a dessert or at tea time.

MF VEG*   JUDY'S BREAD STICKS

Another way to use any dough you may have over from bread making is to make bread sticks.

Preheat oven to 400–425°F/gas mark 6–7/200–220°C.

Roll out the dough thinly and spread with yeast extract spread (optional). Cut into thin strips about 20cm/8 inches long. These can be twisted or left flat. Leave to rise for 30 minutes.

Brush with egg* and sprinkle with sesame or poppy seeds as preferred. Cook for 15–20 minutes.

Easy finger food to accompany soups and other dishes, or use to serve with dips (see page 166–8).

MF VEG   MUFFINS

Muffins are best eaten fresh and warm, as they dry out quickly.

Make a slack bread dough; allow to rise once in the bowl. Knock down and knead lightly in the bowl. Roll out flat on a board and cut into 8cm/3inch rounds. (If you have no cutter, you can use a glass.) Dust with maize flour (polenta) all over and leave for about 15 minutes.

Heat a griddle or a large heavy frying pan over low heat. Transfer the muffins carefully to the griddle and cook slowly for 8 minutes per side. They shoud be browned (but not blackened) top and bottom. Keep the first batch warm in a low oven while you cook the next.

To eat, split open around the sides with a fork. Any left over can be toasted on another occasion.

As an oven is not needed, these can be made in the simplest conditions, even with a gas ring or camping cooker. (Take care the heavy pan does not topple over.)

MF GF YEAST-RISEN SPICE LOAF

350g/12oz wholewheat flour
5g fresh yeast/1 teaspoon dried yeast/½ teaspoon Fermipan
50g/2oz currants
25g/1oz candied peel
50g/2oz raisins
1 teaspoon cinnamon
½ teaspoon nutmeg
½ teaspoon mixed spice
210ml/7fl oz warm water
2 tablespoons oil

In a small bowl place dried yeast (or fresh), oil, dried fruit, water and spice. Leave in a warm place until the yeast begins to bubble. (Fermipan can be mixed with the first half of the flour.) Add the activated yeast mixture to half the flour and the candied peel (chopped). Beat this batter well and leave covered with a polythene bag until doubled in size. A warm but *not* hot place will speed up this stage. Beat again whilst slowly adding the remainder of the flour. You may not need all the flour, the dough should be soft. (Different flours absorb varying amounts of liquid.) Shape into an oiled 1kg/2lb loaf tin. Leave to rise in the polythene bag again. In about 20 minutes the loaf should have doubled in size.

Whilst the dough is rising preheat the oven to 450°F/gas mark 7/220°C.

Bake the loaf, when risen, for 25–30 minutes at this temperature, until hollow-sounding when tapped, but still soft in texture.

If wished the top may be glazed with rice syrup whilst still hot.

Other fruit loaves and tea breads are given in the home-baking section on pages 146–7.

Pizza dough is on page 84–5.

Soups

Soups are a good way to vary the presentation of vegetables on your menu. They can provide a substantial simple meal with a wholemeal roll, or a course in a larger meal. Perhaps a person who does not like vegetables would find soups an acceptable way to eat more of them.

The more adventurous can try soups using Japanese seaweeds. These can be obtained from Wholefood shops, and are very nutritious. 'The mineral and trace element composition of sea water and of the plants that grow in it, is similar to that of human blood. The sea vegetables are therefore an ideal source of the minerals and trace elements required by the body', say the authors of *Cook Yourself a Favour* (see Booklist).

Kombu is used here to make stocks. Others available include wakame, arame and nori.

When your baby is about 7–8 months old, he or she will enjoy many of these soups puréed, or with pieces of bread added to mop up the liquid. There are more ideas in *Growing Up With Good Food*.

After the basic stocks and garnishes, the lighter soups are given first, graduating through thicker soups to the hearty pulse soups. Cold soups follow at the end of the section.

BASIC SOUP RECIPE

Allow approximately 500g/1lb vegetables to 500ml/1pint liquid. How you chop them will depend on whether or not you are going to purée them. Sweat the vegetables in butter or oil for a rich soup. For a thick consistency, add some cereal such as flour or cereal flakes (millet and oats often go well) and let it absorb any excess fat. Then add the stock or water and cook the vegetables until tender. Serve as is or puréed. If adding milk or cream do this at the end and reheat until not quite boiling. A knob of butter or butter mixed with flour makes a good liaison for puréed pulse soups made with split peas, lentils or beans.

GF use potato or millet flakes to thicken a soup, or gluten-free flour.
VEG MF use oil or whey-free margarine for sweating the vegetables and ground cashews or soya milk in place of milk, and meat- or bone-free stock for vegans.

Most of the soups in this section are variations on this method. Try your own mixtures of vegetables based on these recipes. There are many possibilities, interesting, subtle or adventurous – depending on taste.

GF MF VEG*   CLEAR STOCK

1 litre/2 pints cold water
(bones or chicken carcass – optional)*
leek tops
carrots (any oddments left over can be used)
celery tops
an onion (stuck with a clove)
other vegetables you have to spare, but not from the brassica family (cabbage, cauliflower etc)
bay leaf, parsley and thyme
various kinds of Japanese seaweeds especially Kombu can be used to add flavour

The secret of a clear stock is to start with cold water and to skim it often. Simply cover your ingredients with the water and bring to the boil skimming frequently. Simmer on a low heat, partially covered for an hour. Reduce the stock if it is not tasty enough. Add a little yeast extract spread or tamari if you prefer. Baking the onion in the oven first until the skin is brown will also make the soup tastier and give a good brown colour. Strain and allow to cool.

THICK STOCK

You can use all the same vegetables, but for the liquid you may use water from cooking pulses, grains or potatoes. Make up with fresh water to the quantity above. It is still good to skim the stock, but it will not matter if it is cloudy as you will add this stock to a cream soup or root vegetable soup.

MF* VEG*   CROUTONS

A tasty garnish to many soups and a good way to use stale bread. Allow a small slice per person. Cut into 2cm/inch cubes and toss in butter or oil* until brown all over. Serve immediately very hot so they sizzle in the soup!

Garlic or herbs can be added to the butter for extra flavour.

MF VEG   RICE BALLS

Use freshly cooked or left over rice, preferably short grain.

Make tiny balls by pressing a small quantity into the palm of the hand with the fingers of the other hand. Drop into the soup for a novel garnish.

GF MF VEG*   JULIENNE CONSOMMÉ
---

1 litre/2 pints of stock*
1 medium carrot
1–2 stalks celery
1 fairly thin leek
1 small turnip/swede/parsnip
pepper and salt
herbs for garnishing

The quality of the soup will depend largely on the quality of the stock. A homemade stock is preferable to one made with a stock cube, but vegetarian stock cubes without additives are available for people in a hurry.

As you are heating the stock, cut the carrot, leek and celery into 4 5cm/2 inch lengths and make some chunks of turnip (or substitute) the same size. Then cut very thin sticks like matchsticks and throw them into the boiling stock to seal immediately. If you have a kitchen device which will produce julienne, so much the better. You could use a grater, but the effect is not the same.

Simmer for 5–10 minutes, no longer, so the vegetables are slightly crunchy and still taste very fresh. Season to taste and garnish if you wish with a little fresh chopped chervil or parsley and chives.

GF* MF* VEG*   CELERY SOUP

---

1 litre/2 pints stock*
2 or 3 sticks of tasty celery with leaves or 1 large celeriac root, grated
1/4 teaspoon celery seeds (for extra flavour if needed)
a knob of butter*
pepper and salt

Again you need a good stock to get a good soup. Slice the celery finely and then cut again into smaller pieces if you wish. Melt the butter and let the celery 'sweat' in the pan for 5 minutes. Add the celery seeds and stock, bring to the boil and cook until the celery is tender but not soft.

A cream of celery can be made by adding some flour* and stirring before you add the stock, pouring in the stock gradually to avoid lumps forming. *Some milk or cream (or yogurt) can also be added when the celery has cooked.

VEG* MF* GF*   TOMATO SOUP

450g/1lb tomatoes
1 small onion
a sprig of basil (fresh if available)
½ cup stock* or water
275ml/½pint milk (or more if needed)
1 tablespoon flour*
30g/1oz butter*
pepper and salt

Cook the tomatoes and onion: put in a saucepan and add the basil and enough stock or water to just cover them. When cooked, purée or rub through a sieve. Keep aside. Now melt the butter and add the flour then gradually add the milk to make a thickish sauce. Add the purée of tomatoes and season with salt and pepper. Delicious with home-grown tomatoes.

VEG* MF* GF*   ZUCCHINI (COURGETTE) SOUP

3 cups thinly sliced zucchini/courgettes
½ cup diced onion

1 cup chicken stock* or vegetable stock
basic cream soup
paprika

Basic Cream Soup
30g/1oz butter*
2 tablespoons flour*
salt to taste
pinch Cayenne pepper

1 cup milk*
1 cup vegetable water
1 small bay leaf

Cover the zucchini and onion with the chicken stock (or vegetable stock) and bring to the boil. Cook for about 20 minutes until the zucchini are soft. Sieve or liquidise and keep to one side, while you make the basic cream soup. Melt the butter, stir in the flour, add the milk slowly, stirring all the time. Add the bay leaf and season with salt and Cayenne. Add the vegetable water, stirring to blend well. Bring to the boil and simmer until it thickens. Add the zucchini purée and reheat without boiling. Serve sprinkled with paprika.

Other squashes including pumpkin or marrow will also taste delicious cooked in this way. A potato could be added to thicken the soup instead of the basic cream soup.*

GF MF* VEG*   CAULIFLOWER SOUP

a small cauliflower (a little broccoli can be added for colour)
a small potato grated
275ml/½pint water or stock
275ml/½pint milk* or cashew nut milk

a knob of butter*
pepper and salt and a little grated nutmeg
grated cheese* for optional garnish

Cut the cauliflower heads very finely, having removed any blemishes. The stalks can be added in the cooking for extra flavour. Add grated potato, cover with water and bring to the boil. Simmer gently for 15 minutes. Remove stalks. Season, then add the milk and a knob of butter. Reheat and serve, garnished if you wish.

GF* — MUSHROOM SOUP

150–170g/5–7oz mushrooms
a knob of butter
a tablespoon of flour*
1 cup stock or less if water (make up with milk)
1 cup milk (or part single cream)
pepper and salt

Chop the washed mushrooms finely and cook gently in the butter. Add the flour* (or try cereal flakes, rice perhaps?), then liquid and bring to the boil. Simmer for 5 minutes. Season and leave to stand another 10 minutes for the flavours to infuse. Add milk and reheat. Serve garnished, if you like, with yogurt and parsley.

GF — ARTICHOKE SOUP

500g/1lb Jerusalem artichokes (the root kind)
1 cup water or stock
pepper, salt and a little grated nutmeg
milk as required – about 1 cup

Scrub artichokes and remove blemishes, no need to peel. Cut into even sizes, cover with liquid and simmer until tender, about 20 minutes. Cool and purée. Thin with milk and season. Reheat and serve. A delicious, delicate flavour!

GF* MF* VEG* — CARROT SOUP

500–700g/1–1½lb carrots
1 large onion
2 potatoes
500ml/1pint water or stock
½ cup milk or single cream*
a good knob of butter*
pepper and salt
chopped chervil for garnish or croutons*

Scrape the carrots and wash them. Cut into chunks and toss in a heavy pan in some melted butter. Add the chopped onion and when transparent add the chopped potatoes (no need to peel) and cover with the water or stock. Bring to the boil and simmer until the carrots are tender (20 minutes). Allow to cool and then liquidise with the milk and butter. Reheat and serve with the garnish of your choice.

PARSNIP SOUP

500g/1lb parsnips
1 potato
1 carrot

Liquid and seasoning as for carrot soup

Proceed as for the carrot soup. Try one of these variations if you like.

Mystery flavours you can add

MF* VEG* GF   175g/6oz ground cashews added with the milk* (or with equivalent water or stock for a milk-free soup. Use a sunflower oil instead of butter in this case. Try a little orange juice too.)

GF* MF* VEG*   1 teaspoon curry powder and a clove of garlic added while the vegetables are sweating in the butter, with a little flour* to thicken if necessary.

A soupçon of orange juice added at the end gives an interesting lift to this soup.

GF ## LEEK AND POTATO SOUP

3 medium leeks
450g/1lb potatoes
1 litre/2 pints water or stock

275ml/½pint milk
a knob of butter
millet flakes (if liked)

Wash and scrub the potatoes, remove any blemishes and cube. Cut the leeks lengthwise and wash. Remove outer leaves if necessary and cut off withered ends. Cut into small sections. If using the millet flakes, sweat the vegetables in a little butter and add the cereal flakes to absorb any excess fat. If not using millet, simply cover the vegetables with the water or stock, bring to the boil and simmer for about 30 minutes. Blend or sieve. Add the milk and reheat gently, adding the knob of butter as it comes to the boil. Turn off heat immediately, season, stir and serve.

VICHYSSOISE

Leek and potato soup can be served cold. Add chopped chives sprinkled on top of the chilled soup with a little single cream or yogurt swirled in.

GF* MF* VEG*   POTATO GOULASH SOUP

2 onions	a teaspoon caraway seeds
1kg 350g/3lb potatoes	4 cloves
a tablespoon paprika	pinch Cayenne pepper
a tablespoon flour*	½ teaspoon salt
1 litre/2pints water (more if necessary)	Garnish with yogurt*

Thinly slice the onions and fry gently until soft. Add the paprika and stir for another 2 minutes. Add the water, caraway seeds, cloves and Cayenne. Peel and slice the potatoes and add to the soup with ½ teaspoon salt and the flour mixed with a little liquid from the soup. Bring to the boil and simmer for 40 minutes, stirring occasionally. Serve with a spoonful of yogurt* in each plate sprinkled with a little paprika.

GF MF VEG   PEA AND GARDEN VEGETABLE POTTAGE

1 onion	170g/6oz split green peas
3 cloves garlic pressed	1 litre/2 pints vegetable stock
2 tablespoons sunflower oil	1 bayleaf

A selection of seasonal vegetables from the following: carrots, cabbage, green pepper, runner beans, mangetout peas or shelled peas, leeks, leaf greens, watercress, parsley. Make up to about 250g/½lb weight with four or five different kinds.

Chopped parsley or chives to garnish

Sauté the onion and garlic in the heated oil until soft. Wash the split peas then stir into the oil and cook for a few minutes. Pour in the stock, add the bayleaf and bring to the boil. Skim and simmer for 30 minutes in a covered pan. Prepare the chosen vegetables, chopping finely (except mangetout peas). Add them and cook for a further 15–20 minutes until soft. Serve garnished with a little chopped parsley.

GF MF VEG   BEAN AND BARLEY SOUP

1½ litres/3 pints kombu stock (for preference)
1 onion
1 carrot
1–2 sticks celery
1 turnip or piece of swede (if in season)
125g/4oz butter beans (soaked overnight)
125g/4oz pot barley
salt (added only at end if needed)

Make stock as for basic stock adding a clove of garlic and a 13cm/6inch strip of Kombu seaweed (which can be bought dried at wholefood shops sometimes). Simmer for 2 hours.

Slice onion, carrot, turnip and celery and soften in a little heated oil. Add the stock, bring to the boil and throw in the drained soaked beans and barley. (Pearl barley is polished pot barley, so the latter will have better nutritional value.) Simmer for about one hour or until the beans are soft. Taste and add extra sea salt if needed, then serve.

GF MF* VEG*   LENTIL AND TOMATO SOUP

---

1 cup soaked brown lentils
1 onion
1 carrot grated
1 stick celery
450g/1lb tomatoes (or tinned tomatoes)
a tablespoon tomato purée
25g/1oz butter*
2 cups water or stock

Chop the onion finely and fry gently in butter. Add lentils and 2 cups water or stock. Bring to the boil and simmer for about one hour. Add the grated carrot and finely chopped celery. Cook for 10 minutes. Add the tomatoes and tomato purée. Stir well, heat through and serve.

GF* MF VEG   PUREED FIELD BEAN AND LEEK SOUP

1 cup field beans (soaked overnight)
3 leeks
1 clove garlic
1 litre/1½ pints water or stock
salt and pepper (added at the end)
1 carrot
1 turnip or swede
1 bay leaf
fresh herbs to garnish
garlic croutons*

Cover the field beans with the water or stock and bring to the boil. Add the leeks, carrot, turnip (all washed and chopped) and the bay leaf and garlic. Simmer for about one hour or until the beans are tender. Cool and purée in a blender. Reheat and serve with fresh herbs and garlic croutons.

Field beans are the cheapest bean (often used for animals!). Their thick skins make them more palatable puréed, as in this soup.

FRENCH ONION SOUP

250g/½lb Spanish onions
50g/2oz butter
50g/2oz flour
1½ litres/2½ pints stock or water
A small slice of bread (brown baguette for preference)
50g/2oz cheese (Gruyère is best or Emmental)

Remove the skin from the onions and cut them in half. With the flat side against the chopping board make slices as thin as you can, discarding the base. Heat the butter and fry the onions until golden. Sprinkle with the flour (which can be wholemeal) and season with salt and pepper. Add the stock, bring to the boil and simmer for 10 minutes. In a fireproof dish or individual ramekins place the bread cut fairly thick. Pour the soup over the bread which will then float to the surface. Sprinkle the grated cheese on top and place in a hot oven to brown for 10 minutes. Serve with a warning that it retains heat very well!

COLD SOUPS (see also Vichyssoise p. 68)

GF   CUCUMBER SOUP

600ml/1 pint yogurt
300ml/½pint milk or top of the milk
1 cucumber
½ clove garlic
1 tablespoon fresh chopped mint

Thin the yogurt with the milk and add the cucumber cut into matchsticks. Add the pressed garlic and finely chopped mint (reserve a whole leaf to garnish each serve). Season with freshly ground black pepper and sea salt. Mix well and chill. Serve garnished with a mint leaf on each bowlful. An ice cube can also be added.

RUSSIAN BORTSCH

600ml/1 pint buttermilk or thinned yogurt
2 beetroots (cooked)
1 cucumber
2 slices onion
1 hard-boiled egg

Grate the cooked beetroot, then the cucumber and onion. Add all three ingredients, then the chopped egg, to the cultured milk. Leave to set in the refrigerator for a day before serving.

GF* MF VEG   GAZPACHO

500g/1lb ripe tomatoes
1 green pepper
1 onion
1 cucumber
1 tablespoon olive oil
1 cup consommé or clear stock
extra chilled water or ice cubes
1 clove garlic
pepper and salt
chopped chives, chervil, parsley, basil or tarragon
hot garlic croutons*

For a fine soup, seed and skin the tomatoes and seed and peel the cucumber. A rougher one with whole vegetables tastes good too, and is better for you. As it is all blended, the skins are hardly noticeable. The pepper should always be deseeded. Chop all the vegetables into chunks, place in the blender with the pressed garlic, olive oil and half the consommé or stock. Liquidise for two or three minutes. Turn into serving bowl (previously chilled) and add more liquid to make a fairly thin consistency. A few ice cubes will help chill it. Add the herbs and stir. Serve with hot croutons of bread fried with garlic in a separate bowl. Ice cubes can also be served separately.

If you do not have a blender, the vegetables should be pounded and passed through a tamis or mouli-légumes. It is not so easy to do, so in this case, prepare the vegetables without the skins and seeds.

Hot Dishes

There are four main parts to this section:

1 Flans and pastry savouries, pasta and pizza.
2 Cooking with meat
3 Dishes with beans and pulses, burgers, vegetarian bakes etc.
4 Vegetable dishes

Again, many other recipes may be found in *Growing Up With Good Food*, which would all be suitable for one's diet in pregnancy. The difference here is that the recipes are not restricted to dishes that babies and children may enjoy sharing. Some curries, hot condiments such as fresh ginger and so on, have been included where appropriate. There are also many more ideas on how to present vegetables in a great variety of ways, with the emphasis on vegetables which are particularly valuable in pregnancy (such as those high in folate: broccoli, cauliflower, cabbage, spinach, Brussels sprouts, runner beans, peas, carrots, mung beans for example). Most of the foods also have plenty of all the other vitamins and minerals we need, but which are often lacking in the diet of those who rarely venture away from processed manufactured foods. I hope you will enjoy making and eating these dishes.

FLANS

Some people may find the use of wholewheat flour more acceptable in a pastry base than in bread or other baking at first. The recipes are given as if wholewheat crusts were the norm. However, if you prefer white flour still, use it, or feel free to use the proportions of white and wholewheat that seems best. Even a few tablespoons of wholewheat flour will add to the nutritional value of your pastry. Start even more gently just adding a tablespoon of wheatgerm or soya flour. (See Making the Transition to Wholefoods page 20).

WHOLEWHEAT SHORTCRUST PASTRY

450g/1lb wholewheat flour
  (especially good if freshly
  ground)
100g/4oz butter

1–2 tablespoons seed oil
  (sunflower, safflower, etc)
2–3 tablespoons cold water

Rub the butter into the flour (or mix with electric mixer). Add, bit by bit, the oil until a texture of fine breadcrumbs is achieved. Add the water gradually until the mixture coheres together in a lump. Roll out on a floured board to the thickness required (not more than ½cm/¼inch) and lift gently, suporting it well, into the pie case. Press down carefully into the angle and trim excess around edge.

If you have a flan tin with a removable base, you may find it easier to slide this under the pastry and lift it into the ring that way. Do not worry if cracks appear, wholewheat pastry is easy to repair. But make sure there are no gaps or cracks which could let the flan mixture escape.

Another way (for which you can use less water, or even none) is to distribute the crumbs over your base evenly and to press it down into the tin and around the sides. This does away with the rolling pin and board.

Refrigerate the crust while you prepare the filling.

WHOLEWHEAT SHORTCRUST WITH CHEESE

If you are making a savoury pie or flan, add interest to the crust by adding 50g/2oz finely grated cheese (replacing some of the butter if you are keen to cut down on fat). Make sure to oil the flan case well as this pastry is more liable to stick.

MF   WHOLEWHEAT SHORTCRUST WITH OIL

A shortcrust made with oil alone is more difficult to handle and may be heavier. Be sure to handle it as little as possible (rolling out between two sheets of greaseproof paper helps) and to keep the ingredients cool. Instead of using all oil you could substitute whey-free margarine for the butter.

GF   GLUTEN-FREE SHORTCRUST PASTRY

Use the basic recipe above substituting half rye, half barley flour in place of the wholewheat flour, or try this other recipe.

50g/2oz gluten free flour or millet flour
50g/2oz maize flour (yellow corn meal/polenta)
25g/1oz soya flour
1 teaspoon baking powder
1 beaten egg
50g/2oz sunflower oil
1 tablespoon cold water

Preheat oven to 375°F/gas mark 5/190°C

Cream together half the flour, oil, egg and water until well blended. Mix together the remaining flour and baking powder and add to the creamed mixture. Knead to a soft dough. Wrap in greaseproof paper and chill for half an hour. Roll out as required. If baking blind, bake for 10 minutes.

WHOLEWHEAT FLAKY PASTRY

340g/12oz wholewheat flour
225g/8oz butter (or part oil)
3 tablespoons water

First halve the butter. Rub half into the flour until a breadcrumb texture is reached. Add water until it sticks together in a lump. Roll out on a floured board into a rectangular shape. Cut the remaining butter into small dice and dot evenly over the surface of the pastry. Fold one side over to two thirds the way across and the other side over that. Roll out again into another rectangle. Turn and fold over in the opposite direction into three as before.

Obviously this will not make really light flaky pastry but it will vary the texture from the shortcrust kind and is useful for pasties and pastries.

GREEN QUICHE

250g/½lb courgettes (zucchini)
450g/1lb Swiss chard (or silver beet or spinach)
1 bunch spring onions
3 eggs
125–200g/4–6oz grated cheese (Cheddar, Gruyère)
1 teaspoon dried basil
1 teaspon dried oregano
salt and pepper

250g/8oz shortcrust pastry for a 27cm/11inch flan dish (or a smaller deeper one).

Preheat oven to 350°F/gas mark 4/180°C

Steam the courgettes and spring onions with the greens until just soft. Chop or mash the courgettes and chop the greens and spring onions. Beat the eggs and mix with the grated cheese, herbs and seasoning. Add the vegetables and mix well. Turn into the shortcrust base and bake for 40 minutes until set and the top is going brown. Allow to cool a little before serving. Quiches taste best lukewarm, but may also be eaten cold.

RED AND GREEN PEPPER FLAN

1 red pepper
1 green pepper
1 onion or 4 spring onions
½ cup cooked red kidney beans (optional)
3 eggs
150ml/5fl oz milk
2 tablespoons yogurt
125g/4oz cheese in small dice
pepper, salt and a little paprika

170g/6oz shortcrust pastry to line an 18cm/8inch flan tin. Keep cool while preparing filling.

Preheat oven to 375°F/gas mark 5/190°C

Dice the onion(s) and peppers and cook gently in a little butter until tender but not brown. Mix the eggs with the seasoning and add the milk and yogurt. Dice the cheese and spread over the base. Add the beans (if used) and the peppers and onions, spread evenly. Cover with the egg and milk mixture and sprinkle a little paprika on top. Bake for 40 minutes or until set. Test with a knife in the middle. It should come out clean.

CHEESE AND ONION FLAN

1 large (or 2 small) onions
2 eggs
150ml/5fl oz milk

100g/4oz grated cheese
2 tomatoes for garnish
pepper and salt

170g/6oz shortcrust pastry to line an 18cm/8inch flan tin. Keep cool while preparing the filling.

Preheat oven to 400°F/gas mark 6/200°C

Slice the onions finely into rings and fry gently in a knob of butter. Mix the eggs with the milk and beat together. Add the grated cheese and the onions when soft and transparent. Pour into pastry case and bake for 30 minutes. Fry the tomatoes cut into rounds and when the flan is nearly done, remove from the oven and garnish with the tomatoes. Return to the oven and cook until set.

MUSHROOM ALTERNATIVE

Make the flan as above, but use just one small onion and 100g/4oz sliced mushrooms cooked with the onion.

LEEK FLAN

500g/1lb leeks
1 tablespoon butter
2 well beaten eggs

1 cup single cream or milk
salt and pepper

170g/6oz shortcrust pastry to line an 18cm/8inch flan tin. You can brush the crust with a little egg yolk to help keep it from becoming soggy. Chill the base while preparing the filling.

Preheat oven to 350°F/gas mark 4/180°C

Wash and clean the leeks. You can cut them lengthwise and hold them under the tap to rinse out any soil trapped under the leaves. Remove outer leaves and any old or tough tops and chop the leeks into small pieces, using as much green as you like. Heat the butter and toss the leeks in it until they start to soften. Do not let them brown. Then beat the eggs with the milk (or cream) and seasoning. Spread the leeks over the chilled base and cover with the egg mixture. Bake for about 35 minutes or until it is set and the top is golden.

A little grated cheese could be added but may spoil the delicate flavour of the leeks. The addition of some diced ham works from the gastronomic point of view but is excluded here, not being advisable in pregnancy.

MF*   BROCCOLI FLAN

450g/1lb broccoli spears
3 tasty ripe tomatoes
3 spring onions or a leek
50g/2oz butter*
½ cup flour (white or wholewheat)
½ pint milk (or part single cream) or soya milk*
a squeeze of lemon juice
½ pressed clove of garlic
½ teaspoon basil
pepper and salt

170g/6 oz shortcrust pastry to line an 18cm/8inch flan dish. Chill while preparing the filling.

Preheat oven to 375°F/gas mark 5/190°C

Steam the washed broccoli spears, having removed any thick or tough parts of the stem. A few tender leaves, on the other hand, may be included. When they are soft but still crunchy and bright green remove from the heat and reserve. In a thick pan fry gently the chopped spring onion or leek with the tomatoes and pressed garlic, until just soft. Now make a béchamel sauce with the butter and flour. When the flour has absorbed the melted butter start adding the milk gradually, stirring all the time to prevent lumps forming. If more liquid is necessary to thin the sauce, you can add a little cooking liquid from the steamed broccoli and season with salt, pepper, the basil (or other herbs such as parsley or chives), and the squeeze of lemon juice. The sauce could be made richer with the addition of an egg or egg yolk at this stage, but since the recipe is otherwise suitable for somebody avoiding eggs, it has not been included. Place the broccoli in the pie shell. Add the tomato and spring onion mixture to the sauce, stir and pour

CHICKEN AND PARSLEY FLAN

1 cup diced cooked chicken
50g/2oz butter
½ cup flour (white or wholewheat)
275ml/½pint milk or chicken stock

½ cup chopped parsley
pepper and salt
(50g/2oz sliced mushrooms may be added if liked)

170g/6oz shortcrust pastry to line a 18cm/8inch flan tin which can be baked blind for 10 minutes at 400°F/gas mark 6–7/200°C.

Melt the butter in a heavy based saucepan and add the flour stirring while the flour absorbs the butter. Gradually add the milk or chicken stock (or a mixture of both) stirring all the time to prevent lumps forming. Cook for five minutes on a low heat until a thick béchamel consistency has been reached. Add a little more liquid if necessary and season. Fry the mushrooms in a little butter and spread over the base with the diced chicken. Add the parsley to the sauce, and pour over the chicken. If you are using a precooked crust you will only need to heat the flan gently in a low oven 325°F/gas mark 3/170°C for 15–20 minutes. Otherwise cook in a fairly hot oven at 400°F/gas mark 6–7/200°C for 30 minutes.

SPINACH AND COTTAGE CHEESE TARTLETS

This recipe works well for small tarts, though equally, you could use any of the quiche and flan recipes this way if you want small individual tarts for a picnic or a party.

12 small shortcrust tart bases (6cm/2½inches across)
450g/1lb steamed spinach leaves
3 spring onions

1 cup of cottage cheese
2 eggs
50g/2oz grated cheese
1 teaspoon herbs (basil, oregano, chives)

Preheat oven to 400°F/gas mark 6/200°C

Steam well washed spinach leaves and spring onions until soft. Chop with scissors into a bowl and add herbs. Spoon a teaspoon of cottage cheese into each case, cover with a spoonful of spinach and glaze with beaten egg mixed with the grated cheese. Be careful not to let the filling run over the edge of the case. Bake for 15 minutes or until done.

CHEESE AND SPINACH PASTIES

250g/8oz flaky pastry (see recipe)
250g/8oz soft white cheese (ricotta or Quark, for example)
1 cup steamed spinach leaves
juice of ½ a lemon
pepper and salt
a dash of tamari or shoyu

Preheat oven to 425°F/gas mark 7/220°C

Chop the steamed spinach and combine with the cheese and lemon juice. Roll out chilled pastry fairly thinly and cut into 10cm/5inch squares. Brush around the edges with water. Place a good spoonful of filling into the centre of each square, but do not overfill the cases. Fold over diagonally to make a triangle and crimp the edges together firmly with the fingers to seal. Bake the triangular pasties for 15 minutes. Check after 10 minutes that they are not burning. Can be eaten hot or cold.

You can experiment with other vegetables for the filling. Watercress goes well in place of the spinach. It is also possible to use a shortcrust pastry. If you use the milk-free one with oil only, try rolling it out between two sheets of greaseproof paper. This makes the rather crumbly pastry easier to handle.

PASTA

There are many ways of using pasta in one's cooking, and an increasing number of shapes available for experiment, made from wholewheat flour. If you have a pasta maker you can put exactly what you like in the mixture. Green pasta (made with spinach) and red (coloured with tomatoes) although usually made with white flour may add variety on occasions.

GREEN PASTA BAKE

350g/12oz green pasta shapes (corkscrews preferably)
450g/1lb spinach, Swiss chard or broccoli
2 eggs beaten with a cup of milk
100g/4oz grated cheese
salt and pepper
two teaspoons herbs such as basil, oregano, chives, parsley.
1 clove garlic (pressed)

Preheat oven to 400°F/gas mark 6/200°C

In a large saucepan of boiling water add a little oil and the pasta shapes and cook until nearly done (*al dente*) – tagliatelle will do quicker than the corkscrews, so you will have to judge the time, which will be about 7–15 minutes. Steam the greens until soft but not mushy and shred into thin slices (or small pieces if it is broccoli). Drain the pasta and stir in the greens with a small knob of butter and some pepper and salt. Turn into an open baking dish. Mix the grated cheese into the eggs beaten with the milk, add the herbs and garlic and pour over the pasta and greens. Bake for 20 minutes covered with a lid or tin foil. Uncover to brown for a further 5–10 minutes.

QUICK WAYS WITH PASTA

Many fresh vegetables combine well with cheese and herbs to flavour pasta for a quick meal. Here are a few suggestions:

Grated carrot and cheese Stir into tagliatelle or spaghetti or cut macaroni with freshly ground black pepper and salt.

MF* VEG *Fresh tomato and herbs* Chop some fresh tomatoes into thin slivers with fresh herbs in season, basil is good. Stir into the pasta with a knob of butter* or a spot of olive oil and season with freshly ground black pepper and salt.

Egg with grated cheese and chives Beat the egg with the grated cheese and chives. Drain the pasta, add a little oil or butter to the pan, return the pasta to the pan, and stir in the egg mixture. The egg will cook as you stir it around in the hot pasta. Reheat a little if necessary, but watch carefully or the egg will overcook and may stick to the pan. Season with salt and pepper. Good with pasta shells or macaroni.

MF* *Garlic butter and parsley* Press a good sized clove of garlic and mix into some soft butter or whey-free margarine*. Add a little lemon juice and finely chopped parsley. Place a knob of garlic butter on the bowl of pasta and sprinkle with more parsley, and chives too if available. Season with pepper and salt.

MF* VEG* *Poppy seeds* Toast 2 tablespoons of poppy seeds on a baking tray in a moderate to hot oven for 5 to 10 minutes (check to see they are not burning). Stir into the pasta (tagliatelle are good for this) with a knob of butter.*

Try toasted sesame seeds too. Garlic is a good addition to any of these dishes if you like it. Experiment with your own ideas, green or red peppers, mushrooms or hot greens or whatever and garnish with cress for a change from herbs.

MF — BUCKWHEAT NOODLES (SOBA)

Soba, the buckwheat spaghetti can be purchased from wholefood shops, or made at home.

500g/1lb buckwheat flour	1 beaten egg
1 teaspoon sea salt	125ml/4fl oz water

Place flour and salt in a large bowl. Stir in the egg, mixing thoroughly. Gradually add as much water as required to make a dry dough. Knead for 10 minutes. Roll out the dough on a floured board to a thin rectangular sheet. Fold the ends of the sheet into the middle, then fold again at the middle to divide the dough into quarters. Cut into thin strips with a sharp knife and unroll.

HOT DISHES

Drop the noodles into a large pan of boiling water. Boil for 5 minutes, then remove from heat and allow to stand for 10 minutes. The soba is now ready to use. (The water can be reserved for stock.)

WAYS TO USE THE BUCKWHEAT NOODLES

1. in soups
2. with a sauce (cheese sauce, spaghetti sauce, chickpea sauce)
3. cold in salads
4. stir-fried with mixed vegetables
5. baked in a casserole with tomatoes and cheese

MF* CHICK PEA SAUCE

1 cup cooked chick peas and stock (a tin of chick peas could be used)
2 tablespoons tahini

1–2 tablespoons chopped parsley yogurt, buttermilk or smatana (or lemon juice*)

Blend the chick peas, stock and tahini and parsley together to a smooth paste. Stir in the buttermilk (yogurt or smatana) to the desired pouring consistency. Heat through carefully without boiling.

For those who haven't come across smatana before, it is a cultured milk product made from single cream and can be used as a substitute for yogurt or buttermilk.

This sauce can be served cold too. It goes equally well with baked potatoes in their jackets, bulgur or vegetables.

PIZZA

You can make small individual pizzas tailored to individual tastes. Larger ones can be made in flan dishes or on oven trays to be cut into slices for serving with different toppings to suit preferences among those at your table. Also try making a large grid catering for these tastes – everything in some places, a row of anchovies set apart for those who like them, no olives somewhere else and so on.

Although salami and ham are traditionally used for certain styles of pizza they are not included here as being unsuitable for a pregnancy diet.

PIZZA DOUGH

(Ordinary bread dough can be used but does not reheat as well if any is left over)

500g/1lb wholewheat flour (or part strong white flour)	1 teaspoon salt
	150ml/5fl oz milk
15g/½oz fresh yeast (or equivalent dried quantity) (see page 48)	3–4 tablespoons olive oil
	1 egg

If the flour is freshly ground it will be nice and warm. Otherwise put the flour and salt in your mixing bowl and warm it in a low oven for a few minutes. Add the yeast powder if you are using Fermipan. Otherwise activate dried yeast or, if fresh yeast is used stir to a paste with a little warmed milk from the rest being heated in a pan. Make a well in the flour and pour this yeast (or the activated dried yeast) in and then the warm milk. Break in the egg and add about half of the olive oil. Mix to a dough, adding more oil as needed. It should come away easily from the bowl and can be shaped into a ball. Place the bowl in a large plastic bag and leave to rise in a warm place for a couple of hours. It should then be spongy and have doubled in size. If it rises before you are ready, knock it down, knead it into a ball again and let it rise a second time. When you are ready, take the ball and place on a large oven tray oiled with olive oil, and press out to the edges. You can also roll it out, but make sure it comes right out to the edges of the tray, and has a little bit of rim at the edges to keep the filling in.

TOMATO BASE

1 medium onion, finely chopped
1 clove garlic
250g/½lb chopped fresh
  tomatoes (or tinned tomatoes)

50g/2oz tomato purée
1 teaspoon basil
1 teaspoon oregano or marjoram

Fry the onion in 2 tablespoons of olive oil until transparent. Add the pressed garlic (more than one clove if you like) and herbs. Add the chopped tomatoes and the juice if tinned (or a little water or stock if fresh) and thicken with the tomato purée. Season with pepper and salt and allow to simmer for 10–15 minutes so that it all blends well together. Remove from heat and reserve until dough is ready. Then spread over the dough base, up to, but not over, the edges.

TOPPING

Any or all of the following may be used:

fresh tomato rounds
sliced or diced green and red
  peppers
sliced mushrooms
chopped spring onions

anchovies or sardines
black olives
mozzarella cheese (or thinly
  sliced mild Cheddar)
oregano or marjoram and basil

Preheat oven to 450°F/gas mark 8/230°C

Set these out in a pattern to accommodate different tastes. If everyone likes peppers, they can be scattered across the whole base, for example. Perhaps not everyone likes anchovies or sardines; break them up a little and make a row down one side. Cross it with mushrooms, or some other ingredient and so on. Decorate with olives on the parts where they will be appreciated. It looks attractive if they are placed diagonally across the rectangle. Sprinkle with herbs and cover the whole with the sliced cheese.

Bake for 30 minutes. Turn the tray around and lower the heat to moderate (350°F/gas mark 4/180°C) for another 15 minutes or until the top is bubbling and brown. Do not brown too much if you plan to reheat on another occasion.

Serve with a fresh green salad such as lettuce with cress and cucumber.

MG* GF VEG*   POLENTA PIZZA

½ cup beans (any kind: red kidney, rosecoco, borlotti, pinto all look pretty) (dry weight) soaked
1½litres/2½pints water
400g/14oz polenta (maize meal)
2 tablespoons olive oil

1 small onion
3 cloves of garlic
1 green or red pepper (sliced)
1 cup tomato concentrate
water or stock to thin the sauce

Cook the soaked beans until nearly done (a little less than an hour in most cases). In a separate large heavy pan bring 1½litres/ 2½pints of water to the boil. Then rain in the polenta and stir till thick. Add the beans and mix in. Simmer on low heat for 20 minutes, until the spoon will stand up in it. In a separate frying pan heat the olive oil and fry a small onion, finely sliced and the garlic (pressed), add the sliced pepper (red or green or a mixture), when soft stir in the tomato concentrate. Add enough water or stock so that, while still thick, it is smooth and of a soft spreading consistency. When the polenta is cooked, turn into a buttered oven dish or tray large enough to make it about 3cm/an inch or so thick. Let it stand a minute until a skin forms. Spread the tomato sauce over it and top with grated cheese or Parmesan (or a mixture) or olives* and scatter a few herbs, such as basil and oregano on top if you like. Serve cut into slabs (reheating in oven if necessary first), with a green salad. Something fairly rough and tasty with watercress, nasturtium leaves, new dandelion leaves and a crisp Cos or Batavia lettuce would be good.

COOKING WITH MEAT

Those who enjoy eating meat should continue to do so as they prepare for pregnancy as well as during pregnancy and afterwards. Others who eat meat occasionally can also do so with benefit at this time. The iron in meat is more easily assimilated than that from vegetable sources, vitamin B12 is also present in meat, as is zinc (both less easy to get enough of on a vegetarian diet).

1 ORGAN MEATS

Liver, kidney and other organ meats are rich in many valuable nutrients, but because there could also be some 'anti nutrients' (like lead), it is advisable to take them less often than the more enthusiastic might suggest. Once a fortnight or once a month, rather than once or twice a week is appropriate.

2 FISH

White fish and oily fish both present different ranges of important vitamins and minerals. But again, they too could be victims of the pollution of our waters. It is wiser to select deep sea fish rather than those from coastal waters and to remember that the larger the fish, the further up the food chain it is likely to be (big fish eat lesser fish and so on ad infinitum). It is also better to choose fresh fish than tinned and to avoid cured or smoked fish (kippers are usually dyed). Many trace elements are present in sea foods and sea vegetables (see page 61), and iodine is one which is essential to brain development. It is a pity that one cannot feel safe with such foods as shellfish, crustaceans – lobster, prawns, shrimps etc, and tuna, but these are the ones most likely to be contaminated. A compromise might be to have something 'fishy' once a week or a fortnight, alternating white fish (cod, haddock etc) or cod roe with small oily fish (sardines, anchovies, brisling etc). Trout and upland river fish are no doubt better than estuary fish. There is a recipe for trout on page 178: otherwise (apart from the anchovies in the pizza) there are no special recipes for fish.

Grilling, cooking in milk or baking in foil are always winners. If you fry, use fresh oil and drain the fish well.

3 RED MEAT

It is assumed that you know how you like your meat cooked, and that most of the time you will be making simple grills or roasts. The cheaper cuts of meat take longer to prepare but are just as good nutritionally. Here one is more in need of a recipe. Having chosen from Italian cooking for the pizza and pasta, the recipes continue to come from all around the world with Hungarian goulash, through Greek, North African, Indian and Mexican dishes, and then back to England for a traditional steak and kidney pie.

4 VEGETARIAN VARIATIONS

Many of these traditional dishes have the advantage of using less meat and combining it with pulses or grains to 'stretch it'. In a couple of cases vegetarian alternatives are given using no meat at all (moussaka, curried mung beans, chilli). If you have been in the habit of eating meat at least once a day, it will be of benefit to alternate it with vegetarian meals sometimes. There is a cost advantage here too.

5 POULTRY AND GAME

Chicken, duck and turkey all provide variety to one's diet, but one should pay attention to the manner of raising the birds. On the whole frozen poultry is more likely to be intensively raised. Choose fresh where you can, and favour especially any poultry that has definitely come from a good farm. Do not be shy about asking. We can all help retailers (and then the producers) to know it is worth their while stocking good produce. If you have found a source of free range eggs, the same shop may also sell good poultry.

Game, on the other hand, will have grown in the wild. It is likely to be free of the disadvantages of intensively raised birds and animals. So by all means indulge yourself if you wish and if you are able to obtain it. Because it is relatively rare, no recipes are offered here.

6 PORK AND VEAL

If you can obtain good pork and veal by all means use it, there are lots of lovely ways of preparing it. However, pigs too are often intensively raised and may be fed unsuitable wastes (such as those from sweet factories!), so do find out where the meat comes from and how the animals were fed, if you can. Veal is rare in Britain, and so no recipes are given for it either. Pork can be grilled, roast or casseroled (try just apple and onion with some apple juice or stock in your casserole).

GF MF — HUNGARIAN GOULASH

1–2 onions
350g/12oz stewing beef (or lamb)
1 tablespoon paprika
3–4 tomatoes
1 green pepper
100g/4oz mushrooms
1–2 carrots

Brown sliced onions in a knob of butter until golden but not burnt. Add meat cut into small cubes and sprinkle liberally with red paprika. Simmer for 10 minutes. Add carrots, cut in rounds, chopped pepper, washed mushrooms (whole or quartered depending on size) and quartered tomatoes. Cover and continue cooking, checking liquid after 15 minutes and add a little water if necessary. Cook another 10–15 minutes and test to see if the meat is tender. Cook it a little longer if needed. Serve with plain steamed potatoes and, traditionally, dill pickled cucumbers, but these may be left out if preferred.

This is the kind of traditional dish where you use the vegetables available. Vary them as you please, using green beans, other root vegetables, a little celery or whatever is to hand.

GF — TRANSYLVANIAN CABBAGE

1 medium sized cabbage or
  450g/1lb loose sauerkraut (or large tin)
30ml/½pint sour cream or yogurt
paprika
pepper and salt
1 litre/1½pints goulash

In a deep oven casserole dish place layers of sauerkraut or thinly sliced fresh cabbage, sour cream (or yogurt) and goulash (as above). Finish with a layer of cabbage, cover and bake in a slow oven for an hour or so. When ready add some more sour cream on top and sprinkle with paprika. Serve with plain steamed potatoes and dill pickled cucumbers as with the goulash.

MOUSSAKA

Fresh mince, cooked minced lamb (or beef) or even cooked beans or lentils can be used for this recipe. It is quite rich, so serve with plenty of mashed potato, jacket potatoes or rice and a fresh salad.

2 or 3 aubergines
olive oil for frying
450g/1lb minced meat or 2 cups cooked beans or lentils
2 tablespoons grated onion
2 ripe tomatoes
1 tablespoon chopped parsley
¼ teaspoon cinnamon
¼ teaspoon nutmeg
50g/2oz butter
1 wineglass red wine or stock

1 pint béchamel sauce made with:
50g/2oz butter
2–3 tablespoons flour (white or wholewheat)
2 cups milk
1 or 2 eggs
salt and pepper (and a little extra nutmeg)
50g/2oz grated cheese

Preheat oven to 400°F/gas mark 6/200°C

Slice the aubergines and sprinkle with salt in a colander and leave to drain for 30 minutes. Rinse well and pat dry with a kitchen towel. Heat 4 tablespoons olive oil and fry the aubergine slices a few at a time. When brown on both sides drain off any excess oil by placing them on brown paper. In another pan melt the butter and sauté grated onion and chopped tomatoes. Add raw meat and allow to brown, stirring and turning for 5–10 minutes in the pan. If using cooked mince or beans, add together with the parsley and spices and moisten with the wine or stock. Cook slowly for 20 minutes adding a little more water if necessary, while making the béchamel sauce. Melt the butter and add the flour, stirring while the flour absorbs the butter. Add the milk (heated if you want to hasten the cooking) little by little, stirring all the time to prevent lumps forming. Season with salt and pepper and a little extra nutmeg. Take a spoonful or two of the sauce to add to the mixture in the other pan. Now add the beaten egg to the béchamel and reserve for the top layer of the moussaka.

In a large oven dish make layers of the meat or bean mixture and aubergine slices sprinkled with a little grated cheese. Finish with a layer of aubergines and cover with the sauce. Bake for 45 minutes until golden brown.

MF* GF*   **BUCKWHEAT MOUSSAKA**

500g/1lb aubergines
1 cup buckwheat
2 cups water
1 onion
1 carrot

125g/4oz mushrooms
1 tin tomatoes (or fresh)
1 teaspoon allspice
1 clove garlic

Topping:
1 carton yogurt*
2 eggs

2 tablespoons flour
(Potatoes mashed with soya milk could be used)*

Preheat oven to 350°F/gas mark 4/180°C

Slice the aubergines and sprinkle with salt. Place in a colander to drain for an hour or so. When ready to use, wash away the salt and dry them on a tea towel or kitchen paper towel. Fry for 10 minutes in 4 tablespoons olive oil, adding a little more as necessary. Set aside to drain.

Slice the onion and carrot and sauté with the crushed garlic in oil. Add sliced mushrooms and cook for a further 5 minutes. Add the tomatoes, allspice and water and bring to the boil. Add the buckwheat, cover and simmer for 20–30 minutes until most of the water has been absorbed.

Into an ovenproof casserole place a layer of buckwheat mixture followed by a layer of aubergines, alternating until full.

For the topping, beat the eggs, add to the yogurt and stir in the flour. Cover the casserole with this topping and bake for 20–30 minutes until golden.

MF	COUSCOUS

This North African dish is usually made with lamb, but chicken can be used instead. For a vegetarian version increase the quantity of chick peas and leave out the meat.

250g/8oz chick peas (dry weight)	1 teaspoon ground ginger
350g/12oz lean lamb	2 teaspoons ground coriander
2 carrots	several sticks of celery
2 onions	2 courgettes
2 tablespoons olive oil	2 leeks
2 bay leaves	2 green or red peppers
2 tomatoes	2 aubergines
2 garlic cloves	50g/2oz raisins
1 teaspoon chilli powder (or paprika if avoiding hot food)	450g/1lb couscous grains or bulgur

Soak the chickpeas overnight, discard the water and cook the peas, in fresh water, for about an hour.

If you are using couscous, you will need a steamer, preferably with small holes or lined with some gauze. Bulgur gives a similar result and is much easier to do. The couscous should be laid out on a baking sheet and sprinkled with water, then worked with the fingers to separate the grains. Repeat several times before steaming. The bulgur can be covered with water in a bowl to swell as you are preparing the rest of the dish. Dice the lamb and remove any excess fat. Slice the onion (chunky segments look nice) and cut the carrot into chunks diagonally. Heat the oil and gently fry the onion, meat and carrot for 5–10 minutes, preferably in a large pan which fits under the steamer used for the couscous. Add the chick peas and cover with water, bring to the boil and simmer for half an hour. Add the bay leaves and spices and the rest of the vegetables diced or sliced as you prefer and the raisins, with more water to cover if necessary. Now arrange the couscous or bulgur in the steamer and steam over the stew for 30 minutes. If you have no steamer, you can take some of the cooking liquid for cooking the bulgur in a separate pan. You may have trouble keeping the couscous grains separate if you cook it this way, so it is best to use bulgur if you cannot steam the grains. A little oil added after a while will help to separate the grains. Check the stew from time to time to make sure it is not catching and add a little more water or

LAMB CURRY
GF

- 2 large onions
- 350g/12oz lean lamb (neck of lamb can be used)
- 1 large tin of tomatoes (or 1lb fresh tomatoes)
- 1 teaspoon chilli powder
- 2–3 teaspoons curry powder or cumin
- 1–2 teaspoons turmeric
- 1–2 teaspoons cloves
- 12–15 cardamom seeds (finely ground)
- 1–2 teaspoons cinnamon
- 1–2 teaspoons salt
- 2 cloves garlic (or to taste)
- 1 green pepper (optional)
- 50g/2oz creamed coconut (looks a bit like lard)
- 2–3 teaspoons vinegar
- 1 cup yogurt
- juice of half a lemon
- butter or ghee for cooking

Slice the onions and fry in butter or ghee until they start to brown. Add the meat cut into small cubes and cook for 5 minutes or so until sealed. Then add the spices, garlic and green pepper (if used), stir around in the pan and add the tomatoes (with a little stock if fresh tomatoes are used). Cover and simmer for 30–40 minutes until the meat is tender. Towards the end add the vinegar and cream coconut, stir until melted and taste the sauce. If it is too hot for your taste you can add a teaspoon of sugar and a little more cinnamon. When it is ready add the yogurt, cook for a further 5 minutes and add the lemon juice just before serving.

Serve with a vegetable curry, boiled brown rice and a couple of side dishes and chutneys.

Side dishes
Cucumber Raita Slice half a cucumber finely and dress with yogurt dressing with spices (see Salads, page 116).
Banana and Coconut Slice a banana finely and coat with desiccated (or fresh, grated) coconut. Moisten with the juice of half a lemon and toss in a few raisins or sultanas. Sprinkle a little cardamom and allspice on top.

MF GF VEG* — CURRIED MUNG BEANS

If you are serving this as a vegetable curry you can add the extra vegetables. Alternatively serve with hard boiled eggs* and rice on its own with a side salad with yogurt dressing.

350g/12oz green mung beans (sprouted if you wish)	1 tablespoon fresh grated ginger
1 large onion	freshly ground black pepper to taste
1–2 cloves garlic	1 tablespoon chopped parsley
1 chilli pepper	Extra vegetables:
1 bay leaf	1 carrot
1 teaspoon cumin	1 turnip
1 teaspoon coriander	1–2 sticks celery thinly sliced
1–2 teaspoons turmeric	100g/4oz spinach

If you use sprouted beans they will not need cooking first. Otherwise soak the beans for 2 hours and discard the water. Cover the beans with cold water, bring to the boil and simmer until tender for 20–30 minutes.

Heat some oil or butter (or ghee if available) in a thick skillet or pan and fry the sliced onion and crushed garlic for 5–10 minutes until transparent. Add the cumin, coriander, turmeric and ginger and toss around for a few minutes. Then add the extra vegetables (if used) except the spinach. Then add the mung beans and a little cooking liquid, the bay leaf and the whole chilli (you can remove it before serving or as soon as the dish is hot enough to your taste). Simmer over low heat until the vegetables are tender or for about 20 minutes if you are not using the extra vegetables. Stir in the parsley and season with freshly ground black pepper. Add the shredded spinach (if used), cover and allow to steam for several minutes.

*For the version with hard boiled eggs, start cooking them 20 minutes before the end. Bring to the boil in cold water and simmer for 10 minutes. Drain, cover with cold water and crack the shells. Then peel the shells (under cold running water if necessary), and add the eggs to reheat a few minutes before serving. They can be halved or served whole.

GF — TANDOORI CHICKEN

- 1 small chicken (about 1½kg/3lb)
- 450ml/3/4pint yogurt or buttermilk
- 3 flakes garlic
- 1 tablespoon sliced fresh stem ginger
- 2 green chillis (or 1 teaspoon chilli powder)
- 1 teaspoon cumin
- 1 teaspoon mint
- ½ teaspoon vinegar
- 1 teaspoon salt
- 1 teaspoon garam masala
- ¼ teaspoon turmeric

Garnish with garam masala, chopped onion, lemon and lettuce.

Remove skin from the chicken. (Boil this up with the giblets to make chicken stock.) Make two long cuts in each leg and two cuts each side of the breast. Salt the chicken and leave for one hour. Make up a mixture from the rest of the ingredients (except the garnish) and blend in a food mixer. Spoon over the chicken to marinate for six hours. Return every so often to spoon it over again and make sure it soaks well into the long cuts. If you have a clay chicken roaster this would be ideal for cooking. Otherwise place a large piece of cooking foil in an open oven dish with enough spare at the sides to cover the chicken completely. Line with greaseproof paper to prevent direct contact of the foil with the chicken. Place the chicken in the centre of the dish on the foil and greasproof paper and coat with the mixture (not necessarily all of it). Seal the edges of the foil over the chicken leaving a little room under it. Bake in the oven at 375°F/gas mark 5/190°C for an hour or so. Open the foil case and coat with the mixture and allow it to brown in the oven, increasing the heat a little if necessary.

Serve garnished with a little garam masala (mixed Indian spice) some chopped onion, lemon slices and lettuce on a bed of rice.

MF* GF*   CHILLI BEANS WITH MAIZE PANCAKES
OR TORTILLAS

- 1 onion
- 1 clove garlic
- 1 teaspoon chilli powder (or to taste)
- 1 red pepper
- 1 green pepper
- 1 cup sweet corn or 250g/½lb minced beef
- 1 cup stock or cooking liquid from the beans
- 2 cups cooked red kidney beans
- 250g/½lb tomatoes (or tinned tomatoes)
- 2 tablespoons tomato purée
- pepper and salt

Dice the onion and fry gently in a knob of butter or some oil with the pressed garlic clove. Add the chilli powder; this can differ in strength and tastes vary so make it hot to your own taste. If it becomes too hot you can correct this to some extent by the addition of a little sugar mixed with cinnamon. Dice the peppers and add to the pan with the corn or minced meat. Stir as it cooks for a further 5–10 minutes. Add the cooked beans and tomatoes with the liquid from the cooked beans or tinned tomatoes, other stock or water. Cook until the meat is tender (if you use meat) and the ingredients are well blended (another 10–20 minutes), adding more stock if needed. Then thicken the liquid by stirring in the tomato purée and season.

*Serve as a filling for the maize pancakes or with tortillas **MF**. (Omit for gluten-free version.)

MAIZE PANCAKES

- 1 cup wholewheat flour
- ½ cup maize meal (polenta)
- 1 teaspoon baking powder
- 2 eggs
- a few drops of tabasco (chilli pepper sauce)
- 1 tablespoon corn oil (or corn germ oil)
- 2 tablespoons yogurt
- 1 cup water – or a little more

Mix the dry ingredients and make a well in the centre. Add the eggs, tabasco and oil and stir well until the flour has absorbed all the egg and oil. Stir in the yogurt and add the water gradually until a runny consistency is reached. Grease a thick frying pan and when hot ladle a little mixture on to it, tipping the pan until it has covered the surface. When brown at the edges, turn the pancake to brown on the other side briefly. Then remove with a spatula or egg slice and keep warm while you make the rest of the pancakes.

MF   **TORTILLAS**

Tortillas can be bought ready-made, usually made with fine maize flour. Here is a wholewheat version.

250g/½lb wholewheat flour   150–250ml/6–8fl oz water
½ teaspoon salt

Mix flour and salt. Stir in enough water to make a stiff dough. Knead on a floured surface until smooth and elastic. Break the dough into 2cm/1inch balls (it should make up to 20), and roll out into very thin tortillas. Cook over low heat on a lightly greased griddle or frying pan. Turn to brown on both sides. Serve warm or cold.

MF GF*   **STEAK AND KIDNEY PIE**

350g/12oz stewing steak   wholewheat flour to coat meat
125g/4oz ox or lamb kidney   250g/8oz shortcrust pastry or*
125g/4oz mushrooms   **GF** pastry see page 75

Preheat oven to 400°F/gas mark 6/200°C

Dice the steak and the kidney and remove any excess fat. To coat with flour you can place some flour (or soya flour*) in a paper bag and season it, then toss the pieces of meat in, hold the top closed firmly and shake it all around. Then wash the mushrooms and coat them with flour in the same way. Mix with the meat and fill a greased pie dish, choosing a size in which the filling comes up to the top, or is raised slightly above the top. Add water or stock up to about an inch from the top and wet the edge of the dish. Roll the pastry out to about 1cm/½inch thickness and cover the dish, pressing down well at the edge. Trim and make a hole in the centre.

Decorate with the left over pieces. Stick on the leaves, diamonds or other pastry shapes with a little water. To glaze, brush the crust with beaten egg. If you use milk, apply it just 10 minutes before the end. Bake the pie for half an hour and then reduce the temperature to stew the meat to 300°F/gas mark 1–2/150°C for at least another hour. (Cover with oiled greaseproof paper to prevent browning too much, if necessary.)

Serve with lots of vegetables and potatoes. A 'macedoine' of broad beans, peas, diced carrots and swede looks attractive.

COOKING WITH BEANS AND OTHER PULSES

Dried beans and other pulses (lentils, split peas, chick peas etc) will, in general, expand to double the volume when soaked and cooked. They will usually weigh about twice as much too. This can be a rough guide when estimating how much to measure out for cooking when the recipe calls for cooked amounts.

It is always best to soak in cold water overnight (or at least 12 hours) and to discard the water before cooking in fresh water. However, there is a short cut if you are in a hurry. Bring the dried pulses to the boil in plenty of cold water. Allow to stand for an hour or so. Discard water and cook in new cold water. Abandon this practice if it gives you wind.

As even the quick way still takes a couple of hours or more, you can cook a quantity and keep some in the fridge for a few days in a sealed container for use later on. You can also freeze cooked beans or pulses for up to one month. Then they are ready as a stand by.

Note: Whatever way you cook beans, make sure they are boiling for at least 15 minutes during the cooking. The temperatures on slow cooking pots do not allow the beans to reach boiling point, so they must be boiled separately before or after slow cooking methods.

There are many more vegetarian recipes in some of the titles given in the Booklist, page 232.

BURGERS, RISSOLES AND VEGETARIAN BAKES

GF* MF VEG   TOFU RISSOLES

- 200g/6oz cooked millet or brown rice
- 200g/6oz drained tofu
- 100g/4oz chopped mushrooms
- 50g/2oz minced or grated carrot
- 50g/2 oz minced or grated onion
- 2 tablespoons tamari or soya sauce
- 1 teaspoon sage and chopped parsley
- some wholewheat flour to coat burgers (or sesame seeds)*

Mix all the ingredients together except the flour. Form the mixture into small rissoles and coat with the flour. It helps to keep hands and spoons wet as the rissoles can be sticky. Either fry the burgers in sunflower oil or bake for 25 minutes in a moderate oven.

Cooked rissoles can be frozen.

Serve with a green salad or cooked greens with a jacket potato or bread.

MF VEG*   BULGUR BURGERS

- 1 cup bulgur
- 100g/4oz tofu
- 1 medium onion
- 1 carrot
- 1 clove garlic
- 2 tablespoons oatmeal (or a little more)
- 1 egg (or a tablespoon of oil or soya flour*)
- 1 teaspoon mixed herbs (or garam masala for spicy burgers)
- flour to coat
- oil for frying

Add two cups of boiling water to bulgur and cook for about 10 minutes until all the water has been absorbed. Grate the onion and carrot and mix with mashed tofu. Add crushed garlic and herbs or spice and the beaten egg. Then add enough oatmeal to make a firm mixture. Shape into burgers and coat with flour.

Fry for approximately 5 minutes on each side.

If you make the spicy version you could serve with a cucumber and yogurt salad.

MF VEG — SOYA BURGERS

2½ cups cooked soya beans
½ onion finely chopped
½ cup wholewheat flour
½ teaspoon basil
1 teaspoon oregano

1 clove pressed garlic
salt and pepper
optional addition: ½ chopped green pepper

Soak the soya beans overnight. Discard the water and cook in fresh water. They need plenty of time so a pressure cooker is useful. Use 3 cups water for every cup of soaked beans. Add a drop of oil to prevent the vent getting blocked. Cook for 40–45 minutes at standard 15lb pressure.

Another method is to soak as before and discard the water. Then measure cooking water and reserve in a pan. Freeze the beans for several hours and then bring to the boil in the water without thawing. Simmer for an hour, or until the beans feel soft between finger and thumb.

Without either pressure cooker or freezer you must cook them for several hours to get them soft. It is important that they are thoroughly cooked to be properly digestible.

To make the burgers, drain and mash the beans, adding the rest of the ingredients as you mash. Mix well together. Divide the mixture into eight portions and roll in a ball, then flatten as you coat with wholewheat flour. You can also use sesame seeds to coat the burgers. Fry in oil, turning until nice and brown on both sides.

MF GF VEG — LEAFY TOFU BALLS

1 clove garlic
75g/3oz sunflower seeds
250g/½lb spinach, Swiss chard or spring cabbage
400g/14oz tofu

juice of one lemon
2 tablespoons tamari
3 tablespoons chopped parsley
50g/2oz ground cashew nuts

Preheat oven to 350°F/gas mark 4/180°C

Heat a little oil in a large pan and gently fry the crushed garlic and sunflower seeds. Shred the spinach (or other greens) and add to the pan. Cover and leave to steam for a few minutes over low heat. Stir in the tofu and other ingredients including a little flour if the mixture is too moist. With wet hands form the mixture into balls, flatten and place on an oiled baking sheet. Bake for 20 minutes.

Serve with brown rice or mashed potato and swede.

MF CHICK PEA FRITTERS

170g/6oz dry chick peas
100g/4oz wholewheat flour
1 teaspoon baking powder
1 egg
1 tablespoon soya sauce or tamari

2 teaspoons seed oil
150ml/5fl oz water
salt and pepper

Soak the chick peas in water overnight and discard the water. Cook them in fresh water for an hour or so until done – they take longer than some beans. Drain the peas and reserve while you make the batter. Mix the baking powder with the flour and salt in a bowl (not much salt will be needed as the tamari or soya sauce is salty) and make a well in the centre. Break in the egg and add the oil, soya sauce and water. Mix thoroughly until well blended and leave to stand for 30 minutes or so if possible. Mix in the chick peas and pepper, and heat some oil in a pan. Drop spoonfuls of the batter on to the pan. Cook on both sides and keep warm as you drain them on kitchen paper or brown paper.

Serve with chutneys or a sharp sauce, with brown rice and fresh spring onions.

MF VEG SAVOURY RICE BAKE

2 cups cooked rice
1 onion
1 red or green pepper
1 carrot

1 stick celery
1 clove garlic
1 teaspoon mixed herbs
1 tablespoon chopped parsley

Topping
1–2 tablespoons breadcrumbs
1 tablespoon mixed sunflower and sesame seeds

1 tablespoon chopped or ground peanuts

Preheat oven to 350°F/gas mark 4/180°C

Cut vegetables into fairly small pieces and fry gently in oil until soft. Add the herbs and parsley and mix vegetables with the rice. Turn mixture into an oiled ovenproof casserole. Mix together the topping ingredients and sprinkle on the rice mixture. Bake for 30–40 minutes until the topping is starting to brown.

GF MF VEG   **NUTTY SUNFLOWER ROAST**

- ½ cup millet
- 2 tablespoons peanut butter (unsweetened) or ½ cup chopped cashews
- 1 large carrot
- 1 small apple
- 1 green pepper
- 3 tomatoes
- 1 tablespoon miso dissolved in a little cold water
- 1 tablespoon tahini
- 1 teaspoon basil or oregano
- 1 tablespoon soya flour
- sunflower seeds to scatter over the top

Preheat oven to 375°F/gas mark 5/190°C

Dry roast the millet, either in a thick pan over a low heat on the stove top, or in the oven at a low temperature. Roasting grains gives a lovely nutty flavour. Boil the roasted millet for about 15 minutes in 1½ cups water. Cook until all the water has been absorbed. Cover the pan and do not stir whilst cooking. Grate or mince the carrot, apple and green pepper and chop the tomato finely. Stir these into the millet. Add all the other ingredients except the sunflower seeds and mix well. Grease a flan dish or loaf tin and spoon in the mixture. Scatter sunflower seeds over the top. Bake for 30 minutes.

MF VEG   **CHICK PEA HOT POT WITH THREE SAUCES**

- 2 cups cooked chick peas and stock
- 1 cup bulgur
- 1 large onion finely sliced
- 2 cloves garlic
- parsley
- juice of one lemon
- 1 teaspoon paprika
- a little sunflower oil

Lightly sauté the onion and pressed garlic in the sunflower oil. Stir in the finely chopped parsley, chick peas, bulgur and paprika. Cook gently for a few minutes. Make up the chick pea stock to 2½ cups with extra water if needed and add to the mixture. Cover and simmer for 10–15 minutes or until the stock is all absorbed; add a little more water if necessary.

Serve hot or cold with a selection of sauces.

MF VEG   TAHINI SAUCE

4 tablespoons tahini   juice of ½ lemon

Mix together and add water to make a pouring consistency.

ORANGE SAUCE

½ cup yogurt   1 pressed clove of garlic
½ an orange peeled and diced

Mix together to make a sauce.

FENNEL SAUCE

½ cup yogurt or buttermilk   chopped chives
a small piece of fennel grated   a little white wine (optional)
   finely

Mix together and serve as the third sauce.

MF VEG GF   RED CABBAGE WITH ADUKI BEANS
                           AND CHESTNUTS

1 red cabbage   50g/2oz raisins
1 large cooking apple   1 tablespoon honey (or less)
1 large onion   1 tablespoon vinegar (or to taste)
125g/4oz aduki beans (soaked   preferably apple vinegar
   overnight)   approximately 1 cup water
50g dried chestnuts (soaked
   overnight)

Slice onion and soften in oil in a large heavy based pan. Add sliced or grated cabbage, cover and cook for 10 minutes, stirring occasionally. Add water which should fill about one third of the pan – just enough to simmer ingredients without covering completely. Add peeled and sliced apple, raisins, chestnuts and beans and honey and vinegar to taste. Simmer for about 1 hour, checking every so often to see that it is not boiling dry. Add salt at the end and adjust sweet and sour taste by adding more honey or vinegar if necessary.

Serve with jacket potatoes or brown rice.

VEGETABLE DISHES

These ways of presenting vegetables show how you can vary some ordinary vegetables such as cabbage to provide interesting accompaniments to either meat or bean and grain dishes. In general, wash and scrub your vegetables well, but do not peel them. Cut them at the last minute and cook for the shortest time in little water, or steam or stir-fry them. This will help retain the vitamins and minerals which are the most beneficial contribution the vegetables make to your diet. Root, stem, leaf, flower and fruit all offer different ranges of nutrients, so vary them through the week and the seasons. For these purposes roots include potatoes with carrots, swede, beetroot etc., stems: leek, celery, silver beet stalks etc. Leaf vegetables are easier to identify and very rich in folic acid: cabbage, spinach, cress, sprouts etc. The flower is found in broccoli and cauliflower and fruits include tomatoes, courgettes, peppers, aubergines, pumpkin and marrow.

Fresh homegrown vegetables are by far the best (but do not grow them too near to busy roads), bought fresh vegetables are usually better than frozen, but remember that withered, tired vegetables which have been kept by you or the shop keeper for some days since picking may have lost much of their goodness, and frozen vegetables could have retained more. Tinned vegetables should not be used often, but are very useful stores to keep. Avoid if you can dried or packet vegetables like instant peas and mashed potatoes.

GF MF* VEG*   BROCCOLI AND CAULIFLOWER

250g/½lb broccoli
250g/½lb cauliflower
2 tablespoons sunflower seeds
  (or pumpkin seeds or sesame
  seeds)
50g/2oz butter* or whey-free margarine or oil.

Cut or break the broccoli and cauliflower into small florets. Melt the butter in a heavy saucepan and fry the seeds lightly for a few minutes. Add the washed vegetables and toss in the butter. Close the lid for a minute, then inspect, and add a little water, bring to the boil, turn the vegetables and close the lid for a further 3 or 4 minutes. Test the stems to see if they are reasonably tender, if not ready leave another minute or so in the pan. Serve while they are still crunchy and the broccoli is a nice bright green.

Good with a flan or a bean casserole, or just jacket potatoes with grated cheese.

MF GF VEG   BRUSSELS SPROUTS

You can cook Brussels sprouts in the same way with seeds, or slivered almonds or cashews.

GF MF VEG   CABBAGE

Cabbage can be steamed or boiled in a small amount of water. It is also good stir-fried rapidly, for just a few minutes before serving, sliced finely. Seeds can also be added as above, and a little finely sliced onion or apple added makes a change. Another idea is spiced cabbage.

GF MF* VEG*   SPICED CABBAGE

Shred the washed cabbage finely, cutting it in half first with the flat side against the board. Melt a little butter* or oil in a heavy saucepan or skillet, add some crushed coriander seeds, one or two cardamoms, some finely sliced fresh ginger or a sprinkle of powdered ginger or cinnamon. Then stir in the cabbage, add two tablespoons water, close the lid firmly and let it cook for a few minutes. Serve immediately. Wash out the pan with a tablespoon of apple or wine vinegar and pour over the cabbage for extra piquancy.

GF GREEN BEANS WITH TOMATO

1 onion
450g/1lb runner or French beans
4 or 5 tomatoes
100ml/3–4fl oz sour cream or yogurt
a sprinkle of paprika
black pepper and salt

Preheat oven to 400°F/gas mark 6/200°C

Slice the onion finely and fry gently in an ovenproof dish for 5–10 minutes until transparent. Wash, top and tail and string the beans, leave whole, or cut into 15cm/6inch lengths and blanch in boiling water. Remove onions in dish from heat, lay the beans on top and cover with chopped tomatoes. Cover and bake for 20 minutes or until tender but still crunchy. Drizzle the cream or yogurt over the top and sprinkle with the paprika, pepper and salt. If you are short of beans you could add some green pepper in long slices.

Serve with potatoes or rice. This dish goes well with lamb or pork chops.

MF GREEN BEANS ON TOAST

Allow 125g/4oz runner or French beans per person
a slice of wholemeal toast
yeast extract spread (if liked)
a poached egg per serving

Wash, top and tail the beans and slice diagonally into thin slices. Steam the beans or cook in just enough boiling water to cover until tender. Cook the toast on one side, remove and butter the uncooked side and spread with Marmite, Barmene or other yeast extract, if liked, and replace in griller to frizzle. Poach the eggs to be ready when the beans and toast are. Place beans on toast and egg on top.

A quick and delicious meal.

FLORENTINE EGGS

700g/1½lb spinach
4 eggs
50g/2oz butter

3–4 tablespoons flour
300ml/½ pint milk/spinach liquid
125g/4oz cheese

Preheat oven to 350°F/gas mark 4/180°C

Wash the spinach in several waters to remove all grit. Steam until reduced in size and floppy, but still bright green. Drain well, conserving liquid for sauce, and make little nests in individual ramekins or soufflé dishes (well greased). Break an egg into each one and bake for 10 minutes or until the egg sets. Meanwhile, make the cheese sauce by melting the butter in a pan, adding the flour and stirring until it has absorbed the butter, then gradually adding liquid (milk or spinach cooking liquid) until smooth. Stir in cheese and, when the eggs are ready, pour a little over each egg. Return to oven and increase heat to brown. Serve with jacket potatoes, on a bed of brown rice or with hot wholemeal rolls.

GF MF* VEG*   HOT MACEDOINE DE LEGUMES

The basic ingredients are peas and diced carrots, to which you can add diced swede, turnip, parsnip, celery, fennel or small chunks of green beans. A few chick peas or haricot beans (previously cooked) can also be added. Start by cooking the root vegetables in enough water to cover. Add the peas and beans or other vegetables after 5 minutes, and cooked peas or beans at the end just to warm. Put the lid on as the cooking liquid reduces to steam at the end, and when the liquid is nearly gone add a knob of butter*, pepper and salt and sprinkle fresh chopped parsley, chives or other herbs on the top before serving.

GF   LIMA OR BUTTER BEANS

These beans are delicious served simply with cream and parsley or chives. Cooked beans can also be fried in butter with herbs.

| MF GF VEG | RATATOUILLE |

This quantity makes enough to have some over to freeze as a useful standby. Simply serve with plain boiled brown rice topped with grated cheese as a simple meal.

You can vary the proportions of the different vegetables according to preference or availability, but it works well with roughly equal quantities.

500g/1lb tomatoes
500g/1lb aubergines
500g/1lb courgettes
500g/1lb green or red peppers
500g/1lb onions
2 crushed cloves of garlic

herbs (parsley, thyme, bay leaf or basil)
a few coriander seeds (optional)
3 tablespoons olive oil (or more if liked)
salt and pepper

The vegetables need not be peeled, except perhaps the tomatoes. To do this cut a cross with a sharp knife on the top and pour boiling water over them. Leave for a minute or two, then lift the peel where it is cut and the skins can easily be removed. Dice or slice all the vegetables in fairly chunky pieces to look attractive. Heat the oil in a frying pan and soften the onion and garlic, add the aubergines, courgettes, peppers and finally the tomatoes. Season with salt and pepper and continue cooking covered with some water for 30–40 minutes, and with the herbs and coriander (if used). Alternatively, turn into a casserole dish and bake in the oven at 400°F/gas mark 6/200°C for 30 minutes. Longer cooking is sometimes recommended, but this way it is certain not to be overcooked, if later you wish to reheat some. The dish is also more likely to retain its vitamins with less cooking.

JACKET POTATOES

Cooking potatoes in their jackets is an easy and nutritious way to serve them. Scrub the skins well and remove any blemishes. Blighted potatoes (with black marks through them) should be discarded, as should those which are very green. Small amounts of green can be cut out. The temperature and cooking time can be adjusted to suit your needs. Large potatoes in a moderate oven will take a couple of hours to cook. If you want them done more quickly, cut them in half or use smaller potatoes and raise the temperature to 400°F/gas mark6–7/200°C and they will do in 40 minutes or so. The outsides will go crisper too. You can also reduce the cooking time in the oven if you parboil them for 10 minutes, or put a skewer through them.

Serving suggestions

- **GF** Scoop out the middles and mash with grated cheese, return to halved potatoes and brown in the oven.
- **GF** Serve the potatoes with cream cheese and chives placed in a slit on the top.
- **GF MF* VEG*** A little butter* and some mustard and cress on top is another way to serve jacket potatoes, or mash in some broccoli.

BEETROOT AU GRATIN

A good sized root of beetroot per serving

fresh brown breadcrumbs
grated cheese

Preheat oven to 400°F/gas mark 7/220°C

Clean the beetroot well, but carefully, so as not to puncture the skin. Cook in boiling water until tender. Remove from the water to cool, and then skin them. The skins should rub off in the hands quite easily if you cut the root and top off. Transfer to an ovenproof dish and sprinkle with grated cheese and breadcrumbs. Brown for 10 minutes.

Serve with jacket potatoes with cream cheese and chives and a green vegetable or salad. Potatoes mashed with swede or carrot would also go well, and some fresh water cress.

| GF MF VEG* | CHINESE STIR FRY |

There is considerable flexibility in the vegetables used and their proportions. Here are some suggestions.

- 3–4 leaves Chinese cabbage (you could substitute celery sticks or white cabbage)
- 4–5 spring onions
- 1 cup mung beansprouts
- 1 small carrot (try square flakes)
- 50g/2oz mushrooms (Shitake are superb)
- 1 tablespoon finely chopped fresh ginger (or to taste)
- 1 clove garlic

suitable spices include anise or Chinese wild pepper
Cook in sesame oil for preference.
Serve with a sprinkle of tamari or shoyu sauce and chopped chives

Additional extras: sweet corn, water chestnuts, almonds or cashews, sesame seeds or sunflower seeds, flageolet beans (cooked).

Prepare all the vegetables first, as the key to this method of cooking is to toss all the vegetables in the oil for a short time. Shred the cabbage or chop the celery finely. The spring onions can be chopped finely or cut into lengths with some white and green on. Slice the mushrooms down through the stalk. Cut the carrot into chunks, and then make thin squarish flakes lengthwise. Prepare any other vegetables used so that everything is ready. Now heat a tablespoon of oil in a wok or skillet. Put any seeds or nuts in first to brown, then add the mushrooms and carrot, then cabbage and spring onions and garlic. The ginger (which could also be cut in flakes) and spices can be stirred in next, and beansprouts last. Put the lid on for a few moments to allow the vegetables to steam briefly. Remove lid and stir. The vegetables should be served still nice and crunchy. A few chives could be scattered on top and the tamari or soya sauce served at the table separately.

Serve with plain boiled brown rice, in a separate rice bowl if you like. Meat could also be added to the stir fry – chicken, pork and beef cut in fine strips are all suitable.*

Salads

A raw course with each meal or one raw meal a day is a good general rule for ensuring plenty of vitamins, minerals and fibre. Here are some salads which could form a course on their own (the fresh raw salads) and some others to add if you are serving a salad meal (the staple salads and those based on cooked vegetables).

If it is your habit to shop weekly, you may wonder how you can provide a fresh salad each day. A plan to work from is given below, showing how to start with the vegetables which deteriorate quickest, to move on to those which last better and end up with those which will have ripened during the week (or grown, in the case of bean and seed sprouts), perhaps filling out with some staple beans or grains.

The fresh salad recipes are given in this order. It can only be approximate, as what is ready to use and what needs time to ripen or grow will vary each week. If you are able to grow a few lettuces or other vegetables, the problem of fresh supplies will largely disappear. Even a few herbs in the garden or on the window sill will help vitalise your end-of-week offerings.

Day One   Any green salad based on lettuce or watercress
            Start sprouting some beans and seeds for later on
Day Two   Use up the rest of the lettuce or cress, or reserve a crisp lettuce such as Cos, New York, Batavia etc. for this day. Add more in the way of cucumber, tomato, green pepper if not much lettuce left. Water your bean sprouts.
Day Three Cucumber and tomato salad
            Cucumber and beetroot salad
            Water your sprouting beans or seeds
Day Four Cole slaw
            Red salad
            Water your sprouting beans or seeds

Day Five   Grated root vegetable salads
Celery and walnut salad
Soak beans for next day's salad
Water sprouting beans and seeds

Day Six   Potato salad with peppers, spring onions, parsley
Flageolet and avocado salad
Mixed bean salad with peppers and beetroot
Top these with alfalfa or mung bean sprouts which should be ready now.

Day Seven   Winter salad
Rice salad with left over bits and pieces
Tabbouleh or barley and corn with extra peppers or cucumber and bean or seed sprouts

A shopping list to provide such salads could look like this:

- 1 flat lettuce or bunch of water cress
- 1 Cos lettuce (or other crisp variety)
- 1 celery or 2–3 endives/chicory
- 2 green and 2 red peppers
- 30g/1oz parsley
- 1 ripe avocado and another to ripen during the week
- 500g/1lb tomatoes (ripe) and another to ripen
- 500g/1lb beetroot or a few cooked beetroots
- 500g/1lb carrots
- 1 swede or turnip or parsnip
- a bunch of radishes
- 1 cabbage (white, red or Chinese leaves)
- 1 cucumber
- 2 lemons
- 1 box mustard and cress
- 1–2 bunches of spring onions or some shallots
- optional extras such as some mushrooms, fennel or grapes, some apples (if you like them with cabbage or celery)

Check your store cupboard for the following:

- eggs (to hardboil or for mayonnaise)
- cheese to grate or crumbly white cheese to add with greens
- 50g/2oz walnuts, cashews or almonds
- 50g/2oz sunflower seeds or peanuts
- sultanas or raisins

Check variety in the pulse department – brown and green lentils, red kidney beans, haricot beans, flageolets, rosecocos etc. You can buy tins of precooked beans, sometimes mixed already with three

SALADS

different kinds, for an easy short notice salad. Mung beans, alfalfa or other seeds to sprout

potatoes
rice and other grains
frozen corn or peas

garlic
salad oil

SPROUTING BEANS AND SEEDS

Sprouting beans is easy so long as you remember to rinse and drain them regularly. Hence all the reminders in the weekly list of salads!

Suitable subjects for sprouting include: mung beans, aduki beans, whole lentils (not red ones), alfalfa, sesame and sunflower seeds (for bread too), spicy radish, fenugreek, fennel (good for sandwiches). There are 'salad mixes' and 'sandwich mixes' put out by some seed merchants too, all worth a try. (For wheat see page 34–5.)

You need a large glass jar, a piece of gauze to cover the top held in place by a rubber band.

Scatter the seeds over the bottom of the jar, one or two deep. Fill with water and leave to soak overnight. Cover with the gauze, secure with rubber band and drain in the morning. Fill with fresh water and drain. Leave in a warm dark place. Rince and drain two or three times a day. If you forget, give them two rinses, especially if the water is cloudy or froths. Continue until you see the sprouts emerging. They may be placed in the light now or still kept in the dark until the last day. Some sunlight will improve the vitamins and make the leaves go green.

When ready use or store in a refrigerator.

The seed sprouts should be 1–2 inches long (3–5cm), unless for bread, when the sprouts should be just visible. The bean sprouts should be 1½–3 inches long (4–8cm) for optimum food value.

They will take different times to sprout, usually 3–5 days.

DRESSINGS

One way to lend variety to your salads is to experiment with various dressings. These are best made freshly each time, though left over oil and vinegar dressing can be kept, and yogurt dressing or mayonnaise will keep a day in the fridge.

NOTES ON INGREDIENTS

Oils

It is best to use first pressed, cold pressed or virgin oil when available. Not only does it taste better, but its higher nutritional value is worth the extra cost.

Olive oil gives a flavour many like, but if you want a blander oil, rich in essential fatty acids, use sunflower, safflower or sesame seed oils. Ground nut oil is practically tasteless, but it and corn oil are a little higher in the 'mono' and less high in the poly-unsaturated fatty acids. Avoid anything simply labelled 'vegetable oil' completely.

Lemon juice and vinegars

Prefer lemon juice to vinegar generally, as it gives some vitamin C and prevents oxidisation of cut vegetables (the tendency to go brown). Sometimes vinegar suits the salad better, or you have no lemon. White or red wine vinegar, apple or cider vinegar all taste more pleasant in salad dressings than malt vinegar and rice vinegar is very mild. Malt vinegar should not be used in salad dressings.

Spices and herbs

Mustard will help to emulsify a dressing. Use dry mustard with lemon juice or French mustard with vinegar.

Salt and pepper are usually added; use freshly ground sea salt and black pepper for preference.

Garlic is best squeezed in a garlic press and is a good addition to most dressings provided you like it and can judge when to use just a taste and when to pile it on.

Coriander, cardamom and ginger give a piquancy to yogurt dressings, useful with cabbage or cucumber to provide an anti-flatulent effect.

Chives and parsley go with nearly everything. Basil is regarded as enhancing tomatoes. Dill or fennel tops will lend an anise flavour. Chervil can be used freely. Mint is good with cucumber. All are much better fresh, of course!

FRENCH DRESSING

MF GF* VEG

The traditional dressing is made with one part vinegar and three parts oil. If you are using lemon instead of vinegar, the juice of ½ lemon should be plenty. If wine will be taken with the meal, use a little in the dressing in place of the vinegar (kinder to those drinking the wine, even if you are not).

Dissolve the salt in the vinegar or lemon juice. Then add pepper, mustard*, pressed garlic or other ingredients and oil. Shake well to blend.

Pour a tablespoon or so on to your salad and toss it well before deciding to add more. If there are leaves in your salad, add the dressing just before serving.

MAYONNAISE

MF* GF

The quality and flavour of the oil will be the most important influence in your end result. Equipment and ingredients should all be at room temperature before you start.

Place an egg yolk in a rounded bowl and whisk briskly adding the oil drop by drop. If you are careful only to add more oil when the first has been absorbed, there is little risk of the dressing curdling. (Should it curdle, that is, separate, one way to retrieve it is to start with a new egg yolk in a fresh bowl, and to add your curdled mayonnaise bit by bit, as for the oil. When it is properly emulsified again, continue with the rest of the oil.) Add up to one cupful of oil in total. Then season as you wish with lemon juice, vinegar, herbs, capers, horseradish sauce*, green peppercorn paste, olive paste, tamari, finely chopped hardboiled egg, or whatever goes with your salad. Some cooks suggest adding a tablespoon of boiling water to the finished mayonnaise to lighten it.

MF GF   AÏOLI (for garlic enthusiasts)

Start with 4 pressed garlic cloves. Beat 2 egg yolks into them with a little salt. Add a cup of olive oil, drop by drop, as for mayonnaise. When it has thickened, add ½ teaspoon of cold water and 1 teaspoon of lemon juice. If the aïoli fails to thicken, retrieve it in the way described above. Excellent with cold fish or potatoes.

NOTE These are rich dressings and best reserved for occasional use only. You can add a hot mashed potato to the garlic for the aïoli. This would make it less rich.

GF*   YOGURT DRESSING

1 cup plain yogurt
juice of half a lemon
¼ teaspoon dry mustard*
salt and pepper

Mix all ingredients well. A glass jar with a screw top is suitable and can be shaken to mix the dressing. Any left over is easily stored in the fridge. Add any other flavours for different effects.

For a side dish with curry add crushed coriander seeds, cumin, cardamom, a little chilli powder (a pinch for caution, taste, and add more if wished), ginger powdered or grated fresh root ginger.
For minty cucumber add ½ cup finely chopped mint.
For a grated root vegetable salad (especially if celeriac is included) add 1–2 tablespoons freshly grated horseradish or horseradish sauce, and perhaps some cream.
For cole slaw you can use vinegar instead of lemon juice, add a little paprika and a touch of chilli powder for a hot edge to it.
For a bean salad a mashed or blended avocado pear will make a nice thick sauce when added to the yogurt dressing.

OTHER DRESSINGS

You could use the chick pea sauce (cold) (page 83), or any of the sauces that go with the chick pea hot pot (page 102).

    The tahini sauce would complement the protein in a bean or rice salad. The orange sauce is interesting with the winter salad. All these sauces can accompany the mixed root vegetable salad.

SALADS
FRESH RAW SALADS

GF* MF* VEG*   **GREEN SALAD**
---

lettuce (any sort) to which you can add one or more of:

watercress or mustard and cress
cucumber
green pepper
bean or seed sprouts
finely chopped celery including leaves
finely chopped spinach leaves or cabbage

finely chopped broccoli tops or cauliflower
nasturtium leaves or tender spring dandelion leaves
parsley, chives, chervil or other herbs
spring onions

nutritious extras:* crumbly white cheese in bits, nuts or seeds (raw or toasted), hot garlic croutons (page 63), hard boiled egg chopped finely.

Break the lettuce leaves (never cut them except for occasional shredding). Wash well and shake out, leave to dry or pat with a towel. Add just before serving any shredded greens, chopped extras and dress, toss and serve, sprinkled with herbs or chopped spring onion. If applied too soon a French dressing will make the lettuce 'tired'.

GF MF VEG   **CRESS AND CASHEW AND AVOCADO**
---

1 bunch of watercress (or enough for each person)
1 avocado

½ cup cashew pieces (preferably raw, but salted could be used)
1 spring onion or chives for garnish

The bland cashews and avocado offset the hotter watercress. Slice the avocado into thin fingers and sprinkle with lemon juice, or a lemon based French dressing. Add the cashews and washed and drained cress, toss well and serve with chopped chives or spring onion on top.

Some cold cooked runner beans could be added.

GF MF VEG TOMATO AND CUCUMBER SALAD

250g/½lb tomatoes
10cm/4 inches of cucumber
chives, parsley or basil

French dressing with vinegar base (for preference)

Slice the tomatoes and cucumber finely. Mix well with dressing and herbs.

This salad is good with most flans. Double the quantities if no other salad is served.

GF MF VEG CUCUMBER AND BEETROOT SALAD

2 good sized cooked beetroots
10cm/4 inches of cucumber

French dressing with vinegar

Slice beetroot and cucumber or cut in chunky 'chips' for a different look. Dress with French dressing and top with parsley and other herbs if wished.

GF MF VEG RED SALAD

¼ of a red cabbage
3 or 4 other red vegetables such as:
tomatoes
beetroot (cooked or raw)
red pepper
radishes
carrot
a little onion (red if available)
French dressing

Shred the cabbage finely and add other shredded or sliced vegetables as available (equal in bulk to the cabbage or more). If there is no cabbage, use tomatoes as the main ingredient. Fresh scrubbed beetroot can be grated or shredded in a food processor. Slice the cooked beetroot or make into sticks. Slice and then quarter the tomato, or cut in small wedges. Slice radishes or leave whole if they are tiny. Grate the carrot or cut in fine rounds. Dress the salad 10 minutes before serving, toss again to give it a glossy red colour from the beetroot.

SALADS

GF — **SLAW SALAD**

½ a white cabbage
1 large carrot
½ cup grated celeriac, celery
apple or mung bean sprouts

sultanas or seedless grapes
peanuts or sunflower seeds
celery seeds, caraway seeds or
 dill seeds

Remove the core of the cabbage and shred finely. Grate root vegetables (or shred in a food processor). Apple can be grated or cut into quartered slices. Add other ingredients and toss in a spicy yogurt dressing (with coriander for example). This salad is good with fried foods or pulse casseroles.

GF — **WINTER SALAD**

1 green apple
1 red apple
2 sticks celery
a little shredded cabbage
some thin slices of onion

¼ of a cucumber diced
½ cup bean sprouts
some crumbly white cheese
juice of ½ lemon mixed with cream
 or sour cream

Cut the apple into small pieces and toss in the lemon juice. Add other diced or sliced vegetables and the crumbly cheese broken into small pieces. Stir in 3 tablespoons cream (or yogurt if you prefer). Season if you wish and serve.

GF MF VEG — **CELERY AND WALNUT SALAD**

5 celery sticks
½ cup chopped walnuts

(½ cup mung bean sprouts –
 optional)

Slice the celery and combine with chopped walnuts and bean sprouts. Add a little walnut oil if you have it, or serve with a separate dressing. This makes a good crunchy salad to go with softer staple salads.

WALDORF SALAD
GF MF

1 cup diced celery
1 cup diced apples (red skins look pretty)
1 cup muscatel or champagne grapes
½ cup chopped walnuts
½ cup mayonnaise

Combine all ingredients and mix well with mayonnaise. Add a little more if this amount does not coat everything, but be careful not to add too much.

MUSHROOMS VINAIGRETTE
GF* MF VEG

250g/8oz button mushrooms
6 tablespoons olive oil
2 tablespoons vinegar (tarragon vinegar for preference) or lemon juice
¼ teaspoon dry mustard*
salt and pepper
1 tablespoon chopped parsley
1 tablespoon capers

Use whole de-stalked mushrooms or slice sections through the stalk and all. Make a dressing from the rest of the ingredients in a screw-topped jar and shake till mixed. Pour dressing over the mushrooms and allow to stand an hour for the flavours to blend. Chill before serving.

CARROT AND CHEESE
GF

2 carrots
100g/4oz mild cheddar
parsley to garnish

Grate both carrot and cheese finely (a mouli grater works well), mix together with a little dressing and top with chopped parsley. Good with a lentil salad.

SALADS

GF MF* VEG* MIXED ROOT VEGETABLE SALAD

1 carrot
1 parsnip or turnip
a piece of swede or celeriac
1 fresh beetroot

Grate and mix all the roots together. *Dress with a yogurt dressing, tahini or chickpea sauce (page 116 or page 83).

STAPLE SALADS

These are made from a base of grains, beans, lentils or potatoes. If you are serving a salad meal include at least one from this group and one raw salad, and perhaps a cooked vegetable salad.

MF VEG BARLEY AND SWEETCORN

½ cup pot barley (dry weight)
100g/4oz frozen sweet corn (or equivalent tinned)
½ green pepper
½ red pepper
a box of mustard and cress or chives or parsley to garnish

Cook the barley in plenty of water until tender (about ½ hour). Drain well (keep water for a stock) and tip into the serving bowl and dress with lemon juice and olive oil while hot. When cool, add the thawed sweetcorn and diced peppers and mix well. Cut some cress for the topping or garnish with chopped herbs.

MF VEG* TABBOULEH

1 cup bulgur (dry or 2 cups soaked)
a bunch of spring onions
½ cup chopped fresh mint
2 tablespoons chopped parsley
juice of 1 lemon
olive oil
hardboiled eggs* (optional) – allow ½ per person
whole lettuce leaves to serve it in

green peppers or cress may also be added

Bulgur (spelling varies) is easy to use for a salad as it does not require cooking. Just cover well with cold water and soak for half an hour. Drain it well and squeeze it dry. Rub in the chopped spring onions and lemon juice and leave for 15 minutes to let the flavours mingle. Then add olive oil (about 4 tablespoons) and chopped herbs, season and allow to stand again for 10 minutes or so. Mix well and serve in lettuce leaf cups garnished with chopped hardboiled egg if you like.

RICE SALADS

There are many variations on the base of rice. For a start you can mix brown with white rice, or use either separately. Long grain rice is often favoured for salads, but short grain is good too. Basmati rice (usually more expensive) is nice for a treat and could be used for the salad with tomatoes or the golden rice given here.

Then there is a wealth of variations in the vegetables you combine with the rice – make up your own favourite combinations!

Seeds and cooked beans can be added, or sprouting ones.

Finally, you can get different effects depending on the dressing used, whether French dressing, yogurt, mayonnaise or a tahini or chick pea sauce used as a dressing; and whether you make these plain or tangy (with tamari, tabasco or other spices).

The following suggestions can be varied according to taste, the ingredients available, and how they fit in best with the rest of your meal.

GF MF VEG   **RICE SALAD WITH TOMATOES**

Use a handful of rice (brown or white) per person
3 or 4 tomatoes (depending on size – the large 'beef' tomatoes are especially good for this)

lemon juice
olive oil
a little grated nutmeg, pepper and salt
fresh basil if available

Cook the rice in boiling (but not salted) water. A wedge of lemon in the cooking water will make a white rice extra white (remove after cooking). Salt added before the rice expands will make it go hard. White rice will cook more quickly than brown – about 10 minutes, about 20 for brown. Watch it carefully so it does not overcook and go fluffy. When it is tender, drain well and mix with the lemon juice (½–1 lemon) and olive oil (several tablespoons) and nutmeg. Allow to cool. Place in a shallow serving dish and cover with slices of tomato, season with salt and pepper and sprinkle some fresh basil (chervil or chives) on top. If you are using dried herbs, mix them with the warm rice to help the flavour come out.

GF MF VEG   **MIXED RICE SALAD**

- a handful of uncooked rice per person (½ cup cooked)
- ½ cup sweetcorn
- ½ cup diced peppers (preferably both red and green)
- ½ cup cooked green peas or red kidney beans
- ½ cup diced cucumber or celery
- 1 cup sprouted beans or seeds
- 2–3 spring onions or chopped herbs

If you are using a mix of brown and white rice, start the brown cooking 10 minutes before adding the white. When tender, drain well and tip into the salad bowl with a tablespoon of olive oil in the bottom. Mix and allow to cool. Combine this (or previously cooked rice) with the diced vegetables and toss in a French dressing (skimpy on oil if some is already added to the rice).

GF MF VEG   **GOLDEN RICE**

- a handful of uncooked rice (white or brown) per person
- saffron (for white) or turmeric (for brown rice)
- ½ cup sultanas or seedless raisins soaked in juice of ½ lemon
- 1cm/½inch grated fresh ginger
- a medium carrot grated
- a tablespoon crushed coriander seeds
- 2 or 3 cardamom seeds, crushed
- ½ teaspoon cumin (for a more 'curry' flavour if wished)

Top with roasted peanuts, almonds or desiccated coconut

Dressing made with sultanas and juice, pressed garlic, oil and a tablespoon of watered down tahini (if liked).

Cook the rice with saffron or 1 teaspoon turmeric to turn it golden. Drain and mix with spices and dressing. When cool stir in the grated carrot. Top with hot roasted peanuts or almonds or the coconut.

GF   PINK RICE WITH YOGURT
---

1 cup cooked rice
1 cup chopped tomatoes
1 cup cooked beetroot (diced)
1 cup diced cucumber

Mix together with a yogurt dressing and allow to stand for 15 minutes. Stir again to make it all pink. Top with chives.

MF GF VEG   FLAGEOLETS AND AVOCADO

This is a pretty, delicate, pale green salad.

1 cup dry flageolet beans
1 avocado pear (another for dressing if available)
crisp lettuce (preferably Cos)
watercress to garnish

cooked runner beans may be added

Flageolets, especially the new harvest in Autumn, need less cooking than other beans, so it is unwise to use a pressure cooker, as you will need to watch them. Cook soaked beans until tender. Drain and cool. Combine with avocado cut into slivers. Dress with oil and lemon dressing, with a mashed ripe avocado added, if available. Add lettuce, broken into small pieces, just before serving and garnish with watercress.

GF MF VEG*   MIXED BEAN SALAD

½ cup each of 3 different coloured dry beans (soaked)
1 grated carrot
1 small green and 1 small red pepper (diced)
3 tomatoes (diced)
¼ cucumber (diced)
1 cup beansprouts or seed sprouts
chives or spring onion to garnish

Cook each lot of soaked beans separately. Combine with other ingredients. Dress with French dressing with garlic or try aïoli.* Good with a green salad and a flan.

GF MF VEG   LENTIL SALAD

---

1 cup brown or green dry lentils (soaked)
3 or 4 spring onions
2–3 tablespoons olive oil
parsley or other herbs for garnish

Cook the soaked lentils until tender but not bursting. Drain well. Place a tablespoon of oil in the serving dish and mix it with the hot lentils. Add chopped spring onions, season, mix and leave to cook, or serve lukewarm.

Goes well with the grated cheese and carrot salad or with beetroot.

POTATO SALADS

A variety of different dressings can be used for different effects.

GF MF VEG   WITH OIL

If using freshly cooked potatoes, use oil (olive if you like the taste) and lemon juice, letting them soak in as the potatoes cool. Then add some chopped onion or spring onions and serve warm or cold.

MF GF   WITH MAYONNAISE

Left-over potatoes are good for this salad. Chop them into slices or sticks and add finely chopped onion and parsley, mix well with mayonnaise. If you are fond of garlic, try the aïoli dressing.

Potatoes also form the base of other salads such as the salade russe (page 127). Although connoisseurs insist that potatoes should not be part of an authentic salade niçoise they do combine well with the traditional ingredients.

SALADE NIÇOISE

MF GF

one cooked potato per person
a tin of anchovies
some black and green olives
1–2 hardboiled eggs

1 green pepper
2–3 tomatoes
spring onions or chives
lettuce (if not served in a separate salad)

Cut the cooked potatoes into wedges. Combine with the other vegetables, sliced or in wedges. It should have a chunky look. Add olives and anchovies (sardines could be used instead) and toss in a French dressing with garlic and herbs. Top with rounds of hardboiled egg, or cut them in wedges and arrange in a ring. They will break up if you toss them in with the salad. Serve with lettuce, or with a green salad and a wholemeal roll for a light meal.

COOKED VEGETABLE SALADS

GREEN BEAN SALAD

GF MF VEG

350g/¾lb tender French or stick beans
250g/½lb tomatoes

½ a green and ½ a red pepper
10 black olives (coated in herbs)
French dressing

Top and tail the beans and remove any strings. Steam for 5–10 minutes so they are still bright green and crunchy. Cut into 7cm/3inch lengths and toss in dressing while still hot. When cool, add the tomatoes, cut in wedges, and the peppers in strips the same size as the beans. Coat the olives with oil and fresh herbs (thyme, marjoram, basil) and decorate the salad with them.

CHAMPIGNONS A LA GRECQUE

GF MF VEG

500g/1lb button mushrooms
½ cup dry white wine
¼ cup olive oil
juice of one lemon

1 tablespoon tomato concentrate
1 tablespoon coriander seeds
bay leaf, thyme and parsley
salt and pepper

The tiny button mushrooms are best and can be used whole. Larger ones can be cut and quartered or sliced down through the stalk. Heat the oil in a heavy skillet and toss the mushrooms in it. Add the lemon juice, white wine, coriander, tomato paste, herbs and seasoning and cook on a high heat for 7–8 minutes. Turn into the serving dish and allow to cool. Remove the herbs before serving.

This dish is very piquant, almost like a chutney with cold meat, and needs something bland for balance, such as a tabbouleh potato salad or the rice with tomatoes. A green salad goes well too.

GF MF VEG — CAULIFLOWER VINAIGRETTE

1 small cauliflower
French dressing made with vinegar
chopped parsley

Steam the cauliflower until lightly done and still crunchy. Alternatively, cut first into small florets and blanch in boiling water for a few minutes until just tender. Drain well. Dress the small florets with French dressing while still warm. Leave to cool and serve chilled topped with chopped parsley.

GF MF — SALADE RUSSE

1 cooked potato per person
3 or 4 of the following:
cooked carrot
cooked beetroot
cooked peas or runner beans
cooked cauliflower (lightly done)
fresh avocado
fresh celery
cooked haricot beans

cooked chicken or hardboiled egg could be added
If you like something piquant add:
capers
gherkins
olives
chopped herbs (chervil, tarragon or parsley)

Dice the vegetables (except peas or haricots) and bind with a little French dressing. Then add ½ cup mayonnaise or a little more to coat everything – too much will make it too rich. A little paprika or tiny pinch of Cayenne can enliven the mayonnaise.

Sweet Things

FRUITS AND DESSERTS

By far the easiest and most nutritious dessert to serve is fruit, both fresh and dried, and nuts or seeds.

Depending on what dishes have gone before, cheese and biscuits are often the most suitable savouries to serve at the end of a meal. Choose wholewheat biscuits, rye crackers or oatcakes to suit the cheese. The variety is enormous, from those made from goat's or ewe's milk to the many from cow's milk. Choose those made by traditional methods where possible (often designated 'farmhouse cheese') and avoid processed kinds. There are many pleasing ways of combining soft cheeses with fresh fruit. You can also serve apple with crumbly white cheese, like Cheshire, Wensleydale, white Stilton etc.

Sometimes you will feel like making a dessert because the meal is special or because some seasonal produce invites it. This chapter gives suggestions especially for the summer berry fruits, and the autumn offerings of pumpkin, chestnuts, apples and blackberries. There are several non-seasonal recipes for cheesecakes, tofu sweets and rice pudding. Ice creams and some other ideas may be found in the section on Entertaining (page 183).

Here, as with the recipes in the chapter on Home Baking, (see page 143), the use of sugar has been kept to a minimum. Where possible use the less refined sugars (Muscovado, Barbados, Demerara), and use molasses or treacle in preference to golden syrup (or part of each). Honey or concentrated apple juice can often work well as substitutes for sugar, as can barley malt or maple syrup in baking, or simply use less sugar than the recipe calls for. Dried fruits will add enough sweetness in many cases. These are all good sugar substitutes, but do not let your enthusiasm for reducing sugar lead to the use of artificial sweeteners. They present other hazards and should be avoided in pregnancy.

FRUITS, NUTS AND SEEDS

Dried fruits and nuts can make a significant contribution to the daily need for many minerals (particularly calcium, phosphorous, iron and zinc) as well as some B vitamins (especially folate). The iron is better absorbed when foods rich in vitamin C are taken at the same meal. Nuts and seeds are also good sources of protein, and many contain valuable essential fatty acids, especially sunflower and sesame seeds. The best nuts are almonds, walnuts, Brazils, cashews, peanuts and hazels. Dried apricots, peaches and prunes are rich in many minerals and also contain vitamin A. Figs are rich in calcium and iron. Raisins, sultanas and dates, while less rich in such things, still have a good spread of valuable minerals and vitamins. It is difficult to obtain information on the less common Barcelonas, pistachios and pine nuts, but no doubt such treats are valuable too. There is probably less reason to treasure dried pineapple, papaya, coconut and banana chips, though by all means add them for interest and variety to your mixes. Experiment to find out what combines best.

GF MF* VEG*   HARMONIOUS COMBINATIONS

Satsumas (clementines, tangerines, mandarins etc) and walnuts
Almonds and muscatel raisins
Dried peaches and fresh banana
Dried apricots and hazelnuts or soaked Hunza apricots (remove stone and substitute a hazelnut).
Figs (fresh or dried) with soft white cheese*
Dates (fresh or dried) with cream cheese*
Sticky lexia raisins coated with sesame seeds (shake together in a bag) and fresh apple
Dried pears, cashews and pumpkin seeds
Peanuts, raisins and sunflower seeds
Walnuts and fresh grapes

| GF* MF* VEG* | FRESH FRUIT SALADS |

Almost any three fruits will combine pleasingly to make a refreshing fruit salad. Just use what is available and in season. Allow 1–2 pieces of fruit per person, depending, of course, on whether it is a melon or pineapple that is being considered or a strawberry or grape. If in doubt, think of the bulk of an average pear as a reasonable portion.

As vitamins are lost as soon as you cut fruit, prepare the fruit salad as near to eating time as possible. Add plenty of fruit juice (orange, pineapple, apple or grapefruit) which will help to retain the vitamin C in the cut fruit and prevent it going brown. It tastes good too!

Variety in the colours will make it look attractive. In summer add some halved strawberries, cherries, blackcurrants or grapes. In winter you can use sliced dried fruits, such as apricots, peaches, figs or sultanas to similar effect. Soak them in orange juice for a while to let them soften and expand.

If it is necessary to sweeten the fruit salad you can use a little runny honey (heat in a bowl of hot water if it is solid in the jar) or some concentrated apple juice but not too much as it is rather acid. Another idea is to stew a few figs, with some other dried fruit. When the mixture has cooled mash or liquidise and pour over the fruit salad.

Texture is worth considering. For a crunchy salad add apple, pineapple, passion fruit pips, pomegranate or cashews.

*Serve on its own, or with yogurt, nut cream (page 192), cream or ice cream adding a sweet biscuit or piece of plain cake if desired.

| GF | FRESH FRUIT WITH SOFT WHITE CHEESE |

Summer fruits are particularly delicious with soft white cheese (fromage blanc, Quark). Combine beforehand or serve whole peaches, plums, nectarines, or berry fruit to be prepared at the table with the soft white cheese spooned on to the plate according to individual tastes. Extra sugar should not be necessary when the fruit is ripe.

FRUIT YOGURT

Try making your own flavoured yogurt: whether or not you make the yogurt, you will know that the fruit is fresh, that there are no dyes or other additives. As you will not need to add sugar, it will be much cheaper too. For flavouring ideas, just read the labels on the yogurt counter in your supermarket! All the berries and currants are particularly successful. Raspberry is a favourite.

GF FRESH RASPBERRY YOGURT

500ml/½pint plain yogurt
250–400g/½–1lb fresh raspberries
a squeeze of lemon juice
1 teaspoon honey or sugar (if needed)

Wash the fruit and pick off any stalks or hulls. Remove any damaged fruit. Squeeze a little lemon juice (not more than a segment) over the fruit. Sprinkle with sugar if needed. (If using honey, stir it into the yogurt). Mix thoroughly with the yogurt and leave to stand for half an hour to let the flavours blend. Grate a little hazelnut on top before serving or offer a hazelnut shortbread.

GF YOGURT

There are many ways of making yogurt, but the essentials are the same. The milk is heated to kill off unwanted bacteria. Let the milk cool for about half an hour and introduce the yogurt starter. Then keep warm at the same temperature for 5–8 hours. Chill.

More detailed guidelines
1. *The milk* Use fresh whole milk, pasteurised milk, UHT or sterilized milk. It can be thickened with dried milk up to 25g per 600ml/1 oz per pint. This will give a more junkety yogurt.
2. *Heat but do not boil* A cooking thermometer is a great help in arriving at the right temperature. The milk should be heated to 180°F/80°C.

3. *Containers* A thermos flask will perform both functions of container and hay box. Decant afterwards to store in the fridge. Glass jars (preferably with plastic lids) or earthenware pots can be used. Whatever you choose, the container should be scalded or sterilized. This can be done efficiently by pouring the hot scalded milk straight into the container where it will then cool a little.

4. *Cool to just above blood heat* The milk should be between 105°–120°F/40°–49°C for the most favourable temperature to let the lactic acid bacteria multiply. It should feel hot to the hand.

5. *Introduce the starter* Some fresh yogurt is the best starter, whether homemade or commercial, plain of course. Use ½ teaspoon per 600ml/pint of milk. Take a few tablespoons of the heated milk from the container(s) and mix them with the starter, so that it will blend more easily. Then stir this mixture in to the milk.

6. *Keeping it warm* If using a thermos just put the lid on and leave it for 5–8 hours. Jars or pots can be kept warm in a hay box, or any place which is always warm like a cylinder cupboard, on a storage heater or over a pilot light. An insulated picnic bag can be used, or you can improvise some form of well insulated container. If it has not set when you look at it, put it back for another hour or so, but if it is left too long makes the yogurt become fizzy.

7. *Chill* Before refrigerating the yogurt, remove enough for your next starter and store in a separate container. It should be used again before too long. Eventually it may 'wear out', in which case, buy a new pot of yogurt.

STRAWBERRY SHORTCAKE

2 cups wholewheat flour (sifted to remove bran if preferred)
2 teaspoons baking powder
a pinch of salt
100g/4oz softened butter
about ½ cup milk
250–450g/½–1lb strawberries (as available)
a little sugar

Preheat oven to 400°F/gas mark 6/200°C

Mix the flour, baking powder and salt. (If you sift the bran out of the wholewheat flour keep it for adding to porridge, muesli or bread.) Add butter, working it thoroughly into the flour. Using a fork, lightly mix in the milk – just enough to make a light dough. Divide the mixture in half and pat each portion on the greased base of an inverted cake tin (about 20cm/8inches across). Prick the surface with a fork and bake in the oven for about 15 minutes or until golden. While the shortcakes bake, wash and hull the strawberries. Crush half the berries and sprinkle on a little sugar if required. When the shortcakes are cooked, drain the crushed strawberries (reserving the juice). Stand one shortcake on a baking sheet, or dish, and cover with the crushed strawberries. Place a second shortcake on top and decorate with the whole berries. Return to the oven for 5 minutes, then pour the juice over the top and serve warm with your own fresh strawberry yogurt, plain yogurt or whipped cream.

MF* VEG*	SUMMER PUDDING WITH WHOLEMEAL BREAD

Slices (about ½cm/¼inch thick) of wholemeal bread
500g/1lb red currants (or mixed red and blackcurrants)
250g/½lb raspberries
250g/½lb strawberries
2–3 tablespoons apple concentrate

Wash the fruit and remove any stalks or hulls. Place in a large pan with the apple concentrate, cover the pan and stew the fruit very gently over a low heat for 5–10 minutes, until tender but still whole. Taste and add a little extra apple concentrate if needed.

Line a large basin or glass bowl (1–2litre/2–3pint capacity) with the wholewheat bread, from which you have removed the crusts; this makes it fit together better. Trim to the right shapes if necessary to make sure the bread covers the inside of the bowl completely. Pour in the hot fruit and juice.

To serve hot, allow to stand for 10 minutes or so to let the bread soak up the juices.

To serve cold, cover the top with more bread slices and find a plate or saucer which fits the top of the basin exactly, and can be pressed down a bit further. Put a heavy weight on top and chill overnight. Unmould the pudding on to a plate for serving.

*Serve plain or with yogurt and a sprinkling of toasted nuts, or with almond cream (see next page).

GF MF VEG   ALMOND CREAM

Make as for almond milk (page 192), but use less water – just enough to get a creamy consistency. Hazelnuts or cashews can also be used.

Useful as a topping for many desserts.

GF   GOOSEBERRY FOOL

500g/1lb green gooseberries
2–3 tablespoons sugar (or to taste)

275ml/½pint boiled custard (see below)
275ml/½pint whipping cream

Wash the gooseberries and remove any leaves. The stalks need not be removed if the berries will be sieved. If you prefer to liquidise them in a blender or food processor it is best to cut off the stalks. Cover barely with water in a pan, bring to the boil and simmer a few minutes until tender. Add sugar to taste (it should taste tart) and stir in to dissolve. Leave to cool.

Make a boiled custard and allow to cool.

Sieve the cooled fruit in a tamis or mouli-légumes or liquidise.

When both the custard and the fruit are cool, whip the cream to a stiff consistency. Fold carefully into the custard, and then fold this mixture gently into the gooseberry purée. Turn into a serving bowl and refrigerate 12–24 hours.

GF   BOILED CUSTARD

2–3 egg yolks
1 tablespoon sugar

275ml/½pint milk

The more egg yolks used and the creamier the milk the smoother the custard will be. As it is combined with cream in the fool, it would be rich enough with skim milk.

Use a double boiler if available, or make the custard in a heatproof bowl or jug standing in a pan of boiling water.

Mix the egg yolks with the sugar and beat until creamy. Add a little milk and stir well. Gradually add the rest of the milk (which can be heated to speed the process), stirring all the time. As it thickens, scrape it from the sides and stir frequently to ensure even heating right through. It is done when the custard coats the back of a spoon. This may take 15–30 minutes.

For other purposes a vanilla flavour is pleasant. Add a vanilla pod to the milk as it heats, or use vanilla sugar, or a few drops of essence (preferably pure essence not 'flavouring').

CLAFOUTIS

This French dessert is traditionally made with cherries (big black ones if available). You can also use apples or plums.

700g/1½lb fruit	100g/3oz sugar
3 eggs	½ cup single cream
50g/2oz flour	2 cups milk

Optional tablespoon or so of Kirsch in the case of cherries, apple juice or Calvados can be used with apples.

Preheat oven to 375°F/gas mark 5/190°C

Wash cherries and remove stalks (and stones if desired) or wash and slice apples (remove the core but leave the skins, or halve the plums and remove the stones. Grease an ovenproof dish – a flat oval one is good – and cover with the fruit. Beat the eggs and sugar in a bowl until white and frothy. Add the flour (and an optional pinch of salt). Continue beating while adding the cream and Kirsch etc. Then gradually add the milk, stirring it through. Pour this mixture over the fruit and bake in a fairly hot oven for half an hour. Increase the heat a little to brown the top if necessary. It is done when a knife dipped into the centre comes out clean. Serve hot or cold.

| GF MF VEG* | PLUM JELLY |

500g/1lb plums (red ones look pretty)
1 tablespoon sugar or concentrated apple juice

25g/1oz gelatine or 3–4 tablespoons agar flakes*

Wash the plums and remove stalks. Cover with water and bring to the boil. Cook until tender, testing to see how easily the stones can be removed. Taste and add sugar as required, leaving it to dissolve in the hot liquid. Drain the plums and measure the juice – a little less than 600ml/1pint is all that is needed, so keep any surplus for use as a juice.

Alternatively, make up with cold water to required amount. Place the gelatine in a heatproof container and cover with cold water to soak. Now stone the plums and liquidise in a blender or sieve. Place in a serving bowl. Then heat the gelatine in its container over boiling water until dissolved. If you use agar flakes, these can be dissolved in the liquid brought back to boiling for about 5 minutes. Mix gelatine with the liquid, mix thoroughly, or take liquid with dissolved agar flakes and pour over the plums. Stir to mix. Leave to set.

When cool it can be put in the refrigerator which will help it set more quickly.

Other fruits that can be prepared in this way include dried stewed apricots, rhubarb (nice mixed with strawberries or raspberries) or blackcurrants.

| GF MF | PLUM JELLY MOUSSE |

If you would like to achieve a lighter result, take the plum jelly when it is cool and nearly set and whip with a beater. Beat an egg white separately and fold into the whipped jelly. Leave to set in a cool place as before.

RHUBARB SPONGE

MF*

500g/1lb rhubarb
2 tablespoons concentrated apple juice
2 eggs
50g/2oz sugar (you can use Muscovado, but no lumps!)
50g/2oz flour (wholewheat or sifted to remove some of the bran)
1 teaspoon baking powder

Preheat oven to 425°F/gas mark 7/220°C

Wash and cut the rhubarb into small chunks. Place in a pan and pour a little boiling water over it to soften it just a little. Sweeten with 1–2 tablespoons of concentrated apple juice if necessary, or a little sugar. Whisk the eggs and sugar until very light and creamy. An electric beater makes this task very easy. Mix the baking powder with the flour and fold in lightly with a knife or metal spoon. Grease a flat oven dish and spread the rhubarb over the surface, add enough juice to come up half way. Pour the sponge mixture over the top, the dish should be big enough so that it is just about 2cm/1inch thick. Place in the hot oven and bake for 10 minutes or until the sponge springs back when touched. If it is getting too brown, lower it in the oven.

Serve with yogurt or boiled custard,* or nut cream (page 134).

Instead of the rhubarb you could use apples, sweetened with concentrated apple juice.

BLACKBERRY AND APPLE CRUMBLE

MF*

1 large cooking apple
250g/½lb blackberries
2 tablespoons apple concentrate

Crumble topping

1 cup muesli flakes
½ cup wholewheat flour
1 teaspoon baking powder
50g/2oz corn germ oil or butter
1-2 tablespoons Demerara sugar
a tablespoon of water or milk*

Preheat oven to 350°F/gas mark 4/180°C

Slice the apple and wash the blackberries, removing any stalks or bad bits. Place the apples in a pan with the apple concentrate and

½ cup water. Bring to the boil. Throw in the blackberries and bring back to the boil. Remove from the heat and pour into a greased ovenproof dish, a fairly deep one is best. Mix the crumble topping, rubbing the butter or oil into the dry ingredients. Add a tablespoon of water or milk so it forms small lumps. Sprinkle over the fruit and bake in a moderate oven for 20–30 minutes, until the top has browned.

Serve with yogurt, cream or boiled custard.*

Other fruit can be used with this topping, or mixed with the apple. Try apple and apricots or apple and dates.

MF   **APPLE FRITTERS**

---

1 cup wholewheat flour
1 tablespoon soya flour
1 teaspoon baking powder
1 egg
up to ½ cup apple juice (or diluted concentrated apple juice)

1 sliced cooking apple
1 teaspoon cinnamon mixed with 2 tablespoons sugar to sprinkle on top when serving.

Mix the dry ingredients in a bowl, make a well and break the egg into it. A teaspoon of sunflower oil can be added too. Mix with the flour. Add the apple juice gradually, mixing it in until a stiffish batter is formed. Stir in the finely sliced apple. Drop in spoonfuls on a heated and oiled pan to make fritters a few inches across. Cook on both sides and serve on a plate sprinkled with the sugar and cinnamon.

GF MF* VEG*   **BAKED APPLES**

---

1 apple per person
cloves
cinnamon stick
dates, raisins, chopped dried apricots or nuts

50g/2oz butter
1 cup apple juice

Preheat oven to 350°F/gas mark 4/180°C

Take one good-sized apple for each person. Wash and core it. Cut a ring through the peel around the apple about two-thirds the way up. Place in a buttered baking dish. Stick two or three cloves or pieces of cinnamon stick in the side of each apple. Fill the middles with dates, raisins, chopped dried apricots or nuts. Place a small knob of butter on the top of each apple and pour a cup of apple juice into the base. A few more raisins can be scattered around or some rice flakes. Bake in a moderate oven for 45 minutes. Test with a skewer to check the apples are soft. Return to the oven for a little longer if necessary.

Serve with yogurt, cream, boiled custard or almond cream*.

PUMPKIN PIE

250g/8oz shortcrust pastry (page 74)
2 beaten eggs
⅔ cup brown sugar (Demerara or Muscovado) or 3 tablespoons concentrated apple juice
1½ cups cooked pumpkin
1 teaspoon cinnamon
¼ teaspoon ground cloves
¼ teaspoon ground ginger
½ teaspoon salt
1½ cups milk or buttermilk
small handful of sultanas

Preheat oven to 400°F/gas mark 6–7/200–220°C

Bake the pie shell blind for 10 minutes. Mix all the ingredients together except the sultanas and pour into the pie shell. Drop the sultanas in. Cook in a moderate oven at 350°F/gas mark 4/180°C for about 45 minutes or until set. Allow to cool and serve lukewarm or cold.

GF MF VEG   ## ROAST CHESTNUTS

Something fun to do on a cold autumn evening around a fire or bonfire. If you do not have an open fire you can roast the chestnuts in an oven.

The chestnuts will cook more satisfactorily and stay moist if blanched first in boiling water for 5 minutes or so. It also makes the task of pricking them less hazardous. Prick each chestnut in two or three places, a necessary precaution against explosions!

If you have a chestnut roaster, so much the better. A wire basket can be used or even a fireproof bowl or pot. Roast them in the glowing embers, shaking every so often to get all sides cooked. The skins may burn black, which does not matter, but do not let them get red hot! After 5–10 minutes, depending on the heat of the fire, they should be ready. Let them cool a little to prevent burning fingers as you remove shells to eat them.

For oven roasting preheat your oven to 400°F/gas mark 6–7/205–220°C and spread the chestnuts on a baking tray. Roast for 10–15 minutes.

A bowl of dried figs or other fruits can be passed around while you are waiting between batches of chestnuts.

GF RICE PUDDING WITH NUTS AND RAISINS

500ml/1pint milk
40g/1½oz short grain brown rice
1 teaspoon Demerara sugar

50g/2oz chopped almonds or hazelnuts
25g/1oz raisins or sultanas

Preheat oven to 300°F/gas mark 2/150°C

Heat the milk to boiling point. Add the short rice and a teaspoon of Demerara sugar. Stir off the heat until the sugar dissolves. Place the chopped almonds or hazelnuts and raisins or sultanas in a buttered baking dish. Pour the milk and rice over them – the nuts will float to the top. Place in a slow oven and bake for 2 hours. Serve with stewed fruit. If you use almonds, stewed apple rings go well. Apricots combine nicely with hazelnuts.

If you prefer you can make the rice pudding without fruit and nuts. Stewed prunes are a traditional accompaniment.

Quick method: use cooked rice, and heat on cooker top with less milk and other ingredients.

GF APRICOT CHEESE CAKE

For the base use

A biscuit crumb base made from 300g/10oz crushed digestive biscuits mixed with 2 tablespoons of the sunflower oil. This base requires no cooking.

Or mix 200g/7oz porridge oats with 2 tablespoons sunflower oil and 1 tablespoon of apple concentrate. Bake for 15 minutes and allow to cool.

Or make a wholewheat shortcrust (see page 74) made with 170g/6oz flour, or gluten-free shortcrust* (page 75) or almond pastry (p. 153).

Bake blind and cool.

Preheat oven to 375°F/gas mark 4–5/177°–190°C

Filling

200g/7oz dried apricots soaked overnight
250g/8oz low fat soft cheese (Quark)
250g/8oz cottage cheese
zest and juice of one lemon

Poach the apricots in the soaking water till soft and purée. Cool. Prepare the base in a flan dish while the apricots are cooking. In a blender combine the cheeses and grated rind and juice of the lemon, adding a little milk if the mixture is too solid to blend properly. Stir in the apricot purée (cooled) and spoon into the prepared case. Chill in the refrigerator until firm (1–2 hours). A few whole soaked apricots can be set aside to decorate the cheese cake if wished.

GF*	CURD TART

170g/6oz short crust pastry (page 74) or almond pastry* (page 153)
250g/8oz curd cheese or goat's curds (see below)
50g/2oz butter
50g/2oz sugar
2 eggs
25g/1oz ground almonds (optional)
½ cup currants
milk to moisten (goat's or cow's)

Preheat oven to 400°F/gas mark 8/230°C

Cream the butter and sugar, add beaten eggs and stir in the currants and ground almonds. Mix lightly into the curds and add a little milk to moisten. Fill a shallow pie tin lined with shortcrust pastry. Bake in a hot oven for 10–15 minutes.

GOAT'S CURDS

1 litre/2pints goat's milk
1 teaspoon Epsom salts

1 teaspoon white vinegar

Heat the goat's milk until it just starts to rise. Be careful not to let it boil. Remove from the heat and add 1 teaspoon of Epsom salts and 1 teaspoon white vinegar. Stir well and allow to cool. When it has cooled it will separate into curds and whey, with the curds at the bottom of the pan. Pour the contents of the pan through a sieve (collect the whey for use in bread, pastry and cakes). You are left with the goat's curds. Use or store in the refrigerator.

GF MF* VEG* — **BLACK BAKED BANANAS**

Take one banana for each person (overripe ones can be used). Place on an oven tray or heatproof dish and bake in a moderate oven for 20 minutes. The skin becomes completely black. You can skin the bananas first, or simply serve in their skins, slit lengthwise. *Serve with cream or yogurt and a few chopped nuts if liked. As easy as that, but what a transformation of the ordinary raw banana!

GF — **CITRONA**

1½ cups plain yogurt
½ cup tofu
2 tablespoons date purée

grated rind and juice of 2 lemons
(or just one rind)
2 teaspoons ground almonds

Cook some dates in a little water and mash or liquidise to a purée. Allow to cool. Beat all the ingredients together with a wooden spoon and serve in individual dishes with a twist of lemon peel.

GF MF VEG — **TOFU CREAM**

400g/14oz tofu
100g/4oz chopped blanched
  almonds or cashew pieces

1 cup fruit in season

Liquidise together the tofu, and the almonds or cashew pieces and a cup of fruit in season. Strawberries are delicious and bananas are good too. Add a little water if a lighter texture is preferred.

The cream can be frozen to make an ice; served as it is decorated with a few extra fruits; or piled into a baked pastry case or biscuit crumb base, (see cheesecake page 141). The almond pastry (page 153) would make a good base too.

HOME BAKING

When you are pregnant it is easy to add up everything you eat to see how it contributes to your daily nutritional needs. This may lead you to cut down on cakes and biscuits. In general this could be a good thing, especially when they contain refined flour and a good deal of sugar and fat. In this chapter, the emphasis is on simple ways to bake with wholewheat flour (or oats), sometimes with less fat (or at least 'good' fats) with less sugar or none at all. The use of dried fruits will often add sufficient sweetness, and, of course, lots of valuable minerals. Nuts are used too (100g of walnuts will give you nearly a third of your daily requirement of vitamin B6). Some of the cakes and biscuits could be used to accompany desserts, or as desserts on their own (such as the carob, fig and orange cake). There are plenty of scones and tea breads to make for tea time or when you have visitors. You can also use the fruit loaves for picnics and packed lunches.

Your baking will look and taste different with wholewheat flour, so, as recommended in previous chapters, make the change gradually and use part white flour while you are getting used to the new appearance and flavour.

The recipes which are milk-free, egg-free or gluten-free are marked with their symbol. The asterisk indicates ingredients to exclude or for which to find substitutes.

GLUTEN-FREE BAKING

This baking section has not made special allowance for those on a gluten-free diet. Gluten-free flour can be obtained, but as it is generally of poor nutritional quality, it can be improved by adding a tablespoon of soya flour or seed meal to the recipe.

Commercial baking powder contains gluten, so here is one to make yourself, which is suitable, in fact, for anyone.

GLUTEN-FREE BAKING POWDER

Combine one part arrowroot, one part cream of tartar and one part potassium bicarbonate. Store and use in place of ordinary baking powder in the amounts specified in your recipe. Recipes specifically for those on a gluten-free diet can be found in books in the Booklist.

SCONES

350g/12oz flour
60g/2oz butter
3 teaspoons baking powder

225ml/7fl oz milk (approximately)
1 beaten egg (reserve a little to glaze tops if you wish)

Preheat oven to 450°F/gas mark 8/230°C

If you are going to eat these hot from the oven the egg may be omitted (but you may need a little extra milk). The egg will help the scones to keep. If stale they can be toasted. Try halving the scones, toasting the outsides, then buttering and toasting with a slice of tomato on top.

Stir in the beaten egg and add milk until the mixture is a stiffish dough. You may not need all the milk. Then knead lightly on a floured surface until firm enough to roll out. Roll out to a thickness of 3cm/1 inch or so and cut round shapes. If you do not have a cutter, an upturned glass will do. Another way is to make 3 balls, press each out to required thickness and cut into six segments. This can be done on the baking tray. They will break apart easily when cooked. You can also cut square or triangular shapes from the rolled-out dough. Brush with egg or milk if you wish. Place scones on an oiled and floured baking sheet and bake in a very hot oven for about 10 minutes. They are done when the top is brown and the base is firm. It is not so easy with wholewheat flour to see when the surface is brown from cooking! But you become more practised in judging very soon. Glazing the top also helps one to see a finished look.

This basic recipe can be varied in the following ways.

CHEESE SCONES

To the basic scone recipe add 120–160g/4–6oz grated cheese. Salt and pepper, a little Parmesan, some chopped chives can also be added for different savoury effects. Otherwise proceed as above, but if you wish, halve the amount of butter.

DATE OR FRUIT SCONES

To the basic recipe add 50–100g/2–4oz chopped dates, currants or sultanas, with spice or grated lemon rind for extra flavour. Up to 50g/2oz Muscovado sugar can be added for a really sweet scone, but in most cases the fruit makes them sweet enough. Otherwise proceed as above.

SALLY LUNN SCONES

To the basic recipe add 1 tablespoon sugar (any kind). Roll out thin (about 1cm/½ inch), cut into rounds about 10cm/4 inches across. Fold each one over on itself, glaze top if you wish and bake as above.

MF PUMPKIN SCONES

1 cup cooked mashed pumpkin
2 cups flour
2 teaspoons baking powder
1 beaten egg
25g/1oz butter
50g/2oz sugar (any kind, use less if you like)

Preheat oven to 450°F/gas mark 8/230°C

Beat the butter and sugar to a cream and add the egg, beat again. Add the cooked mashed pumpkin (tinned will do if unavailable fresh), and the flour mixed with the baking powder. Form into a dough quickly and lightly. Roll out on a floured board, cut into shapes and bake in a hot oven for about 10 minutes.

For MUFFINS see Bread section page 59

TEA BREADS

(See also Fruit Plait and Yeast-risen Spice Loaf in the Bread section pages 58–60.)

MF* APRICOT AND ALMOND LOAF

350g/12oz flour
3 teaspoons baking powder
½ teaspoon bicarbonate of soda
pinch of salt
125g/4oz soaked apricots
50g/2oz coarsely chopped almonds

50g/2oz butter* (or whey-free margarine for milk-free version)
2 eggs
150ml/¼pint soya or cow's milk*
50g/2oz honey

Preheat oven to 325°F/gas mark 3/170°C

Soak the apricots overnight in cold water or cover with boiling water and leave for an hour or two until they are swollen and soft.

Mix the flour, salt, bicarbonate of soda and the baking powder.

Drain and chop the apricots. Melt the butter and honey together over a low flame, but do not allow to burn. Add the apricots and chopped almonds to flour mixture. Beat eggs with milk and stir into dry ingredients. Add the honey and melted butter and mix well, but no need to beat. Pour into a greased 2lb loaf tin and bake for 1–1½ hours.

For a shiny top brush with concentrated apple juice when it comes out of the oven.

MF* VEG* DATE AND WALNUT LOAF

50g/2oz honey
80g/3oz molasses or malt extract
50g/2oz butter or whey-free margarine for milk-free version
300ml/½pint milk* or soya milk
(if using a sweetened soya milk you may prefer to reduce the amount of honey)

350g/12oz flour
3 teaspoons baking powder
pinch salt
½ teaspoon bicarbonate of soda
125g/4oz dates
50g/2oz walnuts

Preheat oven to 300°F/gas mark 2/150°C

Put milk, honey, molasses (or malt), and butter in a saucepan and warm over low heat until the butter has melted.

Mix together the flour, salt, baking powder and bicarbonate of soda. Coarsely chop dates and nuts and add to the flour mixture.

Make a well in the middle and pour in the liquid mixture. Stir well and put into greased 2lb loaf tin, smooth the top and bake for 1–1½ hours. Test with a skewer to see if it is done – the skewer should come out clean.

MF* VEG*   **MALT BREAD**

250g/8oz wholewheat flour
2½ teaspoons baking powder
½ teaspoon bicarbonate of soda
60g/2oz sultanas
60g/2oz raisins
60g/2oz chopped dates
3 tablespoons malt extract
150ml/¼ pint milk* (or soya milk)

Preheat oven to 400°F/gas mark 6/200°C

Prepare a loaf tin ready to pour the mixture in immediately it is made. Melt the malt in the milk over heat, but do not boil. Mix the dry ingredients and fruit and stir in heated milk and malt. Stir well and turn into tin. Bake for 40–45 minutes (test with a skewer to check when it is done).

MF VEG   **PLAIN DIGESTIVE BISCUITS**

---

1 cup whole wheat flour
1 cup oatmeal
¼ cup oil (cold pressed corn oil for preference)
½ cup maple syrup or concentrated apple juice
water to mix

Preheat oven to 350°F/gas mark 4/180°C

Mix the dry ingredients, rub in the oil, add the syrup or juice concentrate and enough water to form a dough. Roll out to ½cm/¼ inch thickness and cut in biscuit shapes. Prick with a fork and bake for 20 minutes or a little longer. Spices, dried fruit, sesame or sunflower seeds can be added to this recipe for variety. If using apple concentrate, try adding ½ cup grated apple (and carrot).

MF* VEG* GINGER ROOT SNAPS

340g/12 oz wholewheat flour
1 tablespoon ginger powder
1 tablespoon grated root ginger
2 tablespoons chopped preserved ginger or candied peel
50g/2oz Muscovado or Demerara sugar
225g/½lb black treacle or molasses
80g/3oz butter* or whey-free margarine
a little milk* or soya milk to mix

Preheat oven to 325°F/gas mark 3/150°C

Mix the dry ingredients in a bowl. Heat the butter, and when just melted stir in the treacle or molasses and mix well. Add to the dry ingredients and knead to a paste, adding a little milk (the more you add the softer the biscuits will be; without milk they will be very hard, so judge according to taste, 1–2 tablespoons should be enough). Shape into walnut-sized pieces, place on a greased baking sheet and flatten. Bake for 30 minutes in a moderately slow oven.

MF* VEG* CAROB SHORTBREAD

350g/12oz wholewheat flour
70g/3oz sugar (Muscovado for preference)
3 tablespoons carob powder
200g/7oz butter*
25g/1oz melted butter*

Preheat oven to 325°F/gas mark 3/165°C

Sift the flour and carob powder together and mix in the sugar, pressing out any lumps. Rub in the butter and put the 25g/1oz in a pan to melt. (It should not burn, but it can brown very slightly to give a nutty flavour). Mix in the melted butter and knead until smooth.

For thick fingers: press into a tin about 30cm/11 inches by 18cm/7 inches. When baked mark into fingers before the shortbread cools, and leave to cool in the tin.

For wedges: Divide mixture into four balls. Press out each part with the fingers until the size of a small plate. Smooth with a knife and cut into 8 pieces. Place on greased baking tray. Prick the shortbread with a fork at intervals and mark with the flat part of the fork on edges. Bake for 25 minutes. Allow to cool before removing from tin to store.

Special decoration As soon as the carob shortbread comes out of the oven it can be decorated with finely grated carob bar. Either make stripes of the grated carob, about four lengthwise, so that each bar will have two. Or, cover completely with grated carob. Then, after a few minutes when it has had the chance to melt a little, make stripes with the flat blade of a knife. Each bar will have rough and smooth stripes when you cut them.

Will one of these substitute for the chocolate coated candy bar you crave? You can only try one and see! Perhaps a Chunky Florentine will fill the bill.

MF* VEG*   WALNUT OR ALMOND SHORTBREAD

Replace the carob powder with 50g/2oz chopped walnuts or almonds. Otherwise proceed as above.

MF* VEG*   CHUNKY FLORENTINES

- 2½ cups rolled oats
- ½ cup flaked almonds or chopped cashews (part coconut if wished)
- 1 cup currants and sultanas, mixed
- 1 cup candied peel/chopped cherries/ginger, mixed
- 2 tablespoons golden syrup or concentrated apple juice
- ⅔ cup melted butter*
- extra corn or seed oil to mix
- carob or chocolate* to decorate

Preheat oven to 300°F/gas mark 2/150°C

Mix the rolled oats with the chopped or flaked nuts, dried and candied fruit and add the melted butter mixed with the golden syrup or concentrated apple juice (you could use one tablespoon of each). Mix well and add a spoonful or so of oil until the mixture sticks together well. This can be made in a tray like flapjack, but to get a closer imitation of a Florentine, take teaspoonful and place on a greased oven tray, flatten out to a small round shape and bake for 15–20 minutes until golden at the edges (25–30 minutes if baked as a whole pressed into a tin). Leave to cool for at least 10–15 minutes before handling. (The omission of any sugar from this recipe makes breakages more likely).

The traditional Florentine is coated on one side with chocolate. You can do this by melting the chocolate* or carob bar in a container (glass or stainless steel for preference) over or in boiling water. A double boiler can be used too, off the heat once the water has boiled. Coat the flat side of the biscuit and make wavy lines with a fork. You can cover the top of the Florentines baked in a tin this way, and mark out the squares before the carob or chocolate dries completely.

An alternative, using less carob or chocolate, is to grate it over the top while the Florentines are still warm, so it melts and adheres. A diagonal criss-cross pattern looks attractive, or use more chocolate and make wavy lines with a fork in the traditional way.

If you use chocolate, find a good quality make rather than cheap couverture which may have more additives. Sugar-free carob bars are the more healthy choice, of course!

MF* VEG* **ORANGE CAROB OAT BARS**

---

3 cups rolled oats
1 teaspoon baking powder
½ cup Muscovado sugar
1 cup currants (optional)

½ cup chopped candied citrus peel
¾ cup melted butter*
2 tablespoons corn germ oil (or seed oil)

Preheat oven to 350°F/gas mark 4/180°C

After baking: an orange flavoured carob bar (about 50g/2oz)

Mix the dry ingredients together (but if the Muscovado sugar is hard, it is better mixed with the melted butter). Add the dried fruits, and mix in the melted butter and oil. Press into a baking tin (approximately 30cm/12 inches by 23 cm/9 inches) and bake for 30 minutes, until the edges are browning.

Allow to cool for 10 minutes, then score into small bars. When cool, cut and remove from tin. Have ready the carob bar melted in

MF* WALNUT CHEWS

Base:
1 cup flour
1–2 tablespoons Demerara or Muscovado sugar
½ cup butter*

Top:
2 eggs (separated)
1 cup sugar
¼ cup coconut
½ cup chopped walnuts
2 tablespoons flour

Preheat oven to 350°F/gas mark 4/180°C

Mix the ingredients for the base first; the sugar with the flour and then rub the butter in. Press into a tin approximately 28cm/11 inches by 18cm/7 inches, or a flan tin. Bake for 12 minutes.

While it is cooking you can make the topping. Get all the ingredients ready, walnuts chopped etc, because the mixture should not stand waiting, as it contains beaten egg whites. When you are ready, separate the eggs and beat the whites stiffly. Fold in the beaten yolks, sugar, coconut and walnuts and flour mixing carefully. Pour over the base. Return to oven (same temperature) and bake for about 20 minutes. Do not overcook or it will not be 'chewy' as the name indicates it should be. When cool cut into wedges or squares.

This may also be served as a tart for dessert. A ring of walnut halves on top is decorative.

MF* HAZELNUT OR WALNUT CAKE OR GATEAU

125g/4oz butter*
125g/4oz sugar (Muscovado or Demerara)
250g/8oz wholewheat flour
2 teaspoons baking powder
4 eggs (separated)

250g/8oz toasted hazelnuts, grated, chopped or ground in a food processor or coffee mill; or finely chopped walnuts
a pinch of salt and ½ teaspoon vanilla essence (optional)

Preheat oven to 300°F/gas mark 2/150°C

Beat the butter until light and fluffy. Add the flour, baking powder, egg yolks, sugar and nuts, (and salt and vanilla if used). Beat the egg whites separately to a snowy stiffish consistency and fold in to the mixture.

Bake in a large tin or in two smaller, flatter tins for a gâteau, for 45 minutes–1¼ hours (depending on shape of tin). Allow to cool in tin for a while before turning out to finish cooling on a rack.

For a delicious gâteau with the hazelnuts, fill the centre with whipped cream mixed with some crushed raspberries, and top with more cream (or soft white cheese) and cover with fresh (or frozen) raspberries.

The walnut version combines well with apricots, made in a similar way. Decorate with a few walnut halves among the apricots on the top. (To use dried apricots, soak for a few hours or overnight in orange juice.)

Alternatively, serve slices of either cake with stewed fruit.

MF* FIG AND ORANGE CAROB CAKE

150g/5–6oz butter or equal quantities of butter* and sunflower oil blended together
2 eggs
225g/8oz wholewheat flour
100g/4oz carob powder

225g/8oz chopped soaked figs (see below)
50g/2oz chopped blanched almonds
the juice and rind of 2 oranges
3 teaspoons baking powder

Preheat oven to 350°F/gas mark 4/180°C

Soak the figs overnight in 275ml/½ pint orange juice. Chop and reserve liquid for adding to the mixture. Chop almonds (skins need not be removed if they are not already blanched). Grate rind of oranges and squeeze the juice. Cream all ingredients together, mixing well. Line an 18cm/7 inch loose bottomed cake tin with greased paper and spoon the mixture in. Smooth the top and bake for an hour or until firm.

To make an impressive-looking gâteau, add 50g/2oz chopped stem ginger (and have some pieces of ginger for the decoration). Bake the cake in 2 or 3 shallower sandwich tins (for which it may not need so long in the oven), and check after 30–40 minutes.

Sandwich the layers together, when cool, with 100g/4oz cream cheese* (or soft white cheese) mixed with a tablespoon of honey or a mashed banana. Place a small dob of the cream cheese at intervals around the top (so there will be one on each slice) and flatten with a piece of preserved ginger.

CINNAMON TEA CAKE

50g/2oz butter
75g/3oz sugar
1 egg
170g/6oz flour
2 teaspoons baking powder
85ml/3½fl oz milk
butter, sugar and cinnamon for topping (see below)

Preheat oven to 350°F/gas mark 4/180°C

Cream butter and sugar. Add beaten egg and then flour mixed with baking powder, and finally the milk. Mix well and turn into an oiled sponge tin. Bake for 25 minutes. While still hot, spread a little butter on top and dust with ½ teaspoon cinnamon mixed with 2 teaspoons sugar. Serve warm.

GF ALMOND PASTRY

125g/4oz ground almonds (or 75g/2½oz ground almonds and 50g/1½oz rice flour)
yolk of 1 egg
a little grated lemon rind
1–2 tablespoons buttermilk or yogurt thinned with milk
rice flour for rolling out

Preheat oven to 375°F/gas mark 5/190°C

Mix all the ingredients together adding buttermilk as necessary to make a soft dough. Pat out the dough on the board floured with a little rice flour.
  Line a pie plate and bake for 15 minutes until just golden.
  Add to this a filling of your choice (such as that for the apricot cheese cake page 140 or the tofu cream, page 142), or use the pastry to make the mince slice or spicey apple slice below.

MINCE SLICE

225–350g/8–12oz shortcrust or almond pastry

225g/8oz mincemeat

Preheat oven to 375°F/gas mark 5/190°C

Divide the pastry in two and roll out one half to the right size for your baking tray. Spread with the mincemeat (add some drained stewed apple if you wish). Roll out the rest of the pastry and cover the top. Bake for 20–30 minutes.

SPICEY APPLE SLICE

225–350g/8–12oz shortcrust or almond pastry
450g/1lb cooking apples
½ cup sultanas
½ teaspoon cinnamon
2 or 3 cloves
a little allspice or mixed spice
½ cup water

Heat the water with the spices and when boiling add the finely sliced apple (skins on or off as preferred). Cover and bring back to the boil, then simmer for a few moments, but without letting the apples go mushy. Turn off heat, add the sultanas, stir in and leave them to soak up the juice. When cool, taste, and add a little concentrated apple juice if it is not sweet enough. Drain off excess juice.

Make the fruit slice as for mince slice, using this mixture in place of the mincemeat.

Other combinations with apple (instead of sultanas and spice) are blackberries, blackcurrants, apricots, rhubarb or mincemeat (spread on the pastry base).

MINCEMEAT

4 lemons — weigh them and use equal amounts of the following:
apples (preferably Cox's), peeled and cored
raisins
currants
candied peel
sugar (any kind)
brandy (optional)

Boil the lemons until tender. Remove the pips and cut in pieces. Mince them with all the other fruits, adding the sugar to the mixture and a glass or two of brandy (optional). Sterilise screw-topped jars with boiling water and fill with the mincemeat. Store in a cool place until required.

Picnics and Packed Lunches

What you provide for a picnic and packed lunch will depend on those who will eat it and how many, whether it will be eaten at a table or on the ground, whether it is to be prepared in a proper kitchen or in camping conditions and on how it will be transported (by car, on public transport, or by carrying it some distance on foot).

PICNICS

Picnics where there is a mix of generations from young children to grandparents are usually easiest on a table, whether your own or in a picnic area. Take a cloth (plastic coated if you have one) to cover a public table which may not be too clean.

You may find it convenient to take a pack for each person. Each can choose the contents, or just put what will appeal. A communal salad container can be passed round with fresh vegetables to go with the sandwiches. Likewise, with cake or biscuits, dried fruits and nuts or other 'afters', these can all be in one container. It is nice to have something to hand around if you are meeting another group of friends, even if they are providing their own picnic.

Drinks are best brought in containers with replaceable stoppers or individual cartons.

If you are walking some distance with your picnic, the compact, the light and the non-squashable will be priorities. Plenty of salad and fruit may make it unnecessary to carry drinks. Dried fruits are a good choice, compact and full of energy!

PACKED LUNCHES

Taking a packed lunch to work enables you to choose what you eat instead of relying on a cafeteria or local sandwich shop. It is likely to work out much cheaper too. Look for things that are quick to prepare in the morning, or which will keep overnight in the fridge. Bread freezes well, so if you have a freezer, make a quantity of buttered rolls, taking one out each night to defrost in the fridge overnight, to be filled in the morning, or just take the frozen roll, a slice of cheese or hardboiled egg, and a tomato or piece of fruit. The roll will doubtless defrost by lunchtime in a heated building.

Early in the morning, ideas are likely to be at a low ebb, although it is ideal to have some variety for lunches. Make a poster to pin up in the kitchen or on the back of the pantry door, listing all the sandwich fillings you like. Alternatively, on the weekend, make a sandwich spread which will last all week. Many of the dips in the Entertaining section (page 166–8) would be suitable, and there are more spreads in *Growing Up With Good Food*. Try also to start sprouting some seeds or beans which will be ready at the end of the week when other supplies are running low. Sprout different ones each week from mung beans, aduki beans, alfalfa seeds or 'sandwich mixes' provided by some merchants. (See Sprouting Beans and Seeds, page 113.) The virtue of sprouts is that they keep growing until you eat them, so it does not matter how long in advance you prepare your sandwich or salad.

Suddenly you find there is no bread in the house. What can you do? You could use wholewheat biscuits or similar, or make your own sesame triangles (see page 170). Scones are another suggestion (recipes are on page 144-5). Is there some leftover flan or pizza? If you feel like making something specially, recipes can be found in the Hot Dishes section (page 76–80, 83–6). Why have bread or bread substitutes anyway? You could make a rice or potato salad to take in a small container (see Salads section, page 122–6). Another lunch without bread could consist of celery sticks filled with peanut butter or soft white cheese (make your own by hanging yogurt in muslin overnight), with a packet of potato crisps, extra salad vegetables or fruit, or dried fruits or fruit cake.

A look through the ideas for picnic lunches may provide further ways of varying your daily packed lunch.

SANDWICHES

There are lots of interesting breads on the market and many kinds to make yourself (see Bread section, page 44). If your bread has added seeds or seed sprouts, soya flour, milk or the like, it will be a good food in itself and there is less need to provide the nutritious part in the filling. Think of complementing the grain protein with beans or bean spreads, different cheeses or beansprouts if such things have not already been added to the bread.

SANDWICH FILLINGS

The dips on pages 166–8 would all be suitable and could replace butter.

Almost any of the following would be improved with fresh herbs such as chives or parsley, chervil or dill. The more aromatic thyme, marjoram, basil, savoury etc should be used more circumspectly otherwise they may overpower other ingredients.

MF VEG	avocado spread on the bread with alfalfa sprouts and a little lemon juice
GF	cottage cheese or soft white cheese with black pepper and alfalfa
GF	cream cheese with finely chopped red pepper or olives (or olive paste)
MF* GF	scrambled egg* cooked with finely sliced green pepper (and cooled) or mixed with curry powder, or garam masala
GF	cream cheese with celery and walnuts
VEG MF	peanut butter with sandwich sprouts, banana (a few drops of lemon juice will stop it going brown), or sunflower seeds
VEG MF	peanut butter with grated carrot, (perhaps a few raisins)
VEG MF GF	sesame or sunflower spread with beansprouts, add yeast extract spread for a tangy taste
GF	cheese or cold roast meat with home made chutney, or green pepper paste

MF GF VEG	grated carrot with fresh or cooked beetroot and lettuce
GF	sliced hardboiled egg with cress and a little mayonnaise or yogurt
	(gluten-free fillings to be used with gluten-free bread, of course!)

Combine these and other ingredients in different ways remembering that it is good to have something fairly sticky (avocado, soft white cheese, cream cheese, scrambled egg, mayonnaise etc), something crunchy (beansprouts, celery, chopped nuts, grated carrot), and something tasty or tangy (yeast extract spread, a few drops of chilli sauce, herbs, mustard, chutney or pickles) unless the flavours blend so well together this is not needed.

Although they make interesting sandwiches cooked meats such as ham, sausage, liver paté and seafoods, tinned tuna etc have been excluded because they are not part of the pregnancy diet. However, if you really yearn for such things, there is little harm in making the exception and indulging once in a while. It is always the habit that is more important than the odd occasion with diet.

ROLLS, BAPS AND FRENCH STICKS

Obviously you can use any of the sandwich fillings suggested. Big chunky rolls lend themselves to big chunky fillings too. You can eat a whole salad in each bite! The salad fillings are especially appropriate here. Make your own wholewheat rolls (sesame or poppy seeds on top are good), milk and soya flour baps, or wheatmeal French sticks or use bought ones.

PAN BAGNA

Cut a length of French loaf in half for each person. Pour some olive oil onto a plate and place the cut side of each piece of bread on the oil, allowing it to absorb more or less oil as you prefer. Fill each sandwich with three or more of the following: anchovies, sliced hard boiled egg, lettuce leaves, sliced tomatoes, sliced cucumber and olives. Wrap each sandwich in foil and leave some time before eating to allow the flavours to blend.

OTHER SALAD FILLINGS

Make any salad on its own or with cheese, cottage cheese, hard boiled egg, scrambled egg, cold chicken or roast lamb, beef (with horseradish or mustard) or pork, cold poached fish with dill.

Green leaf: any kind of lettuce, preferably whole leaves rather than shredded, crispy Cos lettuce is refreshing, or try watercress, endive, mustard and cress, Chinese leaves, shredded cabbage or spinach.
Root vegetables, grated or thinly sliced: carrot, celeriac, beetroot, radishes.
Stems: celery (try cutting thin long slices for a change), fennel, spring onions.
Fruit vegetables: tomatoes, green or red peppers, cucumber.
Sprouted seeds or beans: alfalfa, mung or aduki beansprouts etc.

Ideally choose one from each group, and add a little mayonnaise, if liked, or use it instead of butter.

STUFFED PITTA BREAD POUCHES

It is possible to find wholewheat pitta breads, or use white ones. They can be messy, but if not overfilled, bits are less likely to drop out as one eats. Pop them under the grill for just a moment to make them easier to open but not hard outside. Cut in half or slit down one side and carefully separate the two sides to make the pouch. You can make a salad filling from the ideas above, or from the following.

PITTA BREAD STUFFINGS

The use of chickpeas, houmous, tahini, kebabs, and a hot sauce in pitta breads captures the Middle Eastern character, but other fillings are good too. Here are a few suggestions:

GF* MF VEG   a grain* salad or sweet corn with houmous and shredded lettuce

GF MF VEG   cooked chick peas, tahini (thinned with a little lemon juice), shredded greens or green peppers and chilli sauce

GF   cooked red kidney beans (or other sorts) with cole slaw

GF   cooked lamb kebabs (some garlic and chilli used in cooking) with shredded cabbage, tomato slices and fresh herbs, or spicy yogurt

GF   shredded spinach, sliced mushrooms, chopped spring onions with some olive oil or avocado blended with lemon juice or yogurt

GF   cucumber, watercress and crumbly white cheese (preferably goat's cheese)

FINGER FOODS AND OTHER DELICACIES FOR A SPECIAL PICNIC

GF   *Celery sticks* can be cut in short lengths and filled with soft white cheese, cream cheese or peanut butter. Place together and separate when you serve them.

GF   *Avocadoes* can be halved, and the stone removed (thrust the blade of a sharp knife on to the stone and lift it out). The cut surface should then be rubbed with lemon juice. Fill with cottage cheese and replace halves together, wrap in cling film for carrying. (Remember to take spoons with you!)

MF GF*   *Cold chicken joints* can be taken to go with salads in individual pots, salad rolls or stuffed pitta breads*.

GF   *Cold spare ribs* cooked with spices or a tasty sauce with salads.

Pancakes spread with sesame spread and/or yeast extract spread and stuffed with alfalfa sprouts, or stuffed with soft white cheese or grated cheese, spring onions and watercress etc can be rolled up and individually wrapped in foil or cling film.

MF *Asparagus rolls* made with thin brown bread without crusts and a touch of mayonnaise are quite a fiddle to make, but very special

MF *Scotch eggs* coated with vegeburger mix can be taken and halved on site (remember the knife and a little board or plate).

Individual salads using any of the recipes in the Salads section (page 111) or your own, in plastic containers with lids. (Take forks!)

Pastry Individual pies, quiches and pasties are easy to eat on a picnic. You can also take large quiches, pizzas (see recipes in the Hot Dishes section pages 76–80, 83–6) or your own pies. Plates and possibly forks would then be desirable. Serve with salads or whole tomatoes, radishes etc. Carry the flans in the cooking tin.

These are just a few suggestions on how to make a picnic more elaborate. But the fresh air and exercise that go with a day by the sea or in the country are to be valued as much as the food. As people often say everything tastes better out of doors anyway, perhaps it is not always worth spending hours in the kitchen first.

MF GF VEG   THE SALAD BOWL

In order to keep the vegetables as fresh as possible, and to avoid vitamin loss, to say nothing of a messy salad bowl, it is a good idea to choose small tomatoes, carrots, radishes, which do not need cutting, just washing. Celery can be cut in sticks, but you could take cucumbers or green peppers whole and slice them on arrival. Lettuce leaves can also be left whole, also stalks of watercress or other greens, and they are best without salad dressing. If you do not have a suitable bowl with a lid, transport the salad in a polythene bag. Hold the top at the sides and twist over and over, so that the air will be caught. Tie it in and it will act as a cushion to protect crushable items.

AFTERS

The simplest dessert is to take healthfood fruit and nut bars, sesame snacks or carob bars, or pieces of fresh fruit (apples always travel well). You could make your own mix of dried fruits and nuts in a container, also useful for snacks at other times during the day. Then there are things you can bake like flapjack, slab cakes, or tea breads or bought biscuits.

HOMEMADE FRUIT AND NUT BARS

Mince together a selection of dried fruits and nuts that you like. Some whole sultanas or raisins, sunflower or sesame seeds can be added. Mix with a little rice flour or oatmeal and lemon or orange juice and press into a baking tray. Line it with rice paper if you wish, and another sheet on top will make the bars easy to handle. Alternatively, coat with coconut. Place in fridge to harden and cut into bars to be wrapped for the picnic.

Entertaining Friends

Three ways to entertain friends are envisaged here:

1 Friends to 'coffee' (though you may serve something other than coffee),
2 'Cocktail Parties' for 20–30 – standing up, chatting and eating bits and pieces (again it is not essential to serve potent cocktails! see Drinks page 188),
3 Dinner parties for 6–8 (scaled down, these could be a special feast for two on Valentine's Day, a birthday or other anniversary).

If you ever spent an entire weekend cooking a special meal for friends, put away such thoughts! Now you have less time, or time interrupted by children's needs, or are trying to take it easy, and such efforts are unrealistic. But it is still good to invite people for a meal, to have houseguests or a family for a weekend lunch with their children (saves babysitters and provides playmates for yours!). There are many suitable recipes in *Growing Up With Good Food*, as these are all meals children may enjoy sharing. A good idea on such an occasion is a buffet-style meal with a smorgasbord array for choice, including some fairly plain things (such as pieces of cheese, salad vegetables individually served to cater for all tastes), or a simple roast.

WAYS OF MAKING IT EASY TO ENTERTAIN

1 Do what you have time and energy to do. Try to make at least one course ahead of the day.
2 Do not be too ambitious – it is the company that counts! Put your effort into one dish, and do easy things for the rest.
3 Some things create a good atmosphere – communal cooking is

one of them. Is this why barbecues are so popular? If you do not have a fondue pot or a Japanese fire pot or bagna cauda set, you can still roast chestnuts or muffins in front of a fire. The vegetable dips or other dips are similar in effect and even a cheese board gives guests something to do

4 The ingredients do not have to be expensive, but it helps if they look pretty. You could also pay some attention to the table by way of flowers, candles and cloth – something quite simple without fuss, but chosen to go with the meal in style or colour.

5 Nutrition does not have to go out the window! There are plenty of healthy snacks to serve at a buffet, and you will feel better for it the next day. But if you want to indulge in something special, the odd occasion is the time to do it, rather than every day. This is the time to serve a creamier dessert than usual or a more elaborate gâteau.

FRIENDS TO 'COFFEE'

If your friends are expecting a baby, expecting to expect or breastfeeding, then have something other than coffee on offer (maybe fruit juice or herb teas).

Only prepare a home-made offering to eat if you feel able to do so comfortably. It is better to be relaxed with your guests and serve bought biscuits, than to be in a flap because the scones are not in the oven yet. If you do want to make something yourself, concentrate on one thing. Anything else can be ready made. Ideas in the Home Baking section (see page 143) suitable to use include the scones, teabreads and fruit loaves, the ginger root snaps, orange carob oat bars, the shortbreads or Florentines. A hot cinnamon tea cake always goes down well! In the Bread section (page 58–60) you will find a yeast-risen spice loaf, muffins and a fruit plait.

COCKTAIL PARTIES AND BUFFETS

Serve mulled apple, grape juice or wine, or a fruit cup (see Drinks pages 196–7), as well as any more alcoholic beverages.

Some party dips are given to serve with vegetables, cheese

straws, sesame triangles or the like. If you have time or help to do something more elaborate, you could use the dips to stuff eggs, tomatoes or mushrooms (just remove the stalk, tomatoes need the top cutting off and seeds spooned out). Toasted seeds and nuts or garlic bread (page 57) are good in winter. If you would like to have something more substantial on offer you could make small quiches in tart moulds, pizza fingers or small pasties (see Hot Dishes, pages 76–80, 83–6). Bits and bobs on sticks (cheese, pineapple, olives, pickles) are good finger food. But if you want to serve something on plates, make your quiches and pizzas larger and have salads to go with them. Pasta dishes also go well on these occasions with green salad. Try a lasagne, which you could make using the meat filling for canelloni, adding a tin of tomatoes or tomato juice, alternated with mozzarella cheese, and finishing with béchamel sauce topped with Parmesan. Or make the green pasta bake (see page 81). Dried fruits and nuts, grapes or satsumas (clementines, mandarins) may suffice for those with a sweeter tooth in place of a dessert.

PARTY DIPS

Dips may be served at a party of any size, passed around at a stand-up party or as a starter at a dinner.

Mashed with hardboiled egg yolk, they can be used to stuff the halved whites of the hardboiled egg, or mushrooms (with the stalk removed) or tomatoes.

GF* MF* VEG*   FRESH VEGETABLE DIPS

Place a bowl containing the dip* in the centre of a large plate or tray. Surround with sticks of fresh vegetables to dip in. The following are all suitable: green and red peppers, celery, cucumber, Chinese leaves, carrots (dip in lemon juice and water to prevent discolouration), courgettes (blanch in hot water briefly), radishes, large mushrooms cut in quarters, florets of cauliflower, or fennel.

| MF* VEG* | INSTEAD OF VEGETABLES |

You can offer cheese straws* (page 169), sesame triangles (page 170), bread sticks (page 59), garlic bread (page 57), oatcakes, or bought crackers or crisps, to go with dips.

| GF | AVOCADO DIP |

1 ripe avocado pear
juice of 1 lemon
1 cup cream cheese or low fat soft white cheese
coriander
Chinese wild pepper or black pepper
chopped chives

Mash the skinned avocado halves and blend with the lemon juice. Combine with the cream cheese and stir together until well blended. Add spices to taste and allow to stand for 30 minutes. Check seasoning and make adjustments before turning into serving bowl. Sprinkle with chives.

| GF | BLACK OLIVE DIP |

1 cup cream cheese (about 100g/3–4oz)
1 teaspoon grated onion
½ cup chopped black olives
½ teaspoon paprika

Blend the cream cheese with a little milk, and stir in the grated onion, chopped olives and paprika. Leave to stand for the flavours to mingle. Serve chilled.

| GF | CURRIED EGG DIP |

½ cup cream cheese or soft white cheese
1 egg
curry powder or garam masala

Heat a little butter in a pan and add egg beaten with a little milk, stir over low heat until cooked. Add the curry powder (or make your own from turmeric, cumin, cardamom and coriander, with a touch of ginger or chilli) or garam masala. Allow to cool. Mix well with the cheese and serve chilled.

DIPS WITHOUT CREAM CHEESE

You can serve houmous as a dip, you can make them with tofu, or try the tapenade.

GF* MF VEG   TOFU DIPS

200g/7oz tofu
1 tablespoon tamari or soya sauce
1 teaspoon mustard*
1 tablespoon sesame seeds
1 teaspoon sesame or sunflower oil

Liquidise ingredients flavoured as suggested below. Add a little cold water if the texture is too thick.

Green dip   Add half a bunch of chopped watercress
Spicy dip   Add ½ teaspoon garam masala.
Onion dip   Add several chopped green spring onions.
Fruity dip   Add 1 peeled and sliced ripe pear. This can be served with raw fruit as well as vegetables.

GF MF   TAPENADE

125g/4oz black olives (without stones)
125g/4oz green olives (without stones)
1 tablespoon capers
10 anchovy fillets
1 hardboiled egg yolk
olive oil to mix

Remove stones (if not already done) from the olives and place in a blender or food processor with the other ingredients and grind them all together, adding enough oil to make a creamy paste, if to be used as a spread, or more to make a softer texture for use as a dip.

PARTY NIBBLES

Although heating nuts and seeds removes some of their nutritional value, they are delicious roasted and no doubt still much better for you than most of the snacks you can buy.

GF MF VEG   ROASTED PEANUTS

Cover a baking tray with peanuts (add a tablespoon of tamari, shoyu, or soya sauce) and roast in a hot oven at 400°F/gas mark 6/200°C shaking every 5 or 10 minutes, until they are crisp and the liquid, if used, is dried up. Jumbo peanuts will take a good deal longer than small redskins, so it is not possible to give a more exact time than between 10–20 minutes. Do not burn. Serve hot.

GF MF VEG   ROASTED SUNFLOWER SEEDS

Treat sunflower seeds in the same way. They will brown more quickly, in 5–10 minutes (depending on whether you add the tasty tamari).

CHEESE STRAWS

170g/6oz wholewheat flour
100g/3½oz butter
40g/1½oz Parmesan cheese (or part grated cheddar)
1 egg yolk or 1 tablespoon soya flour
salt, pepper and Cayenne

Preheat oven to 450°F/gas mark 8/230°C

Rub butter into the flour, add the grated cheese and seasoning and bind with the egg yolk (or a little beaten egg). If soya flour is substituted you will need some more liquid. Add a little water if needed to make a good consistency for rolling out. Roll out into a rectangle and cut into strips. You can glaze with left over beaten egg. Bake for 15 minutes. Serve on their own or with dips.

| MF | BARMENE CURLS |

225g/8oz wholewheat shortcrust pastry (page 74)
Barmene or other yeast extract spread
30g/1oz finely grated cheese (optional)
a beaten egg for glazing

Preheat oven to 400°F/gas mark 6/200°C

Roll out the pastry into an oblong shape. Spread with Barmene. (Add a little grated cheese if you wish). Roll up like a Swiss roll and cut thin slices. Place on a greased baking sheet, brush with a little egg if you wish. Bake for 10 minutes or until done.

Peanut butter could be used as an alternative to make peanut curls.

| MF VEG | SESAME TRIANGLES |

1½ cups wholewheat flour
¼ cup soya flour
¼ cup sesame seeds (preferably ground or toasted and crushed in a pestle and mortar)
1 teaspoon sea salt
½ cup corn germ oil or sunflower oil
water as needed (about ½ cup)

Preheat oven to 350°F/gas mark 4/180°C

Mix together the dry ingredients. If preferred, keep back half the sesame seeds for rolling out, or decorating the tops. Add the oil and mix until well absorbed. Then add cold water as needed to make a soft dough for rolling out thin. Knead into a ball and roll out 3mm/⅛inch thick. Cut into small triangles and decorate with sesame seeds and a little sea salt if wished. Bake for 15 minutes or until golden.

Serve with spreads or with dips.

DINNERS FOR 6–8

If you are serving wine offer mineral water for those not drinking alcohol, or to 'cut' the wine, sparkling or still as preferred.

When constructing a menu, as well as finding things that go well together or make interesting contrasts, it is sometimes fun to choose a theme for the meal (the first menu uses orange in each course) or to select national dishes from a region (an Indian meal is suggested and one with a Ukrainian flavour based on pancakes). The traditional dishes offered in the main section might provide similar opportunities for invention. Make use of any special seasonal foods; the lamb blanquette is good in spring or early summer, the red cabbage dish followed by pumpkin pie is an autumn menu.

Bearing in mind the advice to concentratre on one main dish and to do easy things or something made a day ahead for the other courses, alternatives are offered in keeping with this plan. Simple starters include melon, grapefruit, avocado, carottes râpées (grated carrot), or a soup made a day ahead (most cold soups are better for standing a while and need chilling anyway). Many desserts can be made ahead, while cheese and biscuits, fresh fruit (with soft white cheese if liked), or dried fruits and nuts all require no cooking, but make a good end to a meal.

TEN SUGGESTED MENUS

Menu 1
GF*

Parsnip soup (with a dash of orange) page 67, or carrot soup with chopped chervil on top (page 66), or grapefruit.

* * *

Tarragon chicken with orange (page 174) and rice, accompanied or followed by green salad with almonds and oranges (page 175).

* * *

Pancakes with orange sauce,* or Nesselrode pudding (page 184), or oranges givrées (*Growing Up With Good Food* page 100), or fruit and nuts.

Menu 2
GF*

Avocado, or asparagus (could be served with a soft boiled egg to dip into instead of butter or vinaigrette).

* * *

Lamb blanquette with polenta, page 175.

* * *

Fruit sorbet or Summer Pudding* (page 133) or just strawberries.

Menu 3
GF* MF*

Plat de crudités (grated carrot, cucumber and tomato, and watercress — or whatever you like, quite simple, but with a nice vinaigrette dressing).

* * *

Lamb with almonds and prunes (page 177) with rice.

* * *

Ginger, tutti frutti or praliné ice cream,* (page 186).

Menu 4
GF*

Small red and green pepper flans* (page 76) or green beans with tomato (page 126) or a fresh vegetable dip (page 166).

* * *

Lamb kidneys on skewers (page 177) with rice and watercress.

* * *

Fresh fruit or praliné ice cream* or peach ice cream* (page 186).

Menu 5
GF*

Cold cucumber soup (page 71) or melon.

* * *

Trout with almonds or poached salmon trout (page 178) with hot potato salad (page 125) and watercress.

* * *

Nesselrode pudding (page 184) or strawberries with cream or soft white cheese or gooseberry fool (page 134).

Menu 6

Courgette salad (page 179) or julienne consommé (page 63), or gazpacho (page 71).

* * *

ENTERTAINING FRIENDS

Canelloni (with ricotta or with meat) (page 180), and a green salad.

* * *

Plum jelly (page 136) or dried fruits and nuts (page 129).

Menu 7
MF* VEG*

Phul Gobi (Indian braised cauliflower) or melon with ginger (p. 181).

* * *

Curried mung beans for a vegetarian meal (with or without* hardboiled eggs) page 94, or the Tandoori chicken* (page 95), both with rice and a side dish of cucumber raita.* Chapattis can be made using the recipe for wholewheat tortillas (page 97), only, when they are made, hold them on a metal fish slice or with tongs over a flame to make them puff out. Instead of serving the cauliflower as a starter, it could accompany the main course.

* * *

Tropical fruit salad (with guavas, bananas, mangoes, pineapple), or Hunza apricots stewed and served with whipped cream* and toasted cashews or almonds, or almond cream (page 192).

Menu 8
GF* VEG*

Mushrooms vinaigrette (page 120) and pink rice* (page 124) or other crudités, or julienne consommé (page 63).

* * *

Red cabbage with aduki beans and chestnuts (pages 103–4).

* * *

Pumpkin pie* (page 139) or roasted chestnuts (pages 139–40).

Menu 9
VEG* MF*

This could be a vegan menu, using ground cashews to thicken the soups and oil instead of butter.
Parsnip soup* (page 67) or cauliflower soup* (page 65).

* * *

A selection of three salads: Red salad (page 118), potato salad (page 125) and lentil salad or one with chick peas made the same way (page 125); or mushrooms a la grècque (page 126), tabbouleh with added cucumber and green pepper (page 121) and green bean salad (page 126); or flageolet and avocado (page 124), celery and walnut (page 119) and rice with tomatoes (page 122). Garnish any of the salads with extra water cress if you wish.

* * *

Dried fruits and nuts or for a non-vegan meal, apricot cheese cake* (page 140), walnut chew tart* (page 151) or fig and orange carob cake as a gâteau with ginger* (page 152).

Menu 10 Russian bortsch (page 71) or caviar (!)

* * *

Barley pancake 'cake' (page 182) with buckwheat kasha and hot greens or a green salad. (Blinis could be an alternative, recipes in many books).

* * *

Cherry kissel (page 184) or fresh fruit.

GF MF*   TARRAGON CHICKEN WITH ORANGE

---

1 jointed chicken (size depending on number of guests, for 8 people you may need two small chickens)
1 medium – large onion
2 tablespoons tarragon
300ml/½pint frozen concentrated orange juice

1 tablespoon cornflour (soaked in 2 tablespoons water or orange juice)
*80ml/3fl oz cream or sour cream (optional)

Allow about 60g/2oz (dry weight) of rice per person to provide the bed of rice on which you serve the chicken.

Preheat oven to 350°F/gas mark 4/180°C

Brown the chicken pieces in 1 tablespoon butter and 1 tablespoon oil. Reserve. Fry the sliced onion until transparent and add the orange juice. Add the tarragon and bring to the boil. Place chicken pieces in a casserole and pour over them the onion, orange juice and tarragon. Place in oven and cook for an hour or until done. After about 45 minutes, cook the rice, drain and make a 'bed' of it in your serving dish. When the chicken is tender (the meat will come away from the bone easily), place the pieces on the rice. Then thicken the remaining sauce with the slaked cornflour, (take a little of the hot sauce to mix with it and the cold water or juice it has been standing in, then return to the rest of the sauce and stir well). Bring to the boil and simmer for 2 minutes. Add the cream if you are using it. Reheat slightly (but do not boil), and pour sauce over the chicken on the rice and serve. A few quartered slices of fresh orange could be used to garnish the dish.

GF MF VEG   **GREEN SALAD WITH ALMONDS AND ORANGE**

This salad would make a pleasant accompaniment or could be served as the next course.

- 1 lettuce (preferably crisp such as a Cos lettuce)
- 1 orange, sliced and quartered
- ½ cup hot toasted almonds or fried in butter with salt and a touch of garlic

Mix these in at the last moment and serve.

GF   **LAMB BLANQUETTE**

- 700g/1½lb lamb (spring lamb is delicious)
- 12 small carrots (scraped and left whole)
- 8 small onions (the size of ping pong balls)
- 500g/1lb petits pois (or small garden peas)
- 3 cloves
- 6 sprigs of parsley
- 6 sprigs of chervil (or 2 teaspoons dried chervil)
- a small sprig rosemary (or ½ teaspoon dried)
- (an optional glass of white wine or a tablespoon white wine vinegar)
- 2 egg yolks
- a cup of sour cream or yogurt
- 1 tablespoon cornflour
- juice of 2 lemons

Cut the lamb into small dice and place in a large saucepan. Cover barely with water and bring to the boil. Simmer for 5 minutes and skim well. Add the wine or wine vinegar (if used), the carrots and onions (one onion stuck with the cloves which you remove before serving) and the rosemary. Cover and cook for an hour on low heat. Check from time to time to skim and to add a little water if necessary. Add the peas and the rest of the herbs, chopped (except for a tablespoonful to use for garnish), and cook a further 10 minutes at most. Meanwhile mix separately in a bowl the cream or yogurt, the egg yolks, lemon juice and the cornflour. Ladle a small amount of the hot cooking liquid on to this mixture and stir well, then pour the whole mixture into the pot and blend in quickly. Reheat, but do not boil. Pour into heated serving dish and sprinkle with remaining herbs. Serve.

This dish would go well with either rice or potatoes, but for an unusual accompaniment, try polenta made with maize meal.

GF   **POLENTA**

---

1 litre/1½ pints water
270g/10oz polenta (maize meal)
a pinch of salt

freshly ground black pepper to taste
25g/1oz butter

In a large heavy-based saucepan bring the salted water to the boil. Sprinkle the polenta in, bit by bit. Simmer on low heat, stirring all the time with a wooden spoon or stick. When it is a thick mass, let it cook for 20 minutes, stirring occasionally. When the spoon stands up in it, it is done. Butter a flat dish and turn the polenta into it. It should be about 3cm/an inch or so thick. Let it dry off a little in the oven for about 10 minutes. Remove from oven, separate the polenta around the edges, cover with a napkin and then a plate. Turn over to unmould. Serve cut in wedges with the lamb blanquette. It will help mop up the sauce. Any left over can be served as polenta pizza (page 86).

GF MF   LAMB WITH PRUNES AND ALMONDS

500g/1lb lean lamb cubed
1 tablespoon butter
½ cup water
50g/2oz blanched almonds
1 tablespoon sugar (optional)
2 teaspoons ground cinnamon
200g/7oz stoned prunes
1 tablespoon cornflour (and a little water)

Brown the lamb in the butter. Add the water, almonds, sugar and cinnamon. Cover and simmer for an hour. Add prunes and simmer for 15 minutes. Taste and add a little salt if necessary. Thicken with the cornflour mixed to a paste with the water. Cook for a further 5 minutes so that the cornflour loses its rawness. Serve with rice.

GF MF   LAMB KIDNEYS ON SKEWERS

Allow 2 kidneys per person
marinade of a taste-free oil, 1 bay leaf per kidney, a clove of garlic, black pepper, (a few juniper berries, optional) and an onion quartered, the layers separated
1–2 handfuls of dry rice per person
green salad of shredded spinach, lettuce, cress with some new (unsprayed) dandelion leaves or nasturtium leaves or capers.

Remove outside membrane (if still present) from the kidneys and cut them in half lengthwise. Then cut out the white vessels in the middle and place kidneys in marinade. If the onion is large, it may be necessary to cut the onion leaves across, about the same size as the kidneys. Leave for 2 hours, turning occasionally. Before your guests arrive make up the skewers, ready for quick grilling at the last moment. Cut the bayleaves across with scissors (or snap them in half before placing in the marinade). Starting and finishing with a kidney, place an onion leaf sandwiched between two bay leaves between each kidney half. Wash salad but leave shredding until the last minute (while the skewers are cooking) and dress just before serving.

When the rice is nearly ready, place the skewers under the preheated grill, or on a cast iron griddle, or over a charcoal grill. Drain rice and arrange in a flat ovenproof dish, season with salt and pepper, and keep warm in the oven with a butter paper over the top. Turn kidneys after 4 minutes and cook on the other side (unless you have an automatically rotating kebab device). When done (in another 4–5 minutes) place skewers on the bed of rice and as you serve each person pull the skewer out through a fork to release the kidneys. The green salad can be eaten alongside or afterwards.

TROUT WITH ALMONDS

One trout per person (preferably from a trout farm near the source of its stream, and preferably cleaned)	1 cup milk
	1 cup flour
	100g/4oz butter
	1 lemon cut in rounds
25g/1oz flaked almonds per trout	1 bunch of watercress for garnish

If you can get your fish merchant to do the time-consuming and messy job of cleaning the fish, so much the better. If not, slit the underside from the hole near the tail end up to the head and empty the innards out, scraping around the inside with a blunt knife. Scrape off any loose scales, but no need to worry too much as the skin will not be eaten. Wash and wipe clean and dry with a kitchen towel. (Remove heads with a sharp knife if they displease you). Dip each fish in milk and coat with flour and fry in a heavy pan in a little butter. When the fish are cooked (test to see if the flesh parts easily from the backbone), heat a little knob of butter per serving in a separate small pan, toss the flaked almonds in the butter until golden and pour over the trout on their serving dish. Surround with the lemon slices and add a branch of watercress on one side.

Serve with a hot potato salad (page 125) or with rice.

GF MF ## SALMON TROUT

Fresh salmon trout is a wonderful treat should it ever come your way. It is expensive to buy (but even more in a restaurant), however as it is so rich and dense the servings can be small. If a whole fish is beyond your means or appetites, ask for a tail end to cook whole.

Allow 100g/3–4oz per person of fish (or a little more)	a little dry white wine (optional)
	cucumber slices or lemon slices
Fresh dill weed and parsley	

Poached

If you have a fish kettle, make a stock from the herbs, wine and some slices of carrot and onion and peppercorns. Poach the fish in the stock for 10 minutes per 450g/lb.

Baked

Preheat oven to 350°F/gas mark 4/180°C. Bring the wine to the boil (the alcohol evaporates). In an ovenproof dish place fish on a generous amount of foil lined with greaseproof paper, lay dill branches over it and cover with cucumber or lemon slices. Grind some black pepper over it, pour on the wine, close foil tightly and bake for 20 minutes per 450g/1lb. Test to see if done by checking if the flesh parts easily from the backbone. (A fish brick – like a chicken brick – can be used for baking too.) To serve, remove skin and discard herbs etc. The skin should peel off easily, then lift off portions of the fish from one side of the bone, remove backbone, and slide fish slice between skin and flesh to serve further portions.

GF MF VEG	COURGETTE SALAD

450g/1lb courgettes
olive oil and lemon juice

thyme, bay leaf, peppercorns, coriander

Scald whole courgettes in boiling water for about 3 minutes. Cut into fine rounds and dry on paper towels. Then place in serving dish, sprinkle with the oil, lemon juice, herbs and seeds and allow to stand for a few hours.

CANNELLONI WITH RICOTTA

A packet of cannelloni pasta (look for green, made with spinach, or wholewheat kinds). About 16 will be used.

Stuffing

700g/1½lb ricotta cheese (goat's curds or soft white cheese could be used)
2 beaten eggs
pinch of salt
1 onion finely chopped or grated
80g/3oz grated Parmesan cheese
a handful of chopped fresh parsley

Tomato sauce

1 onion
1 carrot
1 stick celery
1 clove garlic
1 tin of tomatoes (or 450g/1lb fresh tomatoes and tomato purée)
1 teaspoon mixed herbs
1 bay leaf

White sauce

50g/2oz butter
2 tablespoons flour
600ml/1pint warmed milk
½ teaspoon grated nutmeg

Preheat oven to 400°F/gas mark 6/200°C

To make the tomato sauce, chop the onion, carrot and celery finely, soften in a little oil with the pressed garlic.

If using fresh tomatoes it is best to remove the skins by scoring the tops and pouring boiling water over them. After a minute or two the skins come off easily. Add up to two tablespoons of tomato purée if using fresh tomatoes.

Add tinned or fresh chopped tomatoes and herbs. Simmer for 20 minutes, adding a little water if too thick.

Now make the white sauce. Warm the milk and set aside. Melt the butter and gradually stir in the flour off the heat. Gradually stir in the milk and grated nutmeg, then return to heat and cook for about 10 minutes until thickened.

Stuffing the cannelloni Stir the chopped parsley into the beaten eggs. Mix the ricotta, salt, grated onion and 50g/2oz of the Parmesan. Add the eggs and parsley. Mix well and then stuff the cannelloni with this mixture.

Cover the bottom of a shallow ovenware dish with half the tomato sauce. Arrange the cannelloni on top, then pour over the rest of the tomato sauce. Cover with the white sauce and sprinkle the rest of the Parmesan on top. Bake for about 40 minutes.

CANNELLONI WITH MEAT

Use the same recipe for the sauces, but instead of the ricotta stuffing make one with minced meat (ideally lean meat you have minced yourself). Cook 700g/1½lb minced meat in a frying pan with a finely chopped onion, a pressed clove of garlic and some herbs, such as oregano, thyme, marjoram or basil. Bind with 2 or 3 tablespoons tomato purée, or a beaten egg, or some grated cheese, and stuff the cannelloni with this mixture. Otherwise proceed as above.

A recipe like this is useful when entertaining, because it can be made ready, just waiting to be put in the oven when the guests arrive. If it has become completely cold reheat it slowly for an hour before raising the temperature to brown (as above).

GF MF* VEG ## PHUL GOBI (INDIAN BRAISED CAULIFLOWER)

- 1 large cauliflower
- 25g/1oz clarified butter*
- 2 teaspoons yellow mustard seeds
- 5cm/2 inches ginger root (cut in slivers)
- ½ teaspoon turmeric
- 2 teaspoons cumin powder
- ¼ teaspoon paprika
- ¼ teaspoon freshly ground black pepper
- ½ teaspoon salt

Prepare the aromatics. Break cauliflower into small florets. Heat butter and add mustard seed. When they begin to snap and pop, add the slivered ginger, and sauté on both sides. Add turmeric and stir over low heat for ½ a minute. Add cauliflower, stir and continue to cook over medium heat, seeing that the turmeric colours it all well. Aromatise with cumin, pepper and paprika and cook for another minute, then season with salt. Sprinkle with 1 tablespoon water, bring to the boil and increase heat to build up steam, then cook on low heat. The cauliflower should be ready in 8–10 minutes, and should still be crisp.

Serve as a starter or snack in the fingers, or with the main Indian meal.

BARLEY PANCAKE CAKE

85g/3oz strong flour or wholewheat flour
85g/3oz barley flour (can be ground from pot barley in a flour mill)
15g/½oz fresh yeast (1 tablespoon dried granular yeast or ½ tablespoon of the Fermipan type see page 48)
salt
420ml/¾ pint milk
4 eggs
125g/4oz Cheddar, Lancashire, Wensleydale or Port Salut cheese

Preheat oven to 350°F/gas mark 4/180°C.

Warm about 2/3 of the milk. Mix the two flours together in a bowl; add a teaspoon of salt and mix again (if it is sea salt, add to the milk so it dissolves). Fermipan yeast can be added to the flour mixture, or prepare other yeasts, if used, as appropriate (see page 47). Make a well in the flour and add the milk (and fresh or dried yeast if used) and mix to a batter. Place the bowl in a large polythene bag and leave to rise for an hour or a little longer, until the batter is spongy and bubbly.

Beat in the eggs and then the remaining milk (cold). Cover the bowl again and leave the batter to rise for another hour or longer if necessary, until you are ready to make the pancakes.

In a 7–8inch (18–20cm) pan, melt a bit of butter and pour a scant ladleful of batter, tipping the pan so it spreads evenly and thinly over the surface. Cook over medium heat until small holes appear and the pancake is firm enough to turn with a spatula or egg slice. The second side only needs a few seconds to brown.

Now start to build the 'cake' in an ovenproof gratin dish large enough for the pancakes to lay flat. Between each pancake place two inch-wide (2cm) slices of cheese, some black pepper and nutmeg and keep piling up for 8 or so layers, with a little melted butter on the top. Reheat in oven for 15 minutes and serve, cutting through the layers like a cake.

BUCKWHEAT KASHA

MF VEG

a handful of buckwheat per person
1 chopped onion

4–5 crushed cardamom seeds
water as needed

Wash the grains of buckwheat and fry in a little oil. Add the chopped onion and sauté gently until clear. Add the crushed cardamom and then cover barely with water and continue to cook on a low heat, adding a little more water if needed until the grains are tender. Serve with hot crisp greens (broccoli, spinach or spring cabbage) and the cheese pancake wedges.

DESSERTS

PANCAKES WITH ORANGE SAUCE

1–2 pancakes per person (from 1 cup flour, 1 egg and 300ml/½pint milk), ready prepared.

Orange sauce

2 oranges (grated rind and juice)
50g/2oz sugar or ½ cup maple syrup
90g/3oz butter

Rub oranges with vinegar or lemon juice and dry with a kitchen towel (an attempt to dislodge any mineral oil on the skin). Grate finely. Mix with the sugar or maple syrup. Squeeze the juice and keep ready. Soften the butter and beat into the sugar and orange peel, then add the orange juice gradually. When ready to serve the pancakes, heat this mixture in the frying pan, place each (cooked) pancake in and heat until it begins to bubble, remove and keep warm until all have been done. As each is done, fold in four and place on a serving dish. At the end, heat 2 tablespoons orange liqueur (optional) in the pan, ignite, pour flaming liquid over the pancakes to flambé. Serve immediately.

GF MF* VEG*	CHERRY KISSEL

500–700g/1–1½lb fresh cherries (Morello for preference) or tinned.
1 tablespoon cornflour or potato starch

600ml/1pint water
sugar to taste

Wash and stone the cherries (if necessary). Bring to the boil in the water and cook for a few minutes. Taste and add sugar if needed. Mix the cornflour (arrowroot or potato starch/flour) with a little cold water, then add a little hot liquid and pour into the pan to thicken the juice, stirring well. Simmer until it is all clear and a thick but still liquid juice is achieved. If you use tinned or bottled fruit, make up the juice with water to the required amount, and thicken in the same way: this may not need sweetening.

Serve with a swirl of sour cream.*

ICED DESSERTS

GF	NESSELRODE PUDDING

300ml/½pint custard made with 3 egg yolks (page 134)
300ml/½pint whipping cream
300g/½–¾lb chestnut purée or crème de marrons

2 handfuls raisins (lexias are good) soaked overnight in rum or grape juice

Make the custard as described for gooseberry fool (page 134), but flavoured with vanilla. When cool combine with the chestnut purée and the soaked raisins and fold in the stiffly beaten cream. Freeze in a mould (if you have one) and when frozen, turn out and decorate with whipped cream and marrons glacés (optional). It is perfectly nice just served as an ice cream, with sponge fingers or carob shortbread.

ICE CREAMS

For the ice cream base use equal quantities of custard and whipping cream. You could try the tofu cream (page 142) blended with 1–2 bananas, or either of the ice creams below. The rich ice cream is not especially healthy, but is really easy, gives a good result, and is probably no worse for you than bought ice cream!

GF*   RICH ICE CREAM

275ml/½pint evaporated milk
16 marshmallows (preferably white), or a teaspoon of soaked gelatine could be substituted*

300ml/½pint whipping cream

Heat the evaporated milk and dissolve the marshmallows without letting the mixture boil. Leave to cool. If you use gelatine, soak in cold water, and dissolve in a heatproof vessel standing in boiling water and combine with the evaporated milk, which need not be heated. You will be relying on the sweetness of the milk and the fruits, ginger or praliné powder to sweeten your ice cream, which should be adequate.

Combine with the whipped cream, add flavouring and freeze.

PLAIN ICE CREAM

150ml/¼pint milk
2 teaspoons flour
90g/2½oz sugar
pinch of salt

1 egg yolk
375ml/¾pint single cream (or part yogurt)

Scald the milk. Combine the flour, sugar (you could use part honey or concentrated apple juice for different effects) salt and lightly beaten egg yolk, in a bowl. Pour the heated milk over the mixture, stir and return to pan. Heat gently, mixing until smooth and thick enough to coat the back of a spoon. Cool. Fold in the cream (or cream and yogurt mixture). Freeze for an hour. Then remove, beat in the flavouring and return to freezer. It is a good idea to stir again during freezing, to help break up the ice crystals and keep the mixture smooth.

THREE INTERESTING FLAVOURS

---
1 TUTTI FRUTTI ICE CREAM

A basic ice cream base using one of the above recipes (or your own)

1½ cups (about 250g/8oz) dried fruits selected from: raisins, sultanas, cherries (if possible without added colour), mixed citrus peel, preserved ginger, apricots, figs, peaches, pears, preserved pineapple.	orange or pineapple juice

Chop the larger fruits and soak in the fruit juice overnight. Add enough juice to cover them; they will soak most of it up, but any left can be added to the ice cream. Combine with the ice cream and freeze. The rich ice cream is so smooth it will not need stirring, so you can add the fruit before it freezes. The others should be part frozen before mixing in the fruit.

---
2 GINGER ICE CREAM

A basic ice cream (using one of the above recipes or your own).

60g/2oz chopped preserved ginger	2 tablespoons ginger syrup (from the jar of ginger)

Mix into the ice cream base of your choice, as described for tutti frutti ice cream. Serve with ginger root snaps (page 148) or a plain digestive biscuit or shortbread.

GF*   3 PRALINE ICE CREAM

Ice cream* base using one of the above recipes or your own	Praliné powder made from: 60g/2oz golden granulated sugar 90g/3oz blanched almonds

There is no harm (only good) in using almonds in their skins, only they will not go quite so crisp inside and it is not so easy to see them colour. For the same reason it is easier to use golden granulated sugar than Demerara, but the latter works well too. Hazelnuts can be used in place of the almonds.

Place the sugar in a small heavy saucepan over low heat. Stir it as it heats, so the temperature of the sugar is even throughout. After a few minutes it will begin to melt: keep stirring and if any lumps remain when most is melted, remove from heat to break them up and blend them in. When the colour darkens and if a little smoke starts rising, add the nuts and turn off heat. Stir the nuts in until they are all coated. Turn on to a greased tray or butter paper and allow to cool. When cool, pound to a powder in a pestle and mortar or grind in an electric coffee mill. Mix with the ice cream and freeze. You could make a double quantity and keep half in an airtight jar for another occasion.

GF* FRUIT ICE CREAMS

You can use any of the ice cream* bases and combine with 450g/1lb crushed fresh fruit, such as strawberries, raspberries, blackcurrants, bananas or a fruit salad mix (such as pear, peach, banana and a few strawberries).

Drinks

If you can start getting used to healthy drinks before you are pregnant, it will help later on. During pregnancy and afterwards when you are breastfeeding you may well feel thirstier than usual. Satisfy your thirst rather than drinking a specified amount each day. Try to satisfy it with healthy drinks. Here are some ideas.

See weight gain and water retention (page 211–13).

GF MF VEG   WATER

Water is very cheap if you drink it from the tap. If you do not like your tap water, or worry about what may be in it, you can use bottled spring or mineral water, or use a water filter. A simple filter over a jug can make a big difference and removes the danger of lead in the water. It will cost much less than bottled water. Brita is the name of a widely available brand of filter jug.

MF GF VEG   FRUIT JUICE

It is easy to obtain fruit juice by the litre now. Make sure it is juice and not 'orange drink', which may not be free of additives. Cut your pure juice with water or ice if you think it is too expensive. In any case, there is no need for a great deal each day. One glass is plenty. It is better to eat the fruit itself and get the fibre with it. A diet with lots of fresh fruit and vegetables, such as is recommended here, should not leave you feeling too thirsty anyway.

GF MF VEG   VEGETABLE JUICE

There are also lots of vegetable juices available, and lots more you can make yourself if you have a juicer. Try a glass for a mid-

GF	MILK

Many people recommend pregnant women to drink a pint of milk a day or even more. It is an easy way to add calcium to the diet together with protein. But some do not like it, some are allergic to it and others worry about the amount of saturated fat whole milk contains. These people may be tempted to use skim milk instead. But taking away the fat also removes the fat-soluble vitamins, and some of the vitamin B6 (needed for the body to use protein, among other things). So this is not such a good idea.

Even though a mother may not be allergic to cow's milk, her baby may be. This can show even in the womb with the baby getting hiccups or being restless. Afterwards it may affect the baby by getting into the mother's milk supply and can be one cause of colic. So if you simply do not like milk, or have reason to think either you or the baby may be allergic to it, look for other ways of supplying the food values represented in cow's milk. The section on milk allergy will help you here (p.202). See also milk substitutes at breakfast (page 41). You could try almond or hazelnut milk, a delicious drink for anyone (see page 192).

HERB TEAS AND CAROB – ALTERNATIVES TO CAFFEINE DRINKS

Often you may feel rather tired and in need of a pep. The idea of a coffee or a cup of tea may appeal to you at this moment. There are other things to try. Even just five minutes of complete relaxation can help. The fatigue of pregnancy and the post-natal period is real; pander to it, but try to find things that really help rather than the momentary pep, which may well be followed by a complete collapse! Chewing firm vegetables can re-vitalise you!

In any case caffeine intake should be reduced in pregnancy. Apart from its effects on you (which include binding some nutrients, making them unavailable to you), it is quickly absorbed by the fetus, but is slow to clear. There may be links with congenital anomalies. It also increases blood pressure and can interfere with sleep patterns. Cola drinks and cocoa contain caffeine as well as tea and coffee. Herb infusions are just as easy to make as tea and can be very beneficial. Many aid digestion, and some overcome feelings of nausea in pregnancy. Others are believed to promote fertility or lactation (details are given further on).

Carob drinks can be made as easily as instant coffee and provide a good substitute without the stimulant effect. Decaffeinated coffee is another alternative, or barley cup and other grain drinks.

If you yearn for something fizzy, try the homemade ginger beer or drinks using sparkling mineral water.

ALCOHOL

Alcohol is really worth avoiding if you can. It affects both men and women in their ability to produce healthy sperm and eggs, so it is important to start acting on this prior to conception. It affects an embryo before the placenta is formed, but the placenta is no barrier either, so abstinence should continue throughout pregnancy. Alcohol depletes the body of zinc (needed for healthy sperm, brain and nervous system development) and the B vitamins and vitamin C. But it doubtless has direct toxic effects on the developing baby too. Babies severely affected by alcohol, with 'fetal alcohol syndrome' will be smaller than average, have physical abnormalities and mental handicap, and will also be very susceptible to infection. In one study women taking 10 drinks a week were liable to have babies of lower birthweight. 'Normal social drinking' is no longer regarded as without risk in pregnancy, (see page 220).

Many women develop an aversion to alcohol during pregnancy. It is easier to heed the messages of one's body knowing the wisdom of it as well. Not so easy, perhaps, prior to conception or when you really feel like a drink. When entertaining friends always offer non-alcoholic drinks and do not be embarrassed to ask for something 'soft' when out. You can also use ice or water to 'cut' alcoholic drinks. There are plenty of drivers who will be happy to do this whether or not they are planning a pregnancy or are embarked on one. Recipes for special drinks are offered later on, and may be some compensation for those who regard abstinence as a hardship.

Stout is sometimes suggested as a stimulus for lactation. You will notice it does make the baby woozy. The alcohol is hardly any better for the baby at this stage than earlier. There are other ways to increase your milk supply and to help you relax.

VEGETABLE JUICES

These are easy to make with a special juice extractor. An ordinary blender can be used to pulp the vegetables which can then be strained. Adding some water or prepared juice will help the blender work effectively. Drink the juice within 10 or 15 minutes to get best value from the vitamins.

GF MF VEG **CARROT WITH GREENS**

½ cup carrot juice
¼ cup celery juice (or stick of celery chopped)
¼ cup green juice made from spinach, cress, Swiss chard, parsley.

1 clove garlic
optional additons: 1 green pepper or ½ cucumber

GF MF VEG **SALAD DRINK**

---

1 tomato
juice of ½ lemon
6 leaves of lettuce (or other greens)
2 peppers

½ cucumber
3 stalks celery
1 tablespoon olive oil
optional addition: 1 tablespoon brewer's yeast

You can vary the quantities and proportions of the vegetables to suit your tastes. It can be seen that they are very rich (so many vegetables go to make a little juice), but this is why they can be such a good 'pick-me-up', especially if you have little appetite.

| GF MF VEG | ALMOND MILK |

Cover 200g/7–8oz blanched almonds in a blender with water. Liquidise. As such can be used for almond cream. For the milk add more water to make a thinner consistency and sweeten with honey if wished. You can vary it by blending in lemon juice, sesame seeds, raisins or dates.

Ground almonds can also be used, indeed, if your blender does not grind whole almonds finely enough, you may need to grind them first in a coffee grinder. Unblanched almonds will give a gritty effect. This is not a good idea for babies, but a good way to get even better nutritional value from the nuts. It is very nourishing for pregnant and breastfeeding mothers.

A hazelnut version can be tried. This, mixed with a little oatmeal, is a traditional Scottish food for sickly children.

Cashews are also suitable.

GF MF VEG   HERB TEAS

Moisten the leaves with a little cold water and then pour on boiling water and allow to infuse as with tea. Herb teas can be drunk hot, but many are delicious iced for a cool drink in summer. They may be flavoured with fresh elder flowers, fennel or anise seeds, ginger or cinnamon; or used cold as a base for blackberry, blackcurrant or elderberry syrup.

As you are getting used to the new flavours try just adding a teaspoon of mint or chamomile to your normal pot of tea. Make your own tea blends!

Fresh mint, lemon verbena or raspberry leaves can be used from the garden. You do not have to buy them dried or in sachets.

Special uses for some of the more widely available herb teas are given below. The information is based on *The Illustrated Herbal Handbook* by Juliette de Baïracli Levy (see Booklist page 232), where you can find out how to use less usual herbs too.

For infertility balm, raspberry leaf tea (and raspberries) for men and women; mint is regarded as promoting virility.
For nausea ginger, chamomile (generally soothing too), basil.

For toning up the uterus and reproductive system generally raspberry leaf tea, a cupful a day in the last 3 or 4 months of pregnancy.
Heartburn and indigestion can be eased by chewing a few seeds of caraway or anise before a meal, or mint tea afterwards.
During childbirth raspberry leaf tea can be sipped to ease a difficult birth. It is also said to help a retained placenta. (Putting the baby to the breast releases the right hormones too).
For breastfeeding beneficial herbs include sage, borage, dill but mint can decrease the milk supply.

Herbs can also be taken in bread, see page 56, in salads, soups, stews or fresh with pasta.

GF MF VEG   GINGER TEA (for nausea or indigestion)

25g/1oz ginger root
500ml/1 pint water

optional extras, 1–2 teaspoons honey, juice of ½ lemon, ½ teaspoon cinnamon

Heat the water with the sliced ginger in a pan (not aluminium). Bring to the boil and simmer for 15 minutes. Leave to cool and infuse. Strain and reheat with the other ingredients (if used) and drink a small glassful every 15 minutes until the stomach feels settled.

GF MF* VEG*   CAROB

Carob powder (sometimes known by its misnomer, carob flour) comes from a bean of the locust family, also called St John's bread. It is full of good minerals (including calcium) and a good substitute for cocoa or chocolate having most of the good qualities and none of the drawbacks (such as caffeine). It is naturally sweeter than cocoa and should not need extra sugar. A little honey complements the flavour better in any case. Try different brands until you find a kind you like – they vary.

To make a hot drink, mix the carob powder (a bare teaspoon to a mug is usually plenty) with some cold milk* or soya milk and stir out any lumps. Fill the mug with boiling water, or add more hot milk. A sustaining drink to try in place of morning coffee.

MF VEG — LEMON BARLEY WATER

50g/2oz pearl or pot barley
1–3 teaspoons sugar (optional)

thinly pared rind of 1 lemon
600ml/1 pint boiling water

Cover the barley with cold water and boil for 2 minutes. Discard this water. Place the barley with the lemon rind and sugar (if used) in a heatproof jug. Pour on one pint of boiling water and cover. When cold strain and use.

MF VEG — HONEY BARLEY WATER

This recipe makes a thicker brew which is particularly beneficial for sore throats. More honey can be used in this case.

100g/4oz pot barley
zest of half a lemon

2 tablespoons honey
600ml/1 pint of water

Cover the barley with water, bring to the boil and discard the water. Place the barley in a pan with the lemon zest and the pint of cold water. Bring to the boil and simmer until the barley is tender. Remove from the heat and allow to cool. When the liquid is blood heat, strain and mix with the honey, stirring until it has dissolved.

GF MF VEG — HOMEMADE GINGER BEER

ginger beer plant
8 sultanas
juice of 2 lemons
1 teaspoon lemon pulp

4 teaspoons sugar
2 teaspoons ground ginger
300ml/½ pint cold water

Place ingredients in a large screw top jar and leave to ferment to room temperature for 2–3 days. Then feed daily with 2 teaspoons sugar and 1 teaspoon ground ginger. On the seventh day strain, reserve liquid for the ginger beer. Divide the sediment into two pint-sized jars. Add about 450ml/¾ pint water to each so they are not quite full. Then start feeding again with 1 teaspoon sugar and 1 teaspoon ground ginger 7 times: each day for a week, or every second day if you are not in a hurry for more. Repeat for as long as you want to continue your supply of homemade ginger beer.

You can experiment with different sugars to make it darker (with Muscovado) or not so dark (with Demerara).

GINGER BEER

Reserved liquid from ginger beer plant
juice of 2 lemons

450g/1lb sugar (any kind, or part concentrated apple juice)
450ml/¾ pint boiling water
3 litres/5 pints cold water

Strong airtight bottles for storage

Dissolve the sugar in the boiling water. Add the cold water and pour on to the lemon juice mixed with the ginger liquid. Mix well and store in strong airtight bottles, designed for fizzy drinks. (If you use plastic ones the bottoms go rounded as the fizziness develops and weak glass can explode.) A cellar is a very suitable storage place. The optimum time for maturing ginger beer is 2–3 weeks.

Is homemade ginger beer alcoholic? Only very slightly, but if it helps you cut out more alcoholic drinks, then this is a benefit.

GF MF VEG — APRICOT FIZZ

Often a fizzy drink is just what one wants in pregnancy. The sparkling mineral waters are one option. Bottled fizzy lemonade and other 'pop' is best avoided. Try instead adding the mineral water to fruit juices, or make this delicious apricot drink.

Cook dried apricots in plenty of water when you are using them for another dish. Chill the juice well. Thin with sparkling spring or mineral water (chilled) and add a tang with a dash of lemon juice and a twist of lemon peel.

Try the same with peach or pear juice. A mint leaf added looks pretty too and imparts a pleasant flavour.

GF MF VEG   ICED CANTELOUPE AND PINEAPPLE

1 canteloupe or other melon (an overripe one could be used)
½ cup pineapple juice
½ cup iced water or sparkling mineral water

Skin the melon and remove any soft or bad bits. Cut into pieces and blend pips, pulp and flesh in a liquidiser. Strain the liquid and discard pips etc. Rinse blender and mix the juice with the pineapple juice and iced water, or mineral water with a couple of ice cubes. Chill well, but do not keep for too long. If all the ingredients are chilled before you start, and ice cubes added, it should be cool enough to drink straight away.

GF   ICED MELON CRUSH

1 small honeydew melon
¼ teaspoon ground ginger
150ml/5fl oz yogurt
½–1 cup sparkling mineral water

Remove skin and seeds from the melon and chop the flesh. Put in a blender with the yogurt and ginger. Blend until smooth and chill. Serve with ice and the sparkling mineral water.

GF MF VEG   FRUIT CUPS

You can make your own mixes from the following:

Using orange or apple juice as a base, add a little pineapple or grapefruit juice
a cup of cold rosehip or herb tea
some sliced or diced citrus fruits (orange, lemon, grapefruit)
some halved crushed strawberries
mint leaves or borage
sliced cucumber (goes well with borage)
sparkling spring water
ice cubes

The lemon, grapefruit, cucumber and herb teas such as chamomile or verbena will make it less sweet, the pineapple, orange, strawberries and rosehip will make it more sweet.

Nice for a summer party. In winter, try mulled apple or grape juice.

MULLED APPLE

GF MF VEG

The simple everyday way is to pour boiling water over concentrated apple juice with some cinnamon powder mixed in. Here is a more sophisticated recipe for a party.

Per pint of apple juice (pure juice or made from concentrate) add juice of ½ lemon
1 tablespoon honey (optional)
2 cloves
2cm/1 inch cinnamon stick (or ½ teaspoon powder)
1 eating apple, cored and finely sliced
50g/2oz dried mixed peel or sultanas or raisins

Place all ingredients in a large enamelled or stainless steel pan and bring to the boil, then keep warm until required. Serve with a twist of lemon peel.

If using the dried fruit, it is good to soak it overnight in 150ml/¼ pint of boiling water together with half a fresh lemon pierced with cloves. The number depends on the quantity to be made the next day. For 6 pints (3 or 4 litres) use 10 cloves, but then you need not add more when you heat the mulled apple. Top up with apple juice, if needed, to cover the fruit. Discard the half lemon before heating.

MULLED GRAPE JUICE

GF MF VEG

1 litre/2 pints grape juice (red)
half an orange sliced
5cm/2 inches cinnamon stick (or ½ teaspoon powdered)
3–4 cloves
5–6 allspice corns (crushed in a pestle and mortar) or 1 teaspoon powdered allspice
a small handful of raisins or sultanas

(optional extra to make it sweeter: 1–2 tablespoons blackcurrant syrup, preferably without dyes. Homemade blackberry or elderberry syrup could also be used.)

Even if you do not like cold grape juice, try this. Heating the juice flavoured with the spices transforms it!

Place all ingredients in a stainless steel, enamel or glass pan, and heat gradually. Do not boil. Strain and serve with a quarter of an orange slice, if desired.

If you are serving this at a party, offer a dash of brandy added to the cup or glass of the non-abstainers.

Food Allergies and Special Diets

Allergic reactions show that the immune system is not functioning properly. The body recognises as 'foreign' substances which other individuals can happily accept and assimilate. The body of the allergic person reacts as if this substance were a disease organism. Different systems within the body may all be subject to allergic reactions: the respiratory system (asthmas, hayfever, allergic rhinitis with say, house dust mite), the skin (eczema, dermatitis etc), the gastro-intestinal system (stomach cramps, bloatedness, diarrhoea etc). This is why, although allergies run in families, it is not always the same allergy that one sees. Someone with asthma may have a parent with eczema or a child with food intolerance. The allergies are all related to each other via the way the body's defenses work, our immunological competence.

If you already know what allergy is like, you will know it is worth preventing in your baby if you can. The chances increase if a parent has an allergy and more if both parents suffer from one. Building up your immune status is one way to help your baby.

Preventive measures

1 Stop smoking.
2 Spend as long as possible (5–6 months at least) off the Pill before conceiving.
3 Use a rotation diet prior to pregnancy to help detect food allergies (the *Foresight* booklet, *Guidlines for Future Parents* has one, see Booklist, page 232). You could have desensitising treatment for anything detected.
4 Adopt a good wholefood diet, concentrating on the foods rich in B vitamins, vitamin C and the essential fatty acids.
5 Do all you can to prepare yourself for successful breastfeeding. The good diet will help, also fresh air for your nipples.

FOOD ALLERGIES AND SPECIAL DIETS

Massage by rolling them in your fingers with a little oil or calendula cream or chamomile cream late in pregnancy to make strong and healthy skin.

6 Wean your baby late, if possible not before 6 months of age. Introduce new foods gradually, carefully checking they have been accepted before starting on the next, and leaving any of the foods listed below until the baby is 8 months old and used to a mixed diet. (Fuller guidance is given in *Growing Up With Good Food*.)

The foods most commonly provoking allergies are cow's milk (and related products, even beef and bovine derivatives), wheat (and gluten in other grains – barley, oats and rye), eggs (especially egg whites , maize and corn derivatives such as dextrose), chocolate, bananas, strawberries, tomatoes, oranges, shellfish and foods containing additives (see also notes on hyperactivity page 200).

Special diets free of milk and gluten have been discussed in greater detail. Notes on a vegan diet are also given. As this is free of all animal products, anything suitable will obviously be free of eggs for those wishing to avoid eggs as well.

HIDDEN ALLERGIES

As well as obvious and immediate reactions to certain allergens (e.g. strawberries, pollens, cosmetics), there can be reactions less obvious than a rash, a bout of sneezing, or vomiting, which people just endure and do not attribute to anything in particular. These may include persistent fatigue, depression, irritability, joint pains, back and neck pains, migraine, fluctuations in weight, puffiness of hands, face, stomach, ankles, swollen glands, palpitations, excessive sweating, red eyes, runny or blocked nose. These may be due to very familiar aspects of our environment or diet, such as the air (especially traffic fumes); water (especially where it has too much lead); household gas or other chemicals around us; foods we take every day like coffee, chocolate, bread and so on, especially anything that creates a feeling of addiction.

A properly conducted rotation diet can help find out about food allergies and there are many other ways of investigating the possibility of other allergies, which a specialist can conduct. Those interested can read more about the subject in Janet Pleshette's *Health on Your Plate* and other books in the Booklist, page 232.

PRECAUTIONS AGAINST HYPERACTIVITY

If you have already had a child who is hyperactive, you are likely to be in touch with the *Hyperactive Children's Support Group* (see Address list, page 230). It seems that there may be a connection between families prone to allergy and hyperactivity (although it is rare for there to be more than one hyperactive child in a family).

It could be wise for anyone with any reason to anticipate this problem to take seriously certain measures which, in any case, are sensible precautions in pregnancy.

1. Avoid as far as possible (preferably cut out completely) all colour dyes in food and other additives, especially flavourings, monosodium glutamate, sodium glutamate, nitrites, nitrates, sodium benzoate, butylated hydroxanisole (BHA) and butylated hydroxytolene (BHT) used as antioxidants, also Benzoic acid. (A list of additive-free manufactured foods is available from the *HACSG*.)
2. Keep your diet low in sugar (or eliminate sucrose completely). Concentrated apple juice may not be a good substitute as it contains salicylate; honey would be a better general sweetener.
3. The use of a water filter or filter jug or bottled water may help.
4. It would be wise to be strict about either partner not smoking, and sensible for both to keep off alcohol in the period prior to pregnancy, and for the mother during pregnancy and breast-feeding.
5. Do all you can to promote successful breastfeeding of your baby.

SPECIAL PRECAUTIONS

6. Fruits containing salicylates should perhaps be avoided by someone allergic to aspirin. These include almonds, apples,

apricots, peaches, plums, prunes, oranges, tomatoes, tangerines, cucumber, blackberries, strawberries, raspberries, gooseberries, cherries, currants, grapes, raisins. Otherwise, no need to worry (especially if you have successfully eliminated additives from your diet), but still best to choose freshly squeezed juices as factory-prepared juice may contain traces of dye from citrus peel.

7 If there is a history of allergy in the family, a reduction in cow's milk products, chocolate etc would be wise (see page 202).
8 Write to the *HACSG* for details of what is permitted in their Food Programme, and for advice on the use of Evening Primrose Oil (see Address list, page 230).
9 Check dyes in other substances especially those containing formaldehyde such as most cleaning agents, bubble bath, cosmetics and avoid the use of aerosols and fly catcher strips, solid air cleaners.

GF GLUTEN-FREE DIET

The serious conditions associated with an allergy to gluten are coeliac disease (a malabsorption syndrome) and the skin condition known as dermatitis herpetiformis. The *Coeliacs Society* exists for those who have been medically diagnosed as suffering from this complaint. As fertility can be affected by this condition, it is important to find out if you think you may be a sufferer and to be treated. (Recurrent mouth ulcers, stomach cramps or a feeling of bloatedness after eating, diarrhoea may all be symptoms.) You will be able to find out about the manufacturers who produce a range of gluten-free foods and the cookbooks to match (those by Rita Greer and Hilda Cherry Hills are given in the Booklist, page 234).

Sometimes a person who shows a sensitivity to wheat can find that organically grown wholewheat does not affect him or her in the same way. Here it may be the chemical fertilisers, insecticides and fungicides used in the production of wheat or the additives to white flour which are causing the problem. Such people would benefit by adopting a wholefood diet as organically produced as possible, and reducing the proportion of wheat products in favour of other grains such as rye, oats, barley and rice, in their daily menus. An effort has been made in this book to show how you can introduce a variety of grains to your diet, (see also *Cook Yourself a Favour*, in the Booklist, page 233).

If you know you suffer from an allergy to gluten you will have gone into the whole question thoroughly. Sometimes one finds oneself needing to provide food for a friend in this position and so gluten-free recipes have been marked in this book with the symbol **GF**.

Gluten-free grains are: maize (corn), millet and rice, also sago and tapioca. Gluten-free flours include maize meal (polenta), millet flour, rice flour, potato flour, gram flour (made from chick peas), soya flour (and other flours made from peas and beans). Ground nuts can also replace flour in some recipes, and ground seeds can be used likewise.

Wheat and wheat derivatives crop up in all kinds of edible substances, from whisky and beer to instant coffee and baking powder, so be careful not to use a commercially prepared product for your gluten-free meal, unless you know it is safe. A gluten-free baking powder is given on page 144.

MILK-FREE DIET

Some allergic reaction to cow's milk would appear to be rather common. It may be simply an intolerance to lactose if the enzyme, lactose, stops being produced after weaning (many dark skinned races have this). In this case products where the lactose is converted to lactic acid are fine. These include yogurt, buttermilk, cheese in all its forms from cottage cheese to hard cheese. Goats' milk may be tolerated.

If the reaction is caused by other substances in milk, the allergy may extend to all bovine products (beef, veal, Oxo cubes, Bovril etc). Goats' milk may likewise cause symptoms. A whey-free margarine or oil will be needed, and no manufactured product with skim milk powder, milk solids or casein should be taken. Soya milk and nut milks can be used.

Symptoms include eczema, diarrhoea, vomiting, chronic catarrh and stomach pain. In a baby: unsettled or hiccups in the womb, colic after feeds.

Milk free recipes are marked in the book with the symbol **MF**.

Those with an asterisk as well, indicate that the recipe would be safe if a whey-free margarine or oil were used to replace the butter or if the substitution of soya milk for the cow's milk will be satisfactory. A book by Hilda Cherry Hills, with milk-free recipes, is given in the Booklist on page 234.

Foods rich in calcium include almonds, brazil nuts, dried figs and apricots, dark green leafy vegetables (cress, spring cabbage, spinach etc), small fish with edible bones such as whitebait, sardines, and white fish, eggs, and soya flour, milk or curd (tofu), sesame seeds (and tahini), and carob powder. The vitamins in milk such as riboflavin, A, D and E can all be adequately obtained from other sources. Liver, fatty fish, dark green vegetables, carrots and other yellow fruit and vegetables and broccoli, wheatgerm and wholewheat products, peanuts and many other foods will provide them. Sunlight supplies vitamin D.

A breastfed baby who cries with colic after feeds, has stomach cramps (draws the knees up), diarrhoea or green bowel motions may benefit from the removal of milk products from the mother's diet. Of course food sensitivity is just one possible cause of these symptoms.

The mother of a colicky baby is likely to be lacking sleep and have little time to think about and prepare food. Here are some ideas for home 'fast food'.

MF   **INSTANT NOURISHMENT FOR A BREASTFEEDING MOTHER**

Breakfast

Muesli with soya milk or fruit juice or stewed fruit. Muesli softened (overnight if you like it really soft) with boiling water, when cool serve with grated apple, chopped fresh fruit or berries.

Choose a brand of muesli without added milk powder or make up your own (see page 36).

Porridge made with water only, again, if left overnight it will go very creamy in texture. Try adding currants, sultanas or other dried fruit for sweetening and flavour.

Any (milk-free) breakfast cereal can be taken with soya milk (provided you like it), nut milks (page 192) are delicious too, and fruit juices often acceptable. Another idea is to try Weetabix dry with (whey-free) margarine and honey or yeast extract spread. (See also *milk substitutes*, page 41.)

Toast and peanut butter or tahini (honey too, if you like), or (whey-free) margarine, marmalade, sugar free jam or honey, or with egg, tomatoes, baked beans for a 'cooked' breakfast.

Drinks: Fruit juices, herb or rose-hip teas or tea with lemon to drink. (Some find soya milk satisfactory, especially with carob drink.)

Lunch (cold meals)

A salad or peanut butter sandwich. Try mixing peanut butter with tahini or sunflower spread to make complete protein.

Avocado with lemon juice (and seed oil if wished).

Rye crackers with olive paste and tomatoes, or mashed cooked beans with hazelnut butter (ground to a paste with a little water), or with peanut butter, and watercress.

Many of the salads are quick and easy in the Salads section (pages 111–27). Try the tahini sauce page 103, as a dressing.

Salads with leaves and seeds are good thoughts (rich in calcium and the essential fatty acids needed in breastmilk).

Try a vegetable dip using houmous or another milk-free dip (page 166).

Dinner (hot meals)

Egg dishes eggs any way are quick and easy. Add water to omelettes or scrambled egg, or try eggs scrambled with mashed avocado, chopped tomatoes and chives, or finely sliced green pepper for a nutritious meal with a wholemeal roll.

Soups homemade if you can manage it (make a double quantity and keep some in the fridge for 'instant' use). Otherwise use cans with fewest additives, adding vegetable water for thinning it and some fresh herbs on top. Many of the soups in the soup section can be made in stages, blended when you are ready to eat, and reheated gently.

Rice brown rice with stir fried vegetables is easy. It need not be elaborate, just three vegetables will make a good mix, e.g. mushrooms, beansprouts and spring onions; celery, green pepper and cabbage; leek, carrot and Chinese leaves. Add a little garlic or ginger (if liked) and serve with tamari or shoyu with some sesame seeds on top.

Cooked beans or tinned beans can be reheated with sautéed mushrooms and miso and eaten with rice or in wholemeal pitta breads.

You will probably resort to takeaways too (see page 26). Fish and chips (provided the batter is milk-free), fried chicken and chips, kebabs and pitta breads, Chinese and Indian foods are all likely to be free of milk products (but not pizzas or cheese burgers!) Notice if the Indian food causes a reaction in the baby and do not repeat if it does. Remember that Chinese food nearly always has plentiful monosodium glutamate. Serve with your own brown rice and tamari (soya sauce may have MSG too) and fresh fruit afterwards.

Afters

Fresh fruit, dried fruits (especially figs and apricots), nuts and seeds are all good. Try the combinations listed on page 129 such as the lexia raisins coated with sesame seeds.

Snacks

As well as any of the above, try pieces of vegetable. A celery stick or washed carrot is satisfying to chew and easy to prepare. Oatcakes or crispbreads should be fine, but check manufactured biscuits for milk or milk solids. The contents are not always given, so choose brands which list ingredients.

Drinks

You may well feel thirstier than usual when you are breastfeeding. Do not worry if you cannot drink milk. As already mentioned on page 203, you can get all the nutrients other ways. The Drinks section (page 188) will help you find suitable ways of quenching your thirst. Water, fruit or vegetable juices, carob drink, nut milks and soya milk are all good. Herb teas, lemon tea or carob (with soya milk) are the best choices for hot drinks, but not too much black coffee. Stout is often recommended, but alcoholic drinks should also be kept to a minimum.

Milk-free recipes throughout the book are marked thus: **MF**

VEG   VEGAN DIET (also EGG-FREE)

Vegan parents will find some recipes here marked with a symbol: **VEG**. These will also be useful for those occasionally providing food for vegan friends. Further advice may be had from the *Vegan Society*, see Address list, page 231.

As vegans use no animal products the recipes are, of course, egg free, and therefore useful for anyone with an allergy to eggs. (A tablespoon of soya flour can often be used as a substitute for an egg in cooking.)

Vitamin B12 (mostly found in animal products) can be taken as a supplement. It is added to some yeast extract spreads such as Tastex and Barmene, and to some plant milks such as Plamil. Miso, seaweeds and mung beansprouts are also sources. Vitamin D, apart from sunlight, is available in products it has been added to such as vegan margarines and plant milks.

Nuts, pulses (especially soya products) and wholegrains, dried fruits are all good sources of minerals and other vitamins as are seeds and all the fresh fruits and vegetables.

Common Problems in Pregnancy

PREGNANCY SICKNESS

Although this common complaint is rarely taken very seriously by doctors, it is a misery for those who experience it. Perhaps it is that those doctors who are men have not suffered it, and they can justify their nonchalance because it does not seem to affect the outcome, and there is little they can do besides prescribing drugs. Many women are understandably cautious about taking drugs, and they would like to find other ways of coping with the problem. Herbal and homeopathic remedies are available but do consult a qualified practitioner for advice.

The usual suggestions include taking small meals frequently. Start the morning with something in bed before you get up (see suggestions in Breakfasts page 43). Keep off fatty foods, milk, and anything you consider indigestible or off-putting. Women are often especially susceptible to smells of food. This can be a problem when trying to prepare food for other members of the family – persuade them to cook for themselves or leave the offending dish out of the menu for a while!

If those who will take the meal are not able or willing to do their own cooking, perhaps one idea to follow is to think of meals which do not involve 'smelly' food.

Things cooked in water will make less smell than fried food. So pasta, rice, potatoes or beans could form the staple base of the meal. A tinned or bottled sauce or frozen ratatouille (page 108) could be heated and stirred in at the end with some sunflower seeds or grated cheese for a topping.

Some people find themselves capable of preparing a chicken at arms' length, popping it in a preheated oven, turning on the extractor fan (if available) and going off somewhere else while it cooks. The use of roasting bags could reduce the smell from oven joints also. Some potatoes could be placed in the oven to bake in their jackets. Frozen greens steamed quickly at the last minute would make up an acceptable meal for many families. Fresh fruit or cheese and biscuits, dried fruits and nuts or yogurt and honey could provide 'afters' with no preparation, undue handling of food or cooking smells.

Anyone insisting on chips with everything could get them from the local chippie and preferably eat them on the way home! If you resort to takeaways, see page 26 on how to improve them and balance the meal.

Spending some time while the meal is cooking, just relaxing may help you face the meal. Even ten minutes lying down before the meal could help you feel better. Do not hover about in the kitchen poised to serve the meal, but, if it is ready, turn it off and take your few moments of relaxation elsewhere. In any case it is very desirable that you should spend plenty of time resting and relaxing during pregnancy, especially if you do not feel well.

Reducing stress in your life generally is another aspect on which to work. Try to avoid deadlines where possible, at home or at work. Where they cannot be removed, then try to make them easily achievable. Leave plenty of time for the meal preceding an appointment, meeting or other outing. Getting all the things done you would normally do can tax organisational capacity, the aim is to 'take it easy', so think of ways of making it easy. Dropping some commitments, leaving generous margins of time so that you are not rushed may seem difficult, but you are likely to need to do this anyway when the baby arrives. Do not worry about dropping your standards of housework, cooking or whatever it is. Something has to give if you are leading a busy life, and it is better if it is not you!

It is valuable to have plenty of support. Accept offers of help. Get in touch with sympathetic friends who can share your problems or help distract you from them. Where you can, avoid contact with anyone who rubs you up the wrong way. The right company can be a great morale booster, but try too, to have some time on your own resting. Prop yourself up with pillows so you are not lying on your stomach.

As well as rest, some sort of exercise, not too strenuous, will help your feeling of well-being (see page 227).

It is natural to worry about the baby, but it does seem that such worry is misplaced. The baby is probably coping better than you, especially if you have been well-nourished prior to conception.

Put yourself and your needs first for the time being. It is most likely that your nausea will disappear after the first few months.

If the sickness persists beyond the early months, you are one of the few unlucky ones. You may be helped by reading a booklet prepared by Dr Barbara Pickard, herself a sufferer (see Booklist, page 233). There are detailed suggestions about foods to try and others to avoid. Ideas on how to prepare for your next pregnancy so that you may be able to forestall the sickness before it happens could be worth following up.

Remember that any food is better than none. You may have to abandon your intentions about healthy food at this time and just concentrate on calories from foods you can accept. Sometimes the frequent nibbling of crackers, bread or biscuits keeps the nausea at bay. There are ideas for packed breakfasts and packed lunches for those who go out to work on page 42 and page 156. Ginger may be found helpful in removing nausea. Try the ginger tea (page 193) or the ginger root biscuits (page 148). A nutritious broth can be made using a kombu stock (see page 69). Heat it with some finely sliced carrot, simmered until tender, add some spring onions (if these appeal) and a dash of shoyu. Then grate a small knob of fresh ginger, place in muslin and squeeze the juice into the broth. Nibbling pieces of preserved ginger also helps some people. Other herb teas to try are mentioned in the Breakfasts and Drinks section pages 43 and 188.

Generally speaking, follow your instincts and do not worry about what you think you ought to be eating. Take each day as it comes. There will come a day when you are over this problem. Things are bound to get better!

CONSTIPATION

It is said that during pregnancy the gut becomes more sluggish in its action. Perhaps this enables the body to extract more from the food we eat. Is this the reason that many women complain of constipation when it never used to trouble them before?

Perhaps it is the iron tablets they have been taking? These can have such an effect. If this appears to be so, ask for a different preparation, or reassess your need for an iron supplement (see below).

A good wholefood diet with plenty of fresh fruit and vegetables, especially raw, with wholegrain products should ensure that the risk of constipation is kept at bay. Prunes and figs are often recommended. So is bran, but here one must add a word of warning. Too much bran sprinkled liberally on food or taken in all the many ways that have been devised leads to other digestive problems, especially for a person who has been eating a fairly refined diet before. It can bind some important minerals, including iron, making it impossible for the gut to absorb them. Exercise is also a good remedy for constipation.

Constipation can be a worry for some people after the birth, especially if there has been an episiotomy or stitches. Remember that if you had an enema before the birth, you should not expect a bowel motion for a day or two or three. Just relax and it will come. If a preparation is felt essential try something mild like liquorice tea, or possibly senna, or try other herbal laxatives.

ANAEMIA

Women are often given iron pills because it seems they may become anaemic in pregnancy. It is not certain whether this is as common as once thought. The whole volume of blood is increased when you are pregnant, and so the count of red cells should be adjusted to take the extra fluid into account. The question of supplementation is still problematic, even supposing the need is there.

One study showed that extra iron may so increase the size of the red blood cells that they are unable to cross the placenta. Other doubts concern the best form in which to give the supplement, since iron is usually poorly absorbed by the body. The iron in blood is best absorbed – hence the frequent exhortations to eat red meat and organ meats. It could be that a person with a chronic problem of iron absorption simply taxes her liver more by taking a supplement. Ideally, this would be detected prior to conception and treated, so such a woman starts pregnancy with adequate reserves. Iron tablets can lead to constipation and to nausea and sickness. If you are suffering from either, ask your doctor about it. A different preparation could be tried, or, if there is no special need in your case, the supplement might best be discontinued. Sometimes the iron is combined with folic acid, helpful in preventing neural tube defects. Folic acid is also implicated in some forms of anaemia. Vitamin C helps the assimilation of iron, so it may be recommended to take the supplement with a drink of orange juice, (better still, a fresh orange).

It should be possible to supply the iron one needs from diet alone. Iron absorption increases progressively during pregnancy and there is little evidence that the baby ever goes short. Iron is also required during breastfeeding, so someone with reason to believe they are short of iron, might better take a supplement after the baby is born.

If recommended to take an iron supplement, do make sure that this is good advice for you and get the best preparation prescribed for your individual needs.

Some people think that women today are far more likely to be short of zinc than iron. It is just as important for the developing and breastfed baby, and even more important preconceptually in men to ensure healthy sperm.

WEIGHT GAIN AND FLUID RETENTION

Naturally, weight gain is a normal part of pregnancy. The actual pattern of gain is a very individual matter and little sense can be made of averaging patterns statistically. The amount of weight gain is also variable and there is a wide normal band, even when individual weights at the start of pregnancy, body build, age, height and so on are taken into acccount. So do not take too much notice of precise recommendations as to how much you should gain in which months of pregnancy. A range of 15 to 40lb (7–18kg) gain by the end of pregnancy is perfectly compatible with normal foetal growth and a baby of good birthweight.

One reason your weight is monitored through pregnancy is that it is some guide to how the baby is growing. Besides, sudden fluctuations may indicate fluid retention which, together with other factors, could be a sign that pre-eclamptic toxaemia is developing.

Again, some fluid retention is normal in pregnancy. The increase in the volume of your blood has already been mentioned. Also, rapidly multiplying cells need plenty of fluid, and the amniotic fluid needs to be created. All this means that you will probably find you need to pass water more frequently during pregnancy. In late pregnancy the baby may press against the bladder, requiring you to empty it more often too. This extra fluid which is retained accounts for some of your extra weight, and may explain the wide individual variations. There is extra weight in your breasts, which may come quite early in pregnancy. (Do not be alarmed if your bra size increases a couple of times quite early on, but do get a good supporting bra).

It is quite likely that your doctor will be more concerned about your weight than you are. If you are eating to appetite, and having small meals frequently, your weight gain is most likely to be following the needs of your body and those of the baby. It is not a good idea to try to restrict weight gain during pregnancy. Fasting, even missing breakfast, is not at all helpful to your baby. Nor is it a good idea in general, to control fluid retention with diuretics. Doctors are not so likely to do this now, as they know that many valuable minerals are also excreted when diuretics are used, and that the body needs extra fluid.

If you are uncomfortable with oedema (swelling) of the ankles and hands, try increasing the 'juicy' foods (fresh fruit, salads, soups) and having less to drink, and cutting out drinks with meals. Your appetite is the best guide to what your body needs. Another way to help uncomfortable swelling or varicose veins is to rest as often as possible with your legs higher than your heart. One way to give quick relief to swollen ankles and legs is to lie on the floor, bottom hard against the base of the wall, with your legs up at right angles supported by the wall, which will probably feel nice and cool as well. Five or ten minutes in this position will probably be enough at one time. The fluid will drain back into your body. When you bring your legs down, sit on the floor and make circular motions with your feet to help restore circulation. This and other foot exercises make you feel good, especially when your feet are tired. Find as many opportunities as you can to do the jobs you have to do sitting down. Too much standing is not good for anyone, and especially for those with some swelling.

If your weight gain really seems excessive and you feel you are putting on too much fat on your limbs, just make sure all the food you eat is good food. Cut down, if need be, on the less healthy snacks, replacing them with wholemeal bread or fruit or fresh vegetables. One pattern of eating known to lead to excess weight gain is to have a large meal at the end of the day shortly before sleeping. It is a good idea to leave three hours after your last meal before going to bed. A main meal in the middle of the day is much better, though even spacing throughout the day is better still. There is no need to restrict a reasonable salt intake either.

HIGH BLOOD PRESSURE AND TOXAEMIA OF PREGNANCY

High blood pressure means your heart is working faster to pump the blood around the body, probably because the blood vessels are constricted. If you suffer chronically from hypertension of this kind, you should mention it to your doctor, preferably before becoming pregnant. Good medical care is needed in pregnancy. The constriction of the blood vessels may have a nutritional cause, or may happen as a result of tension. Relaxation is therefore a good first remedy for this problem (see Jane Madders, *Stress and Relaxation*, in the Booklist, page 233).

Many hospitals are now realising that the more they can do to make antenatal visits a pleasant and encouraging experience, the better it is for the pregnancies of the women attending. However, if you find your blood pressure is up at a check-up, and you know you are annoyed at having been kept waiting, or for whatever reason might be more tense than usual, ask to relax for 10 minutes and have it checked again to see if there is a difference. It may save you waiting longer or having to attend for another visit.

When high blood pressure occurs in conjunction with oedema (swelling from fluid retention) and protein (albumin) in the urine, then this is a sign that pre-eclamptic toxaemia could be developing. The latter sign means that your metabolism is not working properly which in turn will affect the functioning of the placenta. This is not likely to happen before the fifth month of pregnancy, but as it can develop quite quickly, it is important that you act at once, especially if you have any trouble with your vision such as blurring or a headache. Your life and your baby's could be at risk if severe eclampsia is not prevented. A premature birth may be the result.

Attention to good nutrition is the best preventive measure to take. Toxaemia is most likely to develop in very young mothers, older mothers and women with their first pregnancy. Those with conditions such as diabetes, high blood pressure, or kidney disorders are also susceptible, as are women carrying twins. If you are in any of these categories, you may wish to contact the *Pre-eclamptic Toxaemia Society (PETS)* (see Address list, page 230). The results from treating the problem through nutrition are very good.

Not Just Nutrition

The effect of good food will be greatly enhanced if you don't smoke or drink, keep pills and potions to a minimum and take plenty of suitable exercise. Here are some notes on these and other health measures to take as you prepare for pregnancy.

GIVING UP SMOKING

1 Why?
Smoking gives your reproductive capacity a multiple handicap. We hear about the nicotine, the tar and the carbon monoxide in smoke, but did you know that 2,350 distinct chemical compounds have been identified in cigarette smoke? Of these 27 are known to be growth retardative and mutagenic (liable to alter the genes) or carcinogenic (capable of causing cancer). Receiving less oxygen, and reducing the rate of DNA synthesis and protein synthesis means that the rate of cell replication is slower in the embryo and fetus. A baby with fewer body and brain cells will be shorter and lighter and have a smaller head.

Smoking reduces fertility in men and women. It also affects the ability of the woman to retain a pregnancy, so she is more likely to suffer bleeding, miscarriage or to have a pre-term birth. The risk of placenta praevia also increases (where the placenta lies over the entrance – or should one say 'exit'? – of the womb), which would make a Caesarean birth necessary.

Smoking impairs one's immune competence. Thus not only are infections of the respiratory system more common in smokers and their children, but it also makes one more susceptible to infections of the urinary system, the vagina and of the amniotic fluid. It casts a long shadow over one's children such that, for example, the number of hospital admissions for children of pre-school age for all reasons is greater for those whose parents are smokers.

Smoking probably also increases the risk of congenital malformation such as defects in the nervous system, digestive system and heart. Maybe some of the malformed fetuses miscarry at an earlier stage and are not counted in the statistics. (This information is based on the review of research in Margaret and Arthur Wynn's *The Prevention of Handicap of Early Pregnancy Origin*, see Booklist, page 234.)

2 *How?*

(a) It is likely that you already knew that smoking is not a good thing. If you simply develop an aversion for it, you are fortunate, heed the message of your body and stick to it! You will feel so much better that your abstinence will carry its own reward.

(b) You can feel intellectually persuaded that your own health will be better, that your prospective baby's health will benefit, that other people around you will be happier without your smoke, and that there is a big financial incentive too, yet there is something more you need to make you take the plunge and give up altogether. There is a leaflet produced by the *Health Education Council*, 'How to Stop Smoking for You and Your Baby' which is readily available at health clinics or GPs' surgeries, or direct. See the Address list, page 230, and other general leaflets on smoking. These could help you with a step by step plan: deciding to stop, giving up and staying stopped. There are different things to work on. Here are some ideas that may suit you.

(i) *Incentives*: promise yourself treats if you stop, or for each day or week you have stopped. Collect the money you would have spent on cigarettes (use it to buy something for your baby, if you like). Tell all your friends you have given up (to make it more difficult to go back on your word). Find someone else who will give up at the same time and give each other moral support.

(ii) *Displacement activities*: when you have worked out the times or occasions when you really wanted a cigarette, find something else to do, such as getting up from the table straight after a meal, doing knitting or handwork when you are watching TV, lying down and practising relaxation or taking a leisurely bath, or playing with 'fiddle beads' when you are trying to collect your thoughts. You could also take up swimming or cycling, and give yourself incentives by seeing how far you can go without puffing. Each time it will be further, and you will remember you could not have done this when you were smoking. Singing or playing a blowing musical instrument would be an alternative activity that will help you feel how much better your lungs are. Drinking fruit juice, water or herb teas at a time when you might have had a coffee and a cigarette may make the absence of the cigarette easier to tolerate. (There may be something akin to the eastern concept of a yin and yang balance here, in that something more soothing does not need the counterbalance of another stimulant.) The same goes for alcoholic drinks, which together with the caffeine drinks are worth giving up as part of your preconceptual programme anyway.

(iii) *Aversion therapy*: There are some really nasty things to do to yourself if the more positive approach has never worked for you! One idea (prior to conception) is to stop smoking for 48 hours. Then chain smoke, lighting each cigarette from the previous one, until you can bear it no longer. This method is said to put most people off for good. If you need further torture, add water to the ashtray containing all those butts, and leave it where you can smell it until you can bear it no longer. The final degree is to get someone to burn the money you would have spent each day on your cigarettes until you plead for mercy! Monday, Tuesday, Wednesday ... it can't go on! You have to stop.

(c) There are many other methods for giving up smoking (as many as the reasons people have for indulging in the habit): support groups, chewing nicotine gum, acupuncture, clinically conducted aversion therapies and so on. Whatever method you choose, remember it is important to get smoking out of the way as soon as possible. You may well need to work on ways of reducing anxiety and stress in your life, but you will find ways of coping without cigarettes, and do give yourself the chance of feeling the benefits of having stopped.

(d) Are there any disadvantages in giving up? Weight gain often follows as smoking depresses the metabolic rate, but on a healthy wholefood diet low in fat and sugar, this should not be a problem for you, and a little extra weight will probably benefit the baby. Bad temper should be temporary. Plenty of understanding and support from those around helps, and a quick relaxation session (even just in the chair or leaning on a table) is a way to help yourself. If you have a sense of loneliness or emptiness, try lighting an open fire for company and comfort, and looking for other comforting things to do, friends to be with, or music to listen to. The main thing is to have confidence that you will be able to cope, even with difficult problems, and possibly better than before.

This topic has been dealt with at some length because smoking is quite a widespread and persistent habit. Of course, all the ill effects are that much worse when associated with other features of poor health and poor nutrition. If all else fails it is still good to cut down on smoking. Babies and smoke really do not mix.

POLLUTION

Some things can be controlled by us, others are all around us in the environment and may be more difficult to avoid. Some of the things to watch out for are:

1. Toxic chemicals at work. These may not be governed by regulations framed to protect reproductive health or a sensitive fetus.
2. Household chemicals, including paint strippers, fly killers (especially strips) and some cleaning fluids (oven cleaners, for example).
3. Garden chemicals and agricultural products such as weed killers (especially anything based on 2,4,5 T), pesticides etc.
4. Lead and heavy metals such as mercury and cadmium, also aluminium.
5. Radiation and X-rays.

Many toxic substances are assimilated readily by the fetus, but only slowly filtered out, as the liver is not mature enough to deal with these things.

Good nutrition can play a protective role. Calcium, for example, is an antagonist for lead. Lead competes with iron and zinc for assimilation into the blood, so a diet high in these is helpful. Protein and vitamin C and the B vitamins (such as folate) also help protect the body from many toxins. High levels of aluminium have been associated with premature rupture of the membranes, so cooking utensils should be looked at too. The most inert substances with heat are glass (and Pyrex) and stainless steel.

Other measures to take against lead include avoiding dense traffic (choose a route by a footpath away from busy roads when you can); removing outer leaves of cabbages etc especially if you know such vegetables have been grown near roads; run the water through the pipes each morning before using any water for drinking or cooking, or use a water filter. Gather blackberries or other wild fruits or herbs at least 100 yards from a road if you can. A hedge higher than the road is safer than one next to the road or lower down from it. It must be hoped that elimination of lead from petrol and paint will take place speedily. (Only use paints which are explicitly non-toxic, especially on items for your baby.)

CONTRACEPTION

The advice to discontinue the oral contraceptive pill for 4–6 months before starting a pregnancy, and for 3 months following immunisation against rubella, means that you should use some other method. Barrier methods such as the sheath or cap are usually recommended for these months. Another to consider is the natural method combining daily temperature and observations of the mucus and the cervix which both change through your cycle. It may seem a bore to do these daily checks, but the advantage is that you become much more familiar with your body. You will know your fertile days as a matter of course when you do want to get pregnant. You can guard against pre-menstrual tension, if this affects you. Like the Pill, this method of contraception is seen to at another time from when you are making love. You can read more about it in the book by Dr Anna Flynn and Melissa Brooks (see Booklist, page 232), but it is always recommended that you should only undertake the method in consultation with a trained counsellor.

One of the reasons for stopping the Pill well in advance of pregnancy is to get your hormones working well. Hormones trigger the various stages of development of the baby and its birth as well as post natal responses. The Pill also affects your metabolism generally and uses up stores of vitamins and minerals. If you have ever had bad side-effects from an oral contraceptive, it is best not to resume its use after the baby is born, but to find another method that suits you.

Even if you are not using the natural method it is important to keep a note of the first day of each period. Then you will be able to notice more quickly when one is overdue, and if you are pregnant, you will be able to calculate the expected date of delivery of your baby by counting on 40 weeks from the first day of your last period.

You can start thinking about the arrangements you would like best for the birth, even prior to conception. Ask your friends or your Community Health Council what is available in your area. If you would like a home birth you may need to do some early groundwork to find a GP who is sympathetic and will attend one.

ALCOHOL

The identification of a specific set of symptoms known as the 'fetal alcohol syndrome' (with characteristic facial features – as recognisable as those of Down's syndrome – low birthweight small length and small heads, mental retardation, hyperactivity and disturbed sleep patterns, frequent other malformations of the hip, heart or palate etc) alerted doctors to the fact that alcohol must be regarded as a teratogen (capable of producing birth defects). Although these babies are usually born to alcoholic mothers, investigations have been carried out to determine whether there are less severe effects from 'normal social drinking', whether there are 'critical periods' in fetal development when effects would be more serious, and whether bout drinking is worse than steady small amounts and so on. These questions have not all been resolved, and, as always, are not easy to determine when so many other factors could be interacting, such as the mother's nutritional status, her general immune status, whether she smokes or takes drugs of any kind and so on. The one thing that is now agreed is the only safe amount is no alcohol. This applies in the pre-pregnancy period as well as during pregnancy. In any case, taking alcohol is a misuse of calories at a time when it is important to get full value from all the day's calories. (See also Drinks, page 190)

PILLS AND POTIONS

If you are in the habit of taking any pills or medicines, even over-the-counter drugs such as aspirin or headache pills, this is something that needs your attention. The general advice is to exclude all drugs. It is best only to take something prescribed by your doctor in the knowledge that you might get pregnant while using it. If your drugs are treating a medical condition, here also it is worth speaking to your doctor as often there is a choice of different preparations.

You will have to think of other ways of coping with the problem for which you use pills. Sleeplessness can be helped by learning relaxation techniques, and engaging in the right kind of exercise. Migraine or headaches may be caused by oral contraceptives. You could find that life without the Pill is headache free. Check for hidden allergies, see page 199.

YOUR GENERAL HEALTH

Before you get pregnant aim to clear up any minor ailments or other health problems. If you suffer from a nagging cough, or keep getting colds and other infections, or if you have skin problems or recurrent headaches, it may be that your general resistance is low or that you have a 'masked allergy' (see page 199). Improving your diet is one way of helping your body recover, but if the problems continue, consult your doctor.

SEXUALLY TRANSMITTED DISEASES

If you are unhappy about any vaginal discharge, irritation or have any reason to wish for a check up, you can visit a hospital clinic completely confidentially, and you do not need a referral from your doctor. Your local hospital can inform you about where to find the clinic nearest you. It is best to clear up any problem, if treatment is needed, before you become pregnant.

RUBELLA (GERMAN MEASLES)

Removing the risk of damage from this infectious disease is an important precaution to take prior to pregnancy. Even if you think you have had it, or once had a vaccination, it is still wise to ask your doctor to do a test to check whether you have antibodies to the disease. If not, one injection should protect you (just check again to be sure it has taken) and then make sure not to become pregnant for 3 months afterwards.

Should you inadvertently find yourself pregnant and in contact with someone with German measles, especially in the first 4 months of pregnancy (when the potential damage could be most severe), tell your doctor as soon as possible. A blood test can be done to check your immunity. If you are not immune a fortnightly check will show whether you have caught the disease. If you have, you will be offered the option of terminating the pregnancy.

OTHER INFECTIONS

Although Rubella is probably the most dangerous common infection to a newly conceived baby, any infection represents some risk, if only because, in diverting your body's resources to dealing with the infection, your baby may get less of what it needs at a critical time. So when you can, avoid anyone with 'flu or any infection, and take good care of yourself if you do catch something around the time of conception or during pregnancy. Taking action immediately, rather than soldiering on, is likely to make the attack less severe. Staying in bed, taking plenty of fluids, (try the barley waters, page 194), and a good dose of vitamin C powder (up to 1g) in some juice as soon as you feel something coming on, will often shake it off in a day or two, so long as you give yourself a quiet day and plenty of rest and sleep the day after. It may also eliminate the need for treatment with prescription drugs. And, as before, if you do see a doctor, remind him or her that you are pregnant or hoping to conceive soon.

Toxoplasmosis, a disease carried by cats, can cause defects in a baby whose mother is infected during pregnancy. Most adults who keep cats are already immune. Postpone getting a cat for the first time if you are going to be pregnant, don't change litter trays etc.

PAST ILLNESSES AND MEDICAL CONDITIONS

If you have a current condition which requires treatment, such as diabetes, asthma, thyroid diseases, heart conditions or high blood pressure, or have had something successfully treated in the past such as coeliac disease, phenylketonuria or you know you have a negative Rhesus factor, it would be wise to discuss this with your doctor before you become pregnant. You will be advised about any checks needed or precautions to take, prior to or during pregnancy.

GENETIC COUNSELLING

Sometimes people are well aware that a hereditary disease runs in the family. Perhaps a relative has recently had a baby with some problem, or an older member developed a condition known to be transmitted by genes. You may even have had, yourselves, a baby with some birth handicap, and be keen to know the chances of it recurring in another pregnancy. Ask your doctor to refer you to a genetic counsellor for a detailed discussion and advice on ways to lessen the risk. However, you may not be aware of any problems in the family if past generations have kept quiet about any abnormalities or infant deaths. It is worth finding out if you can. The list of conditions transmitted genetically is long, but most are extremely rare. It includes muscular dystrophy, cystic fibrosis, Huntingdon's Chorea, haemophilia (affecting boys), certain types of mental illness, also sickle cell anaemia and Thalassaemia (affecting people of Negro or Mediterranean origin).

Explain to your doctor any worry about the possibility of an abnormality, and you may be referred to a genetic counsellor. Getting yourself really healthy, in all the ways described, will help your genes to be given the best chance. It is not known exactly what makes a particular egg mature each month. But if your hormones are functioning well, and good nutrition is providing the best biochemical environment for maturation to take place, maybe it will help your body select a 'good' egg!

BEST AGE TO HAVE A BABY

Physically, it is best to have finished one's own growing before having a baby. Very young mothers have more chance of developing pre-eclamptic toxaemia, of having a premature birth or a baby of low birth weight. It is also important to feel ready emotionally for the demands and joys of parenthood. Many women like to do something with their lives before starting a family, which may postpone pregnancy into their thirties. In fact the majority of births are to women in their twenties and early thirties, and statistics show that between the ages of 23 and 29 is the best time. However, if you are in good health, there is no reason to expect special problems in your early thirties. At a later age the risk of having a baby with Down's syndrome does increase, but even at 40 the risk is no higher than that of the baby dying – in other words, it is not statistically high. An amniocentesis test can be carried out if the mother wishes to check that the baby is normal. This is not without risk and is expensive, so a hospital usually will only offer it when the need is justified.

The best way to guard against the risk of abnormality or of having complications with the birth is to take positive health measures which may balance any disadvantage of being outside the ideal age range for having a baby.

How to space your family is a personal decision for each couple. In the end chance may decide anyway! There are many considerations to take into acccount. Here are some of them.

You need at least a year for your body to recover after nourishing a baby for nine months, and after breastfeeding, which may continue for a year or so. Then you need to consider the best age for that baby to be when another baby arrives. Around two years old is not usually a good time, as children can be very dependent just then. An optimum interval between births, from the point of view of the health of the babies, would appear to be between 2½–4 years. This suggests that it might be best to wait two years before thinking of starting a new pregnancy.

AFTER A MISCARRIAGE

You could give yourself a real advantage if you wait 6 months to a year after a miscarriage before starting again. It is best to leave time to grieve as well as time for your body to recover, and not a good idea to time things so the new baby arrives near the anniversary of the lost baby.

There are many reasons for a high miscarriage rate. It could be that there was something wrong with the baby, it might be that the mother was too tense for some reason, that the body was not ready to sustain a pregnancy, or many other reasons.

If it seems hard to wait, think of positive things to do, either taking advantage of the fact that you are not having a baby just now, or of the extra time to make long-term preparations. A change in the pace of your life may be beneficial and taking up such things as yoga, gardening (grow your own fresh vegetables!), baking (learn to make your own bread!), swimming, walking or just getting out in the open air more may all help.

Attention to your nutrition is important at this time, and will certainly benefit your next baby. There is a leaflet produced by the *NCT* (see Address list, page 230) on this topic, and a good book mentioned in the Booklist by Borg and Lasker which you can read if you want to find out more about coping with a miscarriage. There is also a *Miscarriage Association* (see Address list, page 230).

INFERTILITY

It is said that one in ten couples is infertile. It can also happen that although you experienced no problems on a previous occasion, this time you are finding it hard to conceive.

There are many possible causes which you can read about. (See A. Stanway *Why Us?* in the Booklist, page 235.) Few are irrevocable. Before you resort to drastic measures (such as hormone treatment, surgery or *in vitro* fertilisation) try to get yourselves as healthy as possible. Here are some things you could do.

1 The natural method of birth control is also useful for those who want to promote their fertility. Getting in touch with the female cycle means you know the best time to try to conceive (the period for abstinence when you are wanting to check your fertility). (See Dr Anna Flynn and Melissa Brooks, *A Manual of Natural Family Planning*, Booklist, page 232.)

2. Amenorrhoea (when periods stop altogether) can be caused by inadequate nutrition (through anorexia, dieting or simply insufficient good food). Adopting a good diet and forgetting your weight may well lead to the resumption of normal periods.
3. Diet, here as elsewhere, can help you. The recipes in this book are all based on foods which promote fertility as well as helping a baby, once conceived, to prosper. All the vitamins and minerals are important. Those particularly valuable include, vitamin E, the B vitamins, zinc, the essential fatty acids, vitamin A and C, and protein.

   A 'fertility bread' claimed successful by a GP in Cheshire many years ago (see Lionel Picton, *Thoughts on Feeding*, Booklist, page 233) consists of 2 parts wholewheat and 1 part wheatgerm. The flour and particularly the wheatgerm should be freshly milled and used within 48 hours. This would give a better rise. An egg added would help too. The GP believed this bread could restore deficiencies caused by roller milling and white bread.
4. Herbs believed to be beneficial are mentioned in the section on Drinks, page 192. Further information could be found in many herbal manuals.
5. Cutting out smoking and alcohol and taking regular exercise will help.
6. Checking the home and workplace for lead and other dangerous chemicals (including anaesthetics if you work in a hospital) is a good idea. You can ask to be transferred to a different type of work. Abandon any plans at home for stripping paint, using garden weedkillers and pesticides for the time being. You can ask to have your water checked for lead, and use a water filter for the water you consume. Relegate your aluminium cooking pots to a back cupboard and use instead stainless steel or heat proof glass (these are the most inert substances), enamel and pottery glazes may contain lead or cadmium.

   If you are concerned about possible levels of toxic metals you can have a hair test to check. Contact *Foresight*, see Address list, page 229.
7. Try to feel strong emotionally. This is a frustrating time of unfulfilled hopes and desires. Infertility can be a slight to your

sense of self-esteem. Self-confidence, however, is an important thing to foster. It will be valuable to you as a parent. Try to find friends in whom you can confide and who will value you and what you do. Relaxation, possibly through yoga, will help release any inner tensions too. (See books by Jane Madders and Sophy Hoare in the Booklist, page 233.) Gardening is an activity that may help you transfer your energies to growing things. Eating any fruits or vegetables you may grow will give double benefit! By some sort of magical osmosis it may attune your body to generating life as well.

8 If your infertility persists, it would be wise to consult your doctor with an aim to discover any obvious physical impediment to conception. Psychotherapy of some kind may also be indicated.

All these things will help you decide whether, in your case, it is necessary to be referred to an infertility clinic.

EXERCISE AND EXERCISES

The popularity of jogging and aerobic dance and exercise routines shows our society is becoming more aware of the need for regular exercise and its role in maintaining good health.

In pregnancy it is important to take the right sort of exercise which will help strengthen muscles and enable the body to become supple and relaxed without any strain. Walking, swimming and cycling are all good in this respect (though you may find it necessary to give up cycling after about 6 months of pregnancy). If you always keep within your own limits and do not go beyond to the point of tiredness, there should be no risk involved.

There are some very good books available (as well as records and cassettes) on exercises in pregnancy. It is good to start before pregnancy to get used to them, so they become part of your daily routine and easier to do if you are feeling a little 'off'. Finding time to do exercises will be well worthwhile, not just for toning up for the birth, but for regaining your figure after the birth and feeling fit in the immediate postnatal period.

Yoga is excellent too for achieving suppleness and for toning up your muscles. It is gentle and relaxing too, because the frame of mind plays an important role in yoga.

RELAXATION

Learning techniques for thorough relaxation is very beneficial. It can help reduce stress in everyday life as well as helping you during childbirth. There are plenty of everyday times and places to practise relaxation (see Jane Madders's *Stress and Relaxation*, in the Booklist, page 233). It is not necessary to have an hour to spend, but this will be a good thing to do sometimes too. Even if you are very busy and feel rushed, you will find that tasks become less effort if time is put aside for exercise and relaxation. It will be helpful psychologically as well if you can arrange things so that you are not always in a hurry.

BACK STRAIN

If you suffer from a 'bad back', now is the time to make it better. It could get worse in pregnancy, so look at the way you lift things and carry them, at your posture sitting and standing.

A book on the Alexander technique may interest you (see Barlow's in the Booklist, page 232), and the *Consumers' Association* book on *Avoiding Back Trouble* may also be generally helpful. Some exercises in Dale and Roeber and Elizabeth Noble's books will help strengthen the back and help prevent any trouble.

Useful Addresses

Association of Breastfeeding
  Mothers
131 Mayhow Road
Sydenham
London SE26 4HZ
(01) 461 0022

Association for the Improvement
  of Maternity Services (AIMS)
Christine Rodgers
163 Liverpool Road
London N1 0RF
(01) 278 5628

The Ipswich group of AIMS has
compiled a *Directory of
Maternity and Post-Natal Care
Organisations* which can be
obtained for £1.10 from
Amanda Wade, 76 Suffolk
Road, Ipswich, Suffolk.

Association of Radical Midwives
  (ARM)
Lakefield
8a The Drive
Wimbledon
London SW20
(01) 504 2010

The Birth Centre (London)
(Can give addresses of local
  groups)
101 Tufnell Park Road
London N7
(01) 609 7466

British Homeopathic Association
27a Devonshire Street
London W1N 1RH
(01) 935 2163
(Send an sae for a list of
homeopathic doctors) and
booklets on remedies for mothers
and infants).

Coeliac Society of the UK
PO Box 181
London NW20 2QY

Community Health Councils
Consult your local phone book
under C for Community for your
nearest CHC, which can give
advice on choices available for the
place of birth and other
information on the National
Health Service.

Foresight (The Association for the
  Promotion of Preconceptual
  Care)
Mrs Belinda Barnes
The Old Vicarage
Church Lane
Witley
Godalming
Surrey GU8 5PN
Wormley (042879) 4500

Health Education Council
78 New Oxford Street
London WC1A 1AH
(You can write for the *Pregnancy Book* (free) which includes a useful list with many more helpful organisations.)

The Henry Doubleday Research Association
Convent Lane
Bocking
Braintree
Essex CM7 6RW
(Publishes an *Organic Food Guide* (£2.50) and other useful information on growing food organically.)

Hyperactive Children's Support Group
Sally Bunday
59 Meadowside
Angmering
Littlehampton
West Sussex BN16 4BW

La Leche League (Great Britain)
Box 3424
London WC1V 6XX
(01) 404 5011

The Maternity Alliance
309 Kentish Town Road
London NW5 2TJ
(01) 267 3255
(Send an sae for advice on maternity rights, family benefits etc)

The McCarrison Society
Mrs Margaret Clark
36 Bowness Avenue
Headington
Oxford
The Society studies the relation between nutrition and health, with interesting talks and conferences, and will answer queries on nutrition.

The Miscarriage Association
Dolphin Cottage
4 Ashfield Terrace
Thorpe
Wakefield
West Yorkshire WF3 3DD
(0532) 828946

The Open University
PO Box 76
Milton Keynes MK7 6AN
(For courses on pregnancy, babies and children.)

National Childbirth Trust
9 Queensborough Terrace
Bayswater
London W2 3TB
(01) 221 3833

Pre-Eclamptic Toxaemia Society (PETS)
Dawn James
88 Plumberow
Lee Chapel North
Basildon
Essex SS15 5LQ
0268 42617

The Society for Environmental
 Therapy
Andy Buckingham
31 Sarah Street
Darwen
Lancs BB3 3ET

The Society of Homeopaths
101 Sebastian Avenue
Shenfield, Brentwood
Essex CM15 8PP
(Leaflets available on
Homeopathy in Pregnancy and
Childbirth and on a healthy diet.)

Society to Support Home
 Confinements
Margaret Whyte
17 Laburnum Avenue
Durham DH 4HA
(0385) 61325

The Soil Association
Walnut Tree Manor
Haughley
Stowmarket
Suffolk
(For advice on growing food
organically.)

The Spastics Society
12 Park Crescent
London W1N 4EQ

The Templegarth Trust
82 Tinkle Street
Grimoldby
Louth
Lincs LN11 8TF

The Vegan Society
9 Mawddwy Cottages
Minllyn
Dinas Mawddwy
Machynlleth SY20 9LW
(Leaflets and advice available on
food in pregnancy and for babies.)

The Vegetarian Society (UK) Ltd
Parkdale
Dunham Road
Altrincham
Cheshire WA14 4QG
(Leaflets and booklets available on
diet for mothers and children.)

Booklist

Janet Balaskas, *Active Birth* (Unwin Paperbacks).
Rudolph Ballentine, *Diet and Nutrition – A Holistic Approach* (The Himalayan International Institute, Pennsylvania).
Wilfred Barlow, *The Alexander Principle* (Arrow Books)
Ruth Bircher, *Eating Your Way to Health, The Bircher-Benner Health Guide* (Allen and Unwin)
Gail Sforza Brewer with Tom Brewer, *What Every Pregnant Woman Should Know* – The Truth about Diets and Drugs in Pregnancy (US Penguin).
Diana Carey and Judy Large, *Festivals, Family and Food* (The Hawthorn Press).
Consumers' Association, *Avoiding Back Trouble*.
Michael and Sheilagh Crawford, *What We Eat Today* (Spearman).
Barbara Dale and Johanna Roeber, *Exercises for Childbirth* (Century).
Elizabeth David, *English Bread and Yeast Cookery* (Penguin/Allen Lane).
Juliette de Baïracli Levy, *The Illustrated Herbal Handbook* (Faber and Faber).
Rose Elliott, *The Bean Book* (Penguin) and many other titles in vegetarian cookery.
Edward Espe Brown, *The Tassajara Bread Book* (Berkeley, Shambala Publications).
Dr Anna Flynn and Melissa Brooks, *A Manual of Natural Family Planning* (George Allen & Unwin).
Foresight booklets:
   Guidelines for Future Parents
   Supplementary Chapters to Guidelines for Future Parents (a useful glossary on all the vitamins and minerals, their role in reproductive health and which foods contain them)
   Environmental Factors and Foetal Health: The Case for Preconceptual Care.

BOOKLIST

Ina May Gaskin, *Spiritual Midwifery* (The Book Publishing Co., USA).

Sheila Gibson, Louise Templeton and Robin Gibson, *Cook Yourself a Favour – Help Yourself to Better Health* (Johnston Green Publishing Group).

Health Education Council, *Pregnancy Book – A Guide to Becoming Pregnant, Being Pregnant and Caring for your Newborn Baby* (available from clinics and the HEC, see address list).

Tina Heinl, *The Baby Massage Book* (Conventure Ltd).

Sophy Hoare, *Yoga and Pregnancy* (Unwin Paperbacks).

Sally Inch, *Birthrights, A Parents' Guide to Modern Childbirth* (Hutchinson).

Norman and Ruth Jervis, *The Foresight Wholefood Cookbook for Building Healthy Families* (Roberts Publications).

Hugh Jolly, *Book of Child Care* (George Allen & Unwin).

Betty and Si Kamen, *The Kamen Plan for Total Nutrition During Pregnancy* (Appleton-Century-Crofts, USA).

Sheila Kitzinger, *Birth Over Thirty* (Sheldon Press) and many other interesting titles on childbirth.

Frederick Leboyer, *Birth Without Violence* (Fontana).

Lifespan booklet, *Natural Birth Control* (Townhead, Dunford Bridge, Penistone, W. Yorks.).

Ann Loader (ed.), *Pregnancy and Parenthood* (Oxford University Press paperback).

Geraldine Lux Flanagan, *The First Nine Months of Life* (Heinemann).

Jane Madders, *Stress and Relaxation* (Martin Dunitz).

Peter Mansfield, *Starting Life Well* (Templegarth Trust).

Maire Messenger, *The Breastfeeding Book* (Century).

Ashley Montagu, *Life Before Birth* (Signet/New American Library).

Phyllis Mortimer, *Getting Fit for a Baby* (Family Doctor Booklet BMA).

Lennart Nilssen, *The Everyday Miracle. A Child is Born* (Allen Lane).

Elizabeth Noble, *Essential Exercises for the Childbearing Year – A Guide to Help and Comfort Before and After your Baby is Born* (John Murray paperback).

Michel Odent, *Entering the World* (Marion Boyars).

Michel Odent, *Birth Reborn* (Souvenir Press).

Janet Pleshette, *Health on Your Plate. A complete Guide to Food Therapy – the Natural Way to Fight Disease* (Hamlyn Paperbacks).

Barbara Pickard, *Eating Well for a Healthy Pregnancy* (Sheldon Press).

Barbara Pickard, *Are You Fit Enough to Become Pregnant?* and *Nausea and Vomiting in Early Pregnancy* (Booklets available from Lane End Farm, Denton, W. Yorks.)

Lionel Picton, *Thoughts on Feeding* (Faber and Faber).

Jill Rakusen and Nick Davidson, *Out of Our Hands. What Technology Does to Pregnancy* (Pan Books).

Barbara Richard, *Food, Health and Having a Baby* (Sheldon).

The Boston Women's Health Collective, *Our Bodies, Ourselves*, British Edition edited by Angela Phillips and Jill Rakusen (Penguin).

The Boston Women's Health Book Collective, *Ourselves and Our Children* (British edition by Michèle Cohen and Tina Reid (Penguin Books).

Colin Tudge, *Future Cook – A Taste of Things to Come* (Mitchell Beazley).

Thomas Verny with John Kelly, *The Secret Life of the Unborn Child* (Sphere Books).

Wholefood Cookery School, *Cooking with Sea Vegetables* and many other useful titles from The Wholefood Cookery School, 16/18 Bushloe End, Wigston, Leicester, LE8 2BA.

Cecelia Worth, *Breastfeeding Basics* (Unwin Paperbacks).

Margaret and Arthur Wynn, *Prevention of Handicap and the Health of Women* (Routledge and Kegan Paul).

Margaret and Arthur Wynn, *The Prevention of Handicap of Early Pregnancy Origin. Some evidence for the value of good health before conception* (Foundation for Education and Research in Childbearing, 27 Walpole Street, London, SW3).

Sharon Yntema, *The Vegetarian Baby* (Thorsons).

Other useful titles

James Anderson, *Diabetes, a Practical New Guide to Healthy Living* (Martin Dunitz).

Belinda Barnes and Irene Colquhoun, *The Hyperactive Child* (Thorsons).

Susan Borg and Judith Lasker, *When Pregnancy Fails, Coping with Miscarriage, Stillbirth and Infant Death* (Routledge and Kegan Paul paperback).

Hilda Cherry Hills, *Good Food Gluten-Free* and *Good Food Milk-Free* (Henry Doubleday Research Association, Bocking, Braintree, Essex).

Rita Greer, *Wheat-Free, Milk-Free, Egg-Free Cooking* (Thorsons who publish six other titles in this series on special diets.).

Robert Eagle, *Eating and Allergy* (Futura).

Françoise Labro and François Papa, *Boy or Girl? Choosing Your Child Through your Diet* (Souvenir Press).

Kate Ludeman, Louise Henderson, with Henry S. Basayne, *Do-It-Yourself Allergy Analysis Handbook* (Keats).

National Childbirth Trust, *Miscarriage, Mothers Talking About Postnatal Depression* (and many other useful leaflets and booklets) see address list.

Andrew Stanway, *Why Us? A Common Sense Guide for the Childless* (Granada).

Index

additives, *see* food additives
age, and pregnancy 224
alcohol
    and 'fetal alcohol syndrome' 220; and pregnancy 16, 18, 190–1; and preparation for conception 2, 17–18, 190
allergies 198–200
    and cow's milk 189, 202–5; and gluten 201–2; and hyperactivity 200–1
almonds, *see* nuts
amenorrhoea 226
amino acids 13
amniocentesis test 224
anaemia 210–11
apples, clafoutis 135, sponge 137, crumble 137, fritters 138, baked 138, mulled 197
artichoke soup 66
avocado, dressing 116, salads 117, 124, dip 167

back strain 228
baguettes 56–7
baking, *see* home baking, gluten-free 143–4, baking powder 144
balanced diet 12–21
bananas, baked 142
barley, and bean soup 69, salad 121; pancakes 182; water 194
beans 98, complementing proteins 13; soups 69, 70; dishes 94, 96, 100, 103–4, 106, 107, 124–5; sprouting 113
beetroot, bortsch 71, au gratin 109, salads 118, 121
berries, desserts 131, 132–4, 137
birth 5
    complications 7; optimum interval between 224

birth control, *see* contraception
birth defects
    and hereditary diseases 223; links with age 224; links with alcohol 220; links with nutrition deficiency 11; links with smoking 215–6; preventive supplements intervention 11
birthweight 9
    and nutrition 7–8
biscuits, sweet 147–150; savoury 169–170
blood pressure 213–4
bread 33–4
    croutons 63; 'fertility' 226; ingredients 44–9; making 49–53; pitta 160–1; recipes 53–60; tea breads 58–60, 146–7
breakfast 32–42, 203–4
    and early pregnancy sickness 43; wholefood 20
breast-feeding 9–10
    drinks for 31; food for 29–31, 203–5; and infant illness 8; nipple care 29, 198–9; problems 31
broccoli 15, flan 78, and cauliflower 105, with potato 109, green pasta bake 81
Bryce-Smith D. 11
buckwheat 38, noodles (soba) 82–3, moussaka 91, kasha 183
bulgur, burgers 99; tabbouleh 121
burgers 99–100

cabbage 15, Transylvanian 89–90, red 103, salads 118–9
caffeine, effects of 189–90
cakes and biscuits 146–54
calories, daily needs 21
Canada, pregnancy and nutrition studies 6–8

carob, in baking 148–150, 152, 189–90, 193

carrots, soup 66, salads 120–1, macedoine 107

cauliflower, soup 65, and broccoli 105, vinaigrette 127, braised Indian 181

celery, soup 64, salads 119–20, sticks 161

cell divisions and differentiation 1, 3, 5, 215

cereals 32–3, 34–8
  recipes 176, 182–3

cheese 41, flans 76–77, tarts 79, pasties 80, for breakfast 38, soft white 130, cheese cake 141, curd tart 141, goat's curds 142; straws 169; with pancakes 182

cherries, clafoutis 135, kissel 184

chicken, recipes 79, 92, 95, 174

chick peas, sauce 83, fritters 101, hot pot 102–3; couscous 92

cocktail parties 165–6; recipes 166–70

coeliac disease *see* allergies and gluten

"coffee parties" 165

conception
  contraception and 219–20; diet before 1–3, 10–11; health care before 218–19, 221–3

constipation 209–10

contraception
  and conception 219–20; natural methods 2, 219, 225; *see also* oral contraceptives

corn, on the cob 20, 38; maize pancakes 96; polenta pizza 86; polenta 176

costs 27–8; of manufactured food 27

courgettes, soup 65, salad 179

croutons 63

cucumber soup 71, salads 118

curry, lamb 93, mung bean 94, chicken 95, cauliflower 181

custard, boiled 134, sauce 24

dairy products 14, 15, 40–1

desserts, recipes 132–43, 183–4;; *see also* icecreams

diet
  and allergy prevention 198–9; balanced 12–13, 26–7; changing 22–3; deficiencies 3; and fertility 226; gluten-free 143–4, 201–2; improving before conception 1–3; vegan 206

dinner parties 171–4; recipes 174–87

dips 166–8

Down's syndrome 224

drinks, milk-free 205; recipes 191–7; types of 188–91

drugs, and preparation for conception 2, 11, 221

eggs 41; allergy to 206; recipes 106, 107

embryo 1, 5, 190, 215

"energy" foods 12

entertaining, planning 164–5; *see also* cocktail parties; dinner parties

exercise 208, 227–8

"fast foods" 203–5

fat, in balanced diet 15, 23–4

fatherhood, and diet 2, and smoking 215, and alcohol 190

fish 87; recipes 178; in diet 16

flan recipes 76–80

flour 21–2, 46; and gluten allergy 201–2; wholewheat 73–5, 143

fluid retention 211–13

foetus growth 1, 3, 4–5, 9, 11; and weight gain 211

food additives 16; colour dyes 16–7

food groups 12, 14

food intolerance *see* allergies

Foresight 4

fruit 128
  and allergies 200–1; and nut bars 163; breads 58, 60, 146–7; for breakfast 39–40; dried 129, 143; drinks 195–7; juices 188; salads 130; yogurts 131, *see also* desserts

frumenty 34

garlic bread 57

gazpacho 71

genetic counselling 223

genetic factors 4
German Measles *see* Rubella
ginger, and reducing nausea 193, 209; -beer 194–5
gluten-free diet 201–2; baking 143–4; pastry 75, 153
goulash 89–90
grains 33ff
granola 37–38

health care, during pregnancy 215–23, 227–8
herb teas 190, 192–3
herbs and spices 14; for infertility 226; for salad dressings 114; for sandwich fillings 158
hereditary diseases *see* genetic counselling
high blood pressure *see* blood pressure
home baking 143–155; bread 44–60; pastry 74–5; cheese cake 141, curd tart 141; savoury biscuits 169–70
hyperactivity, and allergy 200–1

icecreams, recipes 185–7
infections, during pregnancy 221–2
infertility 225–7
iron supplements 209–10, 210–11

juice 188–9; at breakfast 39; vegetable juices 191, fruit juice drinks 195–7
julienne consomme 63

kombu 61, stock 69, broth 209

labour, natural 5
lamb 16, red meats 88, 211; couscous 92, curry 93, blanquette 175, with prunes 177, kidneys 177
lead 16, 188, 218–19, 226
leeks, soups 67, 70; flan 77
lentils, soup 69, sprouting 113; salad 125

manufactured foods 25–6; costs 27; and food additives 17; and lack of nutrients 3

meat, 24–5, 86–7, 88–9; recipes 89, 90, 92–3, 95, 97, 175, 177
medical conditions, and pregnancy 223
Mexico, pregnancy supplements study 10
micronutrients 14, 15; *see also* vitamins and minerals
milk 40, 189; allergy 189, 202–3; almond 192; custard 134–5
milk-free diet xi, 202–5; breakfast 41
milk substitutes 41–2
mincemeat recipes 154–5
minerals 3; calcium rich foods 203; in meat 87; supplements 3–4, 209–10, 210–11 *see* toxic substances
miscarriage 3, 224–5
morning sickness *see* pregnancy sickness
moussakas 90–1
mueslis 36–7
muffins 59–60
mushrooms, soup 66; flan 77; vinaigrette 120; champignons a la grecque 126

natural toxins 16
nausea *see* pregnancy sickness
nutrition counselling 8
nutritional deficiency, and birth defects 11
nuts 15, 129, 143; at breakfast 36–7; in soups 62, 65, 67; in salads 117, 119, 123; in baking 151–2, 153; roasted peanuts 169; praline 186; nut milk 42, 192; nut cream 134

oats 35ff; oatmeal bread 53; bars 149–50
oedema 212
offal *see* organ meats
onions, and herb bread 56; soup 70, flan 77
oral contraceptives, and body vitamins 2; and conception 219; *see also* contraception
organ meats 16, 87; recipes 97, 177
organically grown foods 27

INDEX

packed breakfasts 42
packed lunches 157; *see also* sandwiches
pancakes 182, 183
parsnip soups 67
party dips 166–8
pasta 22, 80–3, 180–1
pasties 80
pastry 73–5
pea and garden vegetable pottage 68
peppers, flan 76
perinatal mortality 9; and nutrition 7–8
picnics 156, 161–3
pie shell *see* pastry
pill *see* oral contraceptives
pills *see* drugs
pizza 83–6
pollution, and food contamination 16; and infertility 226; and pregnancy 218–9
porridge 35
potato 12, 14; bread 54; soups 67, 68; "jacket" 108–9; salads 125–6
poultry and game 88; *see also* chicken
preconceptual health 1–2, 10–11, 198–9, 200, 209, 215–228
pregnancy 4–5
  calorie needs 21; contact with Rubella 222; demands of 3; foods to avoid 15–18; health care during 215–23, 227–8; problems 5–6, 207–214; role of nutrition in 6–9
pregnancy sickness 207–9; breakfast suggestions 43
preparing for pregnancy, *see* preconceptual health
pre-pregnancy diet 12–21
protein 13
pulses 14, 15, 98–104
pumpkin, pie 139; scones 145

quiches, *see* flans

ratatouille 108
recipes
  biscuits 147–51; bread 53–60; cakes 151–4; chicken 95, 174; cocktail party 169–70; desserts 132–43, 184; dips 166–8; drinks 191–7; fish 178; flan 76–80; granola 37–8; icecreams 185–7; meat 89, 90, 92–3, 97, 175, 177; muesli 36; pasta 81–3, 180–1; pizza 84–6; porridge 35; pulses 98–104; salad dressings 115–16; salads 117–27, 175, 179; scones 144–5; soups 61–72; tea breads 146–7; vegetable juice 191; vegetables 89, 91, 92, 94, 96–7, 105–10, 126–7, 181; yogurt 131–2
"reference protein" 13
relaxation 208, 227, 228
Rhesus negative factor 223
rice 22; balls 63; bread 54–5; pudding 140; salads 122–4; savoury bake 101–2
Rubella 221
rye 38

saccharin 17
salads 111–13, 162; dressings 113–16; fruit 130; recipes 117–27, 175, 179
salt, in bread-making 48–9; in diet 213
sandwiches 158–60
Scandinavian breakfast 38–9
scones 144–5
seeds 13, 15, 24, 30, 129, 204; in bread 55; sprouting 113; roasted 169; with pasta 82
sexually transmitted diseases 221
shortcrust *see* pastry
smoking, effects of 215–16; giving up 216–18; and preparation for conception 2
soda bread 58; *see also* baking powder
sodium nitrite, and mutagenic potential 16
soups 61–72; broth 209
soya beans, burgers 100
soya flour, 158, as substitute for egg 206
soya milk, *see* milk substitutes
spices *see* herbs and spices

spinach, and cottage cheese tartlets 79, pasties 80, with pasta 81
stock, clear 62, thick 62–3, kombu 69
stress, and infertility 226–7; reducing 208, 213, 228
sugar 12, artificial 17; as a spice 14; in pregnancy 16, 17; reducing intake 23; substitutes 128–9
supplements, and reduction of birth defects 11; in pregnancy 6–8, 9–10, 209–10; types 21; *see also* minerals; vitamins
Switzerland, lack of iodine 11

tofu, burgers 99, balls 100, citrona 142, cream 142, dips 168
tomatoes, soup 64, 69; salad 118
tortillas 97
toxaemia 4, 211, 213–14
toxic substances 16, 218–19; and infertility 226; *see also* natural toxins
toxoplasmosis 222

United Kingdom, pregnancy and nutrition studies 8–9

vegan diet 206
vegetables 14, 15, 73, 104
dips 166–8; flans 76–80; hot dishes 89, 91, 92, 94, 96–7, 105–10, 181; juice 188–9, 191; salads 126–7, 179; soups 63–71; *see also* potato
vegetarianism, and vitamin deficiencies 3
vichyssoise 68
vitamin B.3, 15, 32, 206
vitamin C.3, 12; and infections 22; and iron assimilation 211
vitamins
deficiency and birth defects 11; and effects of oral contraceptives 2; and fertility 226; lack 3; in milk 203; supplements 3–4
vomiting *see* pregnancy sickness

water 188
weight gain 211–13
weights and measures ix–xi
wheat 38
wheatgerm 22
wholefoods, suggested daily menu 20–1
wholewheat flour, 21, breads 44–60; pasta 80–2; pastry 74–5; baking 143–155

yeast 46–7; keeping 47–8
yeast-risen spice loaf 60
yin and yang balance 12, 217
yoga 225, 227–8
yogurt 40; dressing 116; fruit 131; making 131–2

zucchini *see* courgettes